British Railways in Argentina 1857-1914

History: Bloomsbury Academic Collections

This Collection of 23 reissued titles from The Athlone Press and Leicester University Press offers a distinguished selection of titles that showcase the width and breadth of historical study, as well as the interdisciplinary nature of the subject. Crossing over into politics, linguistics, economics, politics, military and maritime history, and science, this Collection encompasses titles on British, European and global subjects from the Early Modern period to the late 20th Century.

The collection is available both in e-book and print versions.

Titles in History are available in the following subsets:

History: British History

History: European History

History: History of Latin America

History: History of Medicine

Other titles available in History: History of Latin America include:

José Martí: Revolutionary Democrat, Ed. by Christopher Abel and Nissa Torrents

Latin America, Economic Imperialism and the State: The Political Economy of the External Connection from Independence to the Present, Ed. by Christopher Abel and Colin M. Lewis

The Rise and Fall of the Peruvian Military Radicals 1968-1976, George D.E. Philip

Government and Society in Colonial Peru: The Intendant System 1784-1814, J. R. Fisher

British Railways in Argentina 1857-1914

A Case Study of Foreign Investment

Colin M. Lewis

History: History of Latin America
BLOOMSBURY ACADEMIC COLLECTIONS

Bloomsbury Academic
An imprint of Bloomsbury Publishing Plc

B L O O M S B U R Y
LONDON • NEW DELHI • NEW YORK • SYDNEY

Bloomsbury Academic
An imprint of Bloomsbury Publishing Plc

50 Bedford Square 	1385 Broadway
London 	New York
WC1B 3DP 	NY 10018
UK 	USA

www.bloomsbury.com

BLOOMSBURY and the Diana logo are trademarks of Bloomsbury Publishing Plc

First published in 1983 by The Athlone Press

This edition published by Bloomsbury Academic 2015

© Colin M. Lewis 2015

Colin M. Lewis has asserted his right under the Copyright, Designs and Patents Act, 1988, to be identified as Author of this work.

All rights reserved. No part of this publication may be reproduced or transmitted in any form or by any means, electronic or mechanical, including photocopying, recording, or any information storage or retrieval system, without prior permission in writing from the publishers.

No responsibility for loss caused to any individual or organization acting on or refraining from action as a result of the material in this publication can be accepted by Bloomsbury or the author.

British Library Cataloguing-in-Publication Data
A catalogue record for this book is available from the British Library.

ISBN: HB: 978-1-4742-4166-3
ePDF: 978-1-4742-4167-0
Set: 978-1-4742-4119-9

Library of Congress Cataloging-in-Publication Data
A catalog record for this book is available from the Library of Congress

Series: Bloomsbury Academic Collections, ISSN 2051-0012

Printed and bound in Great Britain

University of London
Institute of Latin American Studies

12

British Railways in Argentina 1857–1914

BRITISH RAILWAYS IN ARGENTINA 1857–1914

A Case Study of Foreign Investment

by

COLIN M. LEWIS

ATHLONE

Published for the
Institute of Latin American Studies
University of London
1983

First published 1983 by The Athlone Press Ltd
58 Russell Square, London WC1B 4HL

Distributor in the USA and Canada
Humanities Press Inc
New Jersey

© *University of London 1983*

British Library Cataloguing in Publication Data

Lewis, Colin M.
   British railways in Argentina 1857–1914.—(Institute
   of Latin American Studies monographs ISSN 0776-0846; 12)
   1. Railroads—Finance—Argentina—History
   2. Investment, British—Argentina—History—19th century
   3. Investment, British—Argentina—History—20th century
   4. Capital Investment—Argentina—History—19th century
   5. Capital Investment—Argentina—History—20th century
   I. Title   II. Series
332.6′7341082   HE2907

ISBN 0-485-17712-9

US SBN 0-391-02772-7

All rights reserved. No part of this publication may be reproduced, stored in a retrieval system, or transmitted in any form or by any means, electronic mechanical, photocopying or otherwise, without prior permission in writing from the publisher.

Typeset by Inforum Ltd, Portsmouth
Printed in Great Britain at the
University Press, Cambridge

i Elfair

CONTENTS

	Acknowledgements	xi
	Introduction	1
I	The early phase: assumptions, expectations and achievements	5
II	National consolidation	45
III	Crisis and recovery	73
IV	The railway guarantees: a retrospective reappraisal	97
V	Denationalization and reorganization	124
VI	Zonal amalgamation – 1	146
VII	Zonal amalgamation – 2	164
VIII	Integration and prosperity	192
	Conclusion	215
	Abbreviations	222
	Notes	224
	Bibliography	248
	Index	255

TABLES

1	Volume of produce entering the southern market of Buenos Aires	24
2	Principal Argentine exports: relative composition, by value	28
3	Central Argentine: operating data	47
4	BAGS: operating data and dividends declared upon ordinary stock	48
5	Argentine railways: London Stock Exchange quotations of select British-owned companies	49
6	BA&EP: operating data	59
7	Argentine Railways: expansion of the network	68
8	Argentine Railways: density of mileage in select provinces	72
9	BAGS: goods traffic	75
10	BAGS: earnings and expenditure	75
11	BA&EP: operating data	76
12	Argentine Railways: dividends declared on ordinary stocks by select British-owned companies	77
13	Argentine Railways: London Stock Exchange quotations of select British-owned railway securities	78
14	Argentine Railways: guarantee payments, total annual liability	82
15	Service required by national government debt, 1892	83
16	Argentine Railways: net earnings and ordinary dividends of select British-owned companies and global yield	85
17	Argentine exports: select arable products	87
18	Argentine Railways: operating data, BAGS and CA	90
19	BAGS: goods and animal traffic	91
20	Argentine Railways: total nominal investment	95
21	Argentine Railways: ordinary dividends declared by select British-owned companies	96
22	Argentine Railways: working ratios	116
23	Argentine Railways: aggregate guarantee payments	117
24	Argentine Railways: guarantee commutation payments	122
25	BAGS and *Oeste*: gross yield on capital	128
26	Argentine Railways: national government lines, 1889	134
27	Argentine Railways: major systems, 1889	138
28	BAW: distribution of *Oeste* track	139
29	Central Argentine: grain traffic	155
30	BA&R and CA: capital accounts, 1899	157
31	Argentine Railways: tariff schedules, 1897	170
32	Argentine Great Western: capitalization	171

33	Argentine Railways: expansion of British-owned lines	197
34	Argentina: area under cultivation, select arable products	198
35	Argentine Railways: global yield and ordinary dividends declared by major British-owned companies	199
36	BA&P: expansion of system	201
37	Argentine Railways: London Stock Exchange quotations of select British-owned stocks	202–3
38	Argentine Railways: rolling stock ratios of select lines, 1889	205
39	Argentine Railways: rolling stock ratios of select British-owned companies	208–9
40	Argentine Railways: operating data of British-owned companies	213
41	Comparative dividends declared upon ordinary stock by British and Argentine railway companies	218

GRAPHS

1	BAGS: capital account structure	81
2	CA and BA&R: net earnings	158

MAPS

1	The Argentine Railway Network, 1914	xii
2	Expansion of the Argentine Railway system	63
3	Disposal of *FC Oeste* track, 1890	140
4	The consolidation of the Pacific group, 1895–1910	167
5	Railway rivalry and amalgamation in mesopotamia, 1898–1914	181

ACKNOWLEDGEMENTS

It is only appropriate that I acknowledge in this volume, which derives from my doctoral dissertation, the assistance of the librarians, archivists and staff of those public and private institutions in Buenos Aires, London and Exeter who gave me so much of their time when I was gathering data for the thesis. Furthermore, I must mention those who submitted themselves to personal interrogation, relating with gusto, and no little humour, their various experiences as employees and administrators of, or advisers to, the formerly British-owned companies, or as officials of state regulatory agencies. It would be invidious to identify anyone by name, but without their aid and sympathy this study would have proved impossible to complete.

While many colleagues and friends in Great Britain and Argentina have contributed much to the evolution of themes contained within this work, I owe a special debt of gratitude to Professor D.C.M. Platt for his encouragement, criticism and support over many years. Also, I must thank Professor John Lynch for his consideration — not to say forebearance — in the preparation of this volume, and the opportunity to publish the results of my research.

The graphs and maps were compiled by Alison Fisher of the Drawing Office at the London School of Economics and Political Science. Vivienne Stockley and Hazel Leake, Institute of Latin American Studies, and Tess Truman, Department of Economic History, London School of Economics, helped prepare the typescript.

The initial work upon which this study is based was made possible by financial assistance extended by the University of Exeter and the Astor Foundation. Recent revisions have been accomplished due to the generosity of the University of London.

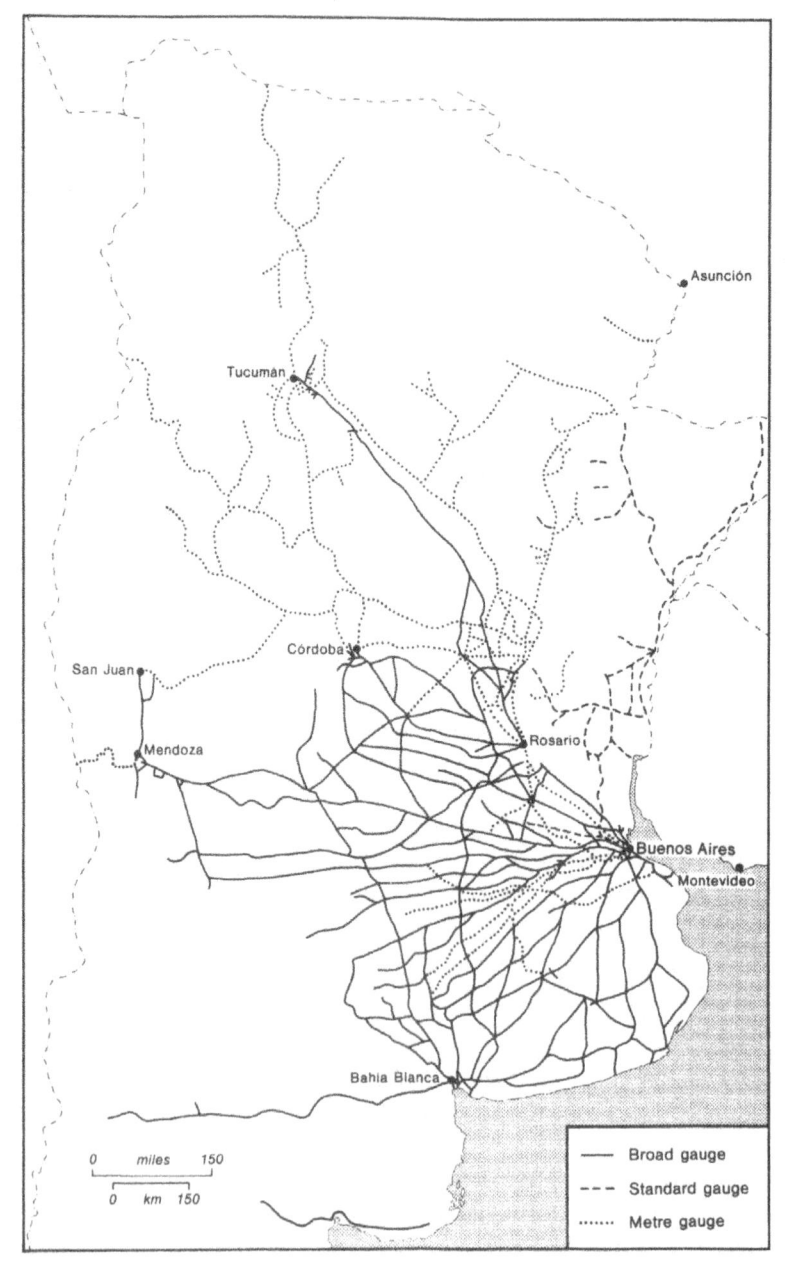

Map 1: The Argentine Railway Network, 1914

INTRODUCTION

The period between the fall of Rosas in 1852 and the election of Yrigoyen in 1916 has long been recognized as critical in Argentine economic history. These were the years which saw the formation of the modern Argentine Republic: the structure of the economy, the nature of society and the pattern of political processes were all clearly established, or profoundly modified, as the country underwent modernization in various forms. Between the mid-nineteenth and the early twentieth centuries Argentina passed from *la época del cuero* almost directly to *la sociedad de masas*, and its capital was transformed from *la gran aldea* of the creole age into the cosmopolitan Paris of South America. These were the years of the consolidation of the state, the expansion of the frontier and the evolution of a political structure sufficiently flexible to cope with the socio-economic changes wrought by rapid export-led growth. Opportunities generated by domestic diversification and the expansion of world demand were predicated upon factor endowment and the ability of the country to absorb those resources not available domestically. One of the key elements in this growth equation was the provision of social overhead capital which, in the Argentine case, was largely financed from external sources. The expanding railway network epitomized this process: not only did the railways express the characteristics of the economy, but the chronology, method and nature of railway construction provides an indication of the complex pattern of relationships which evolved at this juncture.

In part, it may be argued that the formation and evolution of the Argentine railway network between 1854, the date of the inauguration of work on the first line, and the First World War accurately reflect the nature and substance of structural change on a larger scale. The context within which railway companies were floated and operated, the phasing of expansion, the products carried by the lines, the focus of activities – all mirror the dynamics of the growth process. The fortunes of the railways, moreover, represent in microcosm positive and negative aspects of the wider development programme. For the companies, the period possesses a basic unity. The decades between 1880 and 1914 were ones of expansion and, on the whole, prosperity. The economy at large began to grow rapidly during the period in spite of the hiatus of the Baring Crisis; this was followed by the revindication of the preferred development model associated with agricultural diversification, foreign trade and externally-derived factor flows — an environment in which the sheer scale of expansion inhibited any serious discussions concerning distribution and encouraged a facile acceptance of diffusionist tenets. But initial projection and financing of railways demonstrated that the dynamic of export-led growth was not to be easily achieved. As during the expansionist phase, so during the formative epoch, the railway companies' experience was representative, and illustrative, of larger events. The rhetoric and the assumptions associated with original railway concessions mark the contemporary expectations of dominant sectors in Argentine society and the preconceptions of a modernizing elite. In addition, the actual construction of the network and the problems which arose regarding the realization of these objectives, demonstrate the difficulties experienced by that elite in obtaining 'economic progress', albeit sectionally conceived. Essentially, it was a question of striking a balance between internal expectations and the requirements of external interests upon whom the dominant landed groups were dependent for technology, expertise and capital. The resolution of these conflicts, the implementation of a successful *modus operandi*, was the basic pre-condition upon which subsequent growth was founded.

This study is concerned with the nature of railway expansion in an area of recent settlement and the determinants of a pattern of infrastructural development in an agropecuarian economy. It will focus precisely — though not exclusively — upon the broad-gauge pampean companies. It will seek to investigate the nexus of domestic and foreign interests involved, the balance of the momentum for change (as between national opportunities and externalities) and the evolution of these relationships over time within the context of a specific international situation which will be taken as given. In short, this volume considers the problems and profits of railway operations, the expectations of a 'modernizing elite' and the factors promoting and perpetuating a community of interest amongst apparently disparate groups. Railway construction was the catalyst which effected the transformation of the *pampas*. Argentine economic expansion during the late nineteenth and early twentieth centuries owed much to companies' detailed consideration of the infrastructural requirements most appropriate for specific productive sectors. Indeed, it was this concern which permitted individual enterprises to achieve profitable status. Yet the central position which had been acquired by several British-owned entities at the turn of the century contrasted sharply with earlier phases of Argentine railway development when many lines had experienced severe difficulty in establishing themselves upon secure financial bases, and the concept of large-scale external participation in this key area had not been unchallenged. Thus, prior to the First World War, Argentine railway history may be subdivided into a number of clearly identifiable periods: the formative phase of establishment and consolidation; the epoch of conflict and compromise between local and foreign interests; the emergence of a national network; the cataclysm of the Baring Crisis and its aftermath; resurgence and expansion which produced the era of 'golden' prosperity.

I

THE EARLY PHASE: ASSUMPTIONS, EXPECTATIONS AND ACHIEVEMENTS

By the early twentieth century Argentina possessed one of the most extensive, integrated railway systems in Latin America, the greater part of which was British-owned. Whether expressed in terms of route mileage or capitalization, the Argentine network was pre-eminent in the region: it was the tenth largest in the world.[1] Several Argentine railway companies enjoyed an international reputation for the excellence of their service; some had acquired an enviable reputation for financial rectitude and an ability to reconcile the disparate, and apparently contradictory, expectations of shareholders and consumers. During the years immediately prior to the First World War, contemporary opinion held that the Argentine case manifestly demonstrated the dynamic role then ascribed to foreign capital, and the appropriateness of the national railway system to the requirements of the expanding — and already diversifying — pampean economy. The scenario was one of harmony and expansion: of a close, lucrative relationship that had evolved between British capitalists and Argentine producers founded upon co-prosperity. This picture presented a sharp contrast to that of five or six decades earlier when Argentina was poised to enter the railway era. Then an initial optimism respecting railway projects and an enthusiasm for foreign investment had been dissipated by early difficulties. Problems of funding, the long gestation period involved — compounded by the underdeveloped nature of the local economy and political instability — conflicting interests and the often unrealistic expectations of various groups had engendered factious controversy. Notwithstanding original assumptions, it soon became clear that infant companies would require a substantial degree of government support, though no coherent consensus emerged as to the most effective means of according official aid. Confusion and dispute arose concerning the real cost of railway building;

disagreement — between foreign capitalists and the state, amongst promoters and financiers — became the norm as sanguine early expectations were confounded.

Problems and Prospects
Thus the dawn of the railway age in Argentina was far from auspicious, as events surrounding the inauguration of the country's first railway company, the *Sociedad Anónima Camino Ferrocarril al Oeste*, serve to confirm. A few days before 29 August 1857, the date of the official opening, a group of *Oeste* directors commissioned a special train in order to undertake a tour of inspection of the company's seven miles of track. The outward journey from the Buenos Aires terminus at Plaza Parque (Plaza Lavalle), in front of the Teatro Colon, to Flores was safely accomplished and, after suitable refreshments, preparations made for the return trip. Upon the homeward journey the party was somewhat nonplussed when the locomotive, *La Porteña*, left the track and one of their number was injured. Fearful lest knowledge of the accident might depress the earning potential of their company, the directors decided to suppress news of the event. They returned to Buenos Aires chastened by the experience.[2]

Such an incident was perhaps a fitting episode; it illustrates the precarious nature of railway projects then under consideration on the banks of the River Plate. Initial schemes were beset with the problems and difficulties that are usually associated with novel institutions struggling to achieve substance. Yet the concept of the railway as an adjunct of the modern state and the functions which it performed were already recognized in Argentina. The distinguished political philosopher, Alberdi, attributed to the railway an almost mystical symbolism; it was the acme of modernizing influences.[3]

> The railway is the means of over-turning the distorted system established by Spain in this continent. Spain made the heads of our countries where the feet should have been. This system evolved from her isolated and monopolistic perspective; it is lamentable for our expansion and commercial freedom. It is necessary to link the capitals and coast — to bring the littoral to the interior of the continent. Railways conquer distance: they work wonders better than any ruler of the land. The railway

innovates, reforms and modifies — without official decrees and commotions . . . But for the railway, political unity would be impossible in countries where distance impedes the action of central government.

The railway, then, was not merely a metaphysical force but a fundamental pre-condition of political, economic and social change. The railway would open up and develop markets, facilitate the distribution of goods, and encourage migration to sparsely settled regions: it could provide the means of effecting social cohesion, of imparting a sense of community to widely scattered centres of population, and enable the writ of central government to run throughout the state. Little wonder that Alberdi should advocate the cause of the railways with such enthusiasm.

These countries possess abundant means of procuring railways: we can float foreign loans, pledge our income and national wealth for enterprises that will redeem them with interest . . . At the same time we can foster private firms to build railways, heaping upon them all imaginable advantages and privileges . . .

Given Alberdi's influence in mid-nineteenth-century Argentina, it was hardly surprising that these sentiments obtained official recognition in the Argentine Constitution of 1853 which specifically enjoined Congress to provide the means necessary to encourage railway construction.[4] These views, however, were not confined to Argentines, but were shared by most foreign observers with interests in the River Plate at the onset of the railway age. An indefatigable English commentator upon the Argentine scene maintained that 'Railways must be established to drive the countries ahead, or they will recede into a state of semi-barbarism.'[5] Platitudes notwithstanding, there was no apparent lack of economic incentive for the construction of railways. Reporting in 1864, the *Brazil and River Plate Mail* employed terms which were soon to become the norm, although in this instance they referred exclusively to the Central Argentine Railway Company Limited: 'Few projects have ever been launched in the English money market more deserving of support than this railway.'[6]

The construction of railways in Argentina was seen as desirable and necessary by natives and foreigners alike, while the feasibility — in both technical and financial terms — of such projects does not appear to have been doubted: the local terrain was favourable and capital assumed to be abundant. Yet, within the South American community of nations, Argentina was but the fifth to enter the railway age. Brazil, Colombia, Peru and Chile possessed operational railway companies before *La Porteña* first steamed out of Plaza Parque.[7] An immediate explanation for this tardy development is not difficult to discover. The prevailing political situation during the 1850s was hardly likely to favour the fruition of costly railway projects. Given the latent hostility which existed between Buenos Aires and the other provinces of the Argentine Confederation, an antagonism which often resulted in protracted interhecine strife, it is little wonder that large-scale capital-intensive projects were long in the making. Indeed, it was surprising that any progress occurred at all.[8]

However, despite their disagreements and differences, both the merchants of Buenos Aires and General Urquiza's Confederation government recognized the advantages to be obtained from railway development. On the one hand the *porteños* considered the opening up of markets within the province; the national authorities, on the other, saw railways as an instrument for welding their factious and scattered territories together, and also of providing a viable link with the outside world that would circumvent the port and Customs House of Buenos Aires. In this fashion two railways were conceived; the *Oeste* in the province of Buenos Aires, and the Central Argentine, which was to link the Confederation port of Rosario with Córdoba, Tucumán and beyond.

The First Railways
Within weeks of the fall of Rosas, railway projects were under active consideration in Buenos Aires.[9] A plethora of schemes followed during the remaining years of the decade as the recently-installed 'liberal' oligarchy sought to give substance to long-cherished development programmes. The first concession for the *FC Oeste* was awarded in January, 1854.[10] Later the same year the government of the Argentine Confederation authorized an agent, José Buschental, to contract in Europe for the construction of the anticipated preliminary stage, from Rosario to Cór-

doba, of a trunk line to the north-west: the original Central concession was issued in 1855.[11] Further concessions were awarded in Buenos Aires two years later — for the Buenos Ayres and San Fernando Railway Company Limited (later renamed the Buenos Ayres Northern Railway Company Limited) and the Ensenada Port Railway Company Limited, initially known as the Boca Railway.[12] These schemes were not immediately successful: continuing political instability and unrealistic assumptions regarding the costing of railway construction meant that original optimism as to the ease of financing railway development was confounded. The *Oeste*, despite the amenable topography of the province, failed to gain adequate access to local private capital. After the first flush of success in obtaining a franchise, entrepreneurs connected with the project began to doubt their early enthusiasm. Initial forecasts of profitability were revised to such an extent that the company successfully applied for a revision of the concession to enable horses to be employed instead of steam locomotives as originally specified: horses were a cheap local commodity while coal was so expensive.[13]

From its inception the *FCO* relied heavily upon government aid. Although the original stock issue had been readily taken up, subsequent calls for capital were answered less enthusiastically. Consequently, before the line became operational the company had to make further demands on the provincial government. In the first instance, by the Law of 20 August 1857, the Governor was empowered to invest up to $4,000,000 *moneda corriente* in the line: this was additional to the $1,330,000 m/c which the provincial authorities had already subscribed to the *Oeste*'s original capital of $6,900,000 m/c.[14] Yet the province was soon called upon to provide further funds as the company extended its network. A year later the provincial congress authorized the local exchequer to disburse up to $6,000,000 m/c in favour of the company.[15] Thus the railway struggled to survive, becoming increasingly dependent upon official financing. When, in 1861, the main line reached Moreno and the provincial government pressed for continued extension of the network, private interests availed themselves of the opportunity to bow out of the enterprise. It was a logical consequence of the increasing reluctance of private capitalists to commit further funds to the line and the large stake already held by the provincial authorities. Nationalization was effected by the Law of 26 December 1862: the province paid $20,000,000 for stock remaining in private hands.[16]

If the saga of the early history of the *FCO* was not encouraging, events in the Confederation were even less auspicious for the prospect of railway development in Argentina. Unlike the Buenos Aires provincial authorities, the national government was unable to accord its line any financial aid. The only negotiable asset possessed by the Confederation was land, which was offered as an inducement to stimulate investment in the Central. The original concession awarded the railway company, in addition to its right-of-way, a grant of half a league of land on both sides of the track for virtually the whole length of the route from Rosario to Córdoba. Despite this seemingly generous provision, Buschental's scheme aroused little interest in Europe.[17] The project was undoubtedly under-capitalized at £1,000,000, or approximately £4,000 per mile; a fact of which the line's promoters appeared entirely oblivious.[18] Such estimates were greeted with scepticism by European financiers and prospective investors, in whose experience — land grants notwithstanding — railway construction had proved substantially more costly. Although the actual cost of railway construction in Argentina has been hotly contested[19] this figure is out of line with contemporary estimates for other areas of recent settlement and bears little resemblance to the historic cost of railway building in more advanced economies as was demonstrated in official statistics published by the Argentine Railway Board.[20] Several adjustments were made to the original concession during subsequent years, but the most significant was that which occurred in 1862 when the government agreed to guarantee investors a return of 7 per cent per annum on capital placed in the company which was written up to £6,000 per mile.[21] Both of these amendments were critical, particularly the former.

Subsequently a guaranteed return upon investment was to become a feature common to all Argentine railway concessions successfully floated during the ensuing decades. The guarantee, however, was not an outright grant. It was rather a promise to subscribers that the state would ensure a reasonable return upon their investments. The guarantee usually offered by Argentine authorities — national and provincial — was 7 per cent per annum upon a fixed sum calculated at a specified cost of construction per mile, the recognized capital, as inscribed in a company's concession. It was not the intention of the state to subsidize inefficient or otherwise unprofitable concerns. The guarantee was envisaged as a means of attracting and safeguarding investment until an enterprise was capable of proving its profit-earning potential. Moreover, the state not only established a limit on the maximum guarantee allowed but, in addition, provided for repayment by the company of previous advances when earnings achieved a mutually agreed level.

Thus the guarantee may be seen as a major development in the course of Argentine railway history. As the provincial government of Buenos Aires had discovered, attempts to stimulate interest in railway projects could only be expected to bear fruit if the state was prepared to make some financial provisions. The creation of the guarantee system was little more than the realization of this fact. It was an attempt to establish on a formal basis the hitherto *ad hoc* allocation of state funds required to sustain the pace of railway expansion. The guarantee system, as instituted during the early 1860s, was an inevitable response evolved in the face of difficulties experienced by the provincial authorities of Buenos Aires and the government of the Argentine Confederation in the pursuance of their various railway schemes. On the one hand, domestic capital had manifested little real commitment to railway development; on the other, foreign interests had expressed serious reservations regarding the feasibility of railway projects in Argentina as initially costed and promoted.

The implementation of the guarantee system may be interpreted as a recognition on the part of Argentine ruling groups that they were competing for funds in an international market and as such had to apply incentives similar to those being granted by other countries which, lacking sufficient domestic funds to promote social overhead capital projects, had recourse to the world capital market. The experience of countries such as Russia, Brazil, India, and a number of European states indicated that, given the vast sums needed and the long gestation period required in such economies before railways could be expected to yield a reasonable remuneration, foreign investment might be procured only within narrowly-circumscribed conditions.[22] Basically there were two alternatives, though some variation was possible in terms of detail; either a state could obtain funds for the undertaking of such projects and itself bear directly the cost of servicing and amortizing the debts incurred, or private participation might be encouraged by minimizing the risk to be borne, in the first instance, by private capitalists. A guarantee could be offered in the expectation that while the initial charge upon the state might be substantial (as large or possibly larger than that associated with direct borrowing), the sums that it would be required to disburse over time would be dramatically less as railways gradually acquired the ability to meet service and dividend payments from earnings and attract a flow of private finance without further official aid.

The impact of the new guarantee policy may be assessed by a closer examination of the chronology of railway developments in Argentina during the 1860s. Given the insertion of a guarantee clause in the company's concession in 1862, further minor amendments were made in 1863 to provide the Central with an increased land grant. One league of territory on either side of the track was awarded to the company, excepting the terminal cities of Rosario and Córdoba where for four leagues out of each city free land would be granted to the company sufficient only for the requirements of the permanent way. In addition, the land grant would not apply for one league on either side of the towns of San Gerónimo (Frayle Muerto) and Villa Nueva; in each case the company would be provided with only enough state land for the permanent way itself. Nevertheless, despite these exclusions, the company found itself endowed with some 900,000 acres. Also the guarantee of 7 per cent was to be calculated upon a construction cost of £6,400 in place of the previous sum of £6,000 per mile.[23] It was under the terms of this concession, accorded to the North American entrepreneur, William Wheelwright, that the railway was ultimately constructed.

Norberto de la Riestra, sometime Finance Minister of the province of Buenos Aires, considered that the revised Central concession contained all that was necessary to facilitate railway development in Argentina:

> The terms of the concession offer in my opinion all the necessary inducements for foreign capitalists to subscribe to this great undertaking with every prospect of a good return. For the country the benefits of the work will be incalculable, and I sincerely hope that the indefatigable and worthy Mr W.

(Wheelwright) will succeed in soon forming the Company and carrying out his object.[24]

With few modifications the Central concession provided the model for subsequent schemes which were soon to receive congressional approval in recently re-unified Argentina. The only untypical feature of the Central's concession lay in the extensive land grant it was accorded. Other lines were merely provided with sufficient public land to meet the needs of the permanent way, stations, goods sheds, etc. The Central's land grant derived from its peculiar history. The original concession had been drawn up during the period when the province of Buenos Aires had remained outside the Argentine Confederation and when the only inducement which the Confederation government had been able to offer prospective railway concessionists was land.

The situation in Buenos Aires was rather different. There the Buenos Ayres Great Southern Railway Company Limited, soon to emerge as the country's premier line, was projected after the political differences between the province and the Confederation had been temporarily settled on the field of Pavon. It did not share the long gestation period experienced by either the *Oeste* or the Central. The first Great Southern concession was published in 1862.[25] Work on the construction of the line began two years later when President Mitre, who performed the ceremony, declared,

> . . . to turn the first sod of the Great Southern Railway, I feel more pride than in leading on armies to acquire glory on the blood-stained field. How happy I am to have the fortune to inaugurate this railway, where the locomotive with its cheering whistle, will carry hope to the dwellers of the campagna (sic).[26]

Service was commenced the following year when the line was completed from Buenos Aires to Chascomús, some 70 miles.

The conception, formation and flotation of the Great Southern provided a happy contrast to the hesitant beginnings of the *Oeste* and the Central. In part this was due to the fact that the Southern benefited from earlier experiences. By the 1860s the state was convinced of the need to provide viable concessions. Also, the prevailing mood of political stability served to encourage investors, both domestic and foreign. The early years of the company's history were, nonetheless, difficult ones; but its problems were overcome smoothly under the guidance of competent entrepreneurs who never doubted the practicability of their enterprise. Their faith was to be amply rewarded in the years ahead. The major difficulties experienced by the Great Southern during its formative period were personified by William Wheelwright, the driving force behind the Central. Originally it had been anticipated that the Great Southern would be constructed and equipped at a cost of some £700,000, exclusive of the right of way, which was provided free by the provincial government. It was on this basis that the guarantee was advanced at 7 per cent upon a recognized capitalization of £10,000 per mile. Accordingly, the BAGS signed a contract with Messrs Peto and Betts who agreed to construct the line for £651,000.[27] However, it soon transpired that the company had been over optimistic in its original, apparently generous, costing. Consequently, the Great Southern attempted to persuade the provincial government to increase the recognized capital upon which the guarantee would be paid to £750,000. The prospect of such a course of action was not viewed with equanimity by the local authorities. At £10,000 per mile the Great Southern was already the most heavily capitalized line in the country. Moreover, it was at this juncture that the provincial government was negotiating the purchase of the *FCO*. Clearly, the province did not wish to commit itself further. At this stage Wheelwright intervened.

While negotiations with the Southern were pending, Wheelwright had been approached by the Buenos Aires government as to the possibility of constructing the line to Chascomús at a cheaper rate than that which had been agreed with the Great Southern. He was already engaged upon the Central project (which at that stage was costed at some £6,000 per mile) and in addition had acquired from the Buenos Aires authorities the Boca concession which carried no guarantee. Wheelwright rebutted this approach, but not in such a manner as would preclude future contacts, pointing out that he was dependent upon interests associated with the Great Southern for financial support for his own line. He refused to give the provincial authorities any firm undertaking, but intimated that, should the current Great Southern scheme fall through, he would have no difficulty in taking over the Chascomús concession. Whatever Wheelwright's intention, the provincial government undoubtedly gained the impression that it was possible to construct the Great Southern Railway at a much cheaper rate than that proposed by the Great Southern group and probably that Wheelwright himself would prove amenable, provided his position was not compromised.[28]

Wheelwright constituted a double threat to the Great Southern consortium. His action had not only endangered their concession, the ratification of which had been postponed by the provincial governor, but, in acquiring the Boca concession, he had invaded the Southern's zone. Commenting on Wheelwright's activities respecting the Boca line, David Robertson, chairman of the Great Southern, stated that 'it was a great shame and most improper on the part of Mr Wheelwright to interfere about it.'[29] By mid 1863 the Great Southern found itself in a most precarious position. Initial estimates having transpired to be unreliable, the company's request to the provincial authorities for a more generous guarantee was frustrated by the activities of Wheelwright — which had persuaded the Buenos Aires government of the implausible, or even unscrupulous, nature of the Great Southern's appeal for assistance. The gravity of the situation was expressed by Riestra who wrote to Robertson: 'About our Southern railway I have nothing favourable to report — I fear as I mentioned in my last (letter) that this important undertaking will prove a failure.'[30] Throughout, Wheelwright seems to have behaved foolishly, if not worse, and deserving of the epithet 'grasping selfish Yankee' bestowed upon him by Robertson. It appeared, with regard to the Central Argentine, that Wheelwright wished to be both concessionaire and contractor: a questionable procedure to say the least.[31] This behaviour proved to be disastrous for Wheelwright's ambitions. By his actions he had alienated those very interests who had been most likely to support him. His meddling over the Boca concession and the role he had cast for himself as the contractor of the Central occasioned first hesitation and subsequently the withdrawal of Baring Brothers from the Central project. Without such financial patronage Wheelwright's grandiose plans collapsed and he was relegated to a minor position in subsequent railway developments.[32]

Upon Wheelwright's enforced withdrawal from the affair, the question of the ratification of the Great Southern franchise was quickly settled. The provincial government agreed to certain alterations in the concession.[33] A compromise was effected regarding the guarantee. The provincial authorities agreed to extend the cover for the whole capital of £750,000, but a consortium of prominent, local Buenos Aires businessmen would subscribe a sub-guarantee to cover £50,000 of the line's total capitalization. They were to reimburse the province should it ever be called upon to pay a full 7 per cent guarantee upon the £750,000.[34] The sub-guarantors, however, were not required to make such a sacrifice; the contractors agreed to accept £50,000 of deferred stock as part payment for their work. This stock would not be serviced until the requirements of the other shareholders had been met in full.[35] Ultimately, this special stock was repurchased from the contractors for £22,615.[36]

In the final instance the total capital of the Great Southern reached £800,000. These additional sums were required to cover unforeseen costs of certain land purchases, the provision of extra rolling stock and the construction of extra stations and goods depots.[37] But the provincial authorities were never called upon to pay a guarantee above the original estimate, that is £49,000. Its main line apparently highly capitalized, the Great Southern soon proved itself to be one of the most profitable Argentine railway companies. It quickly abandoned its guarantee and by its example indicated the advantages likely to accrue to the country once the state was prepared to frame a realistic concession. Despite its early difficulties the line grew in strength and prosperity, and soon realized the prophecies of its chairman that it was capable of yielding a return of from 10 to 15 per cent.[38] By 1868 the company was already earning over 7 per cent on its capital; the following year some 11 per cent.[39] Within four years of its inauguration the Great Southern's receipts were sufficient to remove the company from dependence upon the government guarantee. Even at this early stage in the company's history its ordinary shares were quoted on the London Stock Exchange at between 15 and 20 per cent above par.

Consequently the company entered into discussions with the Buenos Aires government for the cancellation of the guarantee clauses in its concession. By the Law of 28 October 1869, the provincial congress empowered the local authorities so to negotiate.[40] A final agreement was signed on 13 January 1870. The company was released from its obligations to repay advances which had been made under the guarantee agreement during the years 1866 and 1867, a sum of £34,000. Also, the company was to receive from the province £10,000 representing the arrears of the guarantee for 1867 and 1868. Furthermore, the provincial government was to grant the company a subvention of £500 per mile for extensions which were constructed with provincial approval.[41] Thus the Great Southern became the first railway company in South America to pay a minimum guaranteed dividend upon its capital without recourse to the state. This happy situation was attributed to the 'attention and scrutiny' which the directors applied to the costs of construction; to the close watch which had been kept on expenses; and the policy of encouraging traffic which had been pursued since the opening of the line.[42]

But not all companies were as fortunate as the Great Southern. Work had commenced upon the Central in 1863, and the easy terrain — 'indeed the ground is almost *naturally* ready to receive rails without preparation' [43] — promised rapid completion. But this was not to be the case. Wheelwright's difficulties in raising capital brought about a hiatus in construction and work did not resume until 1865. Subsequently the laying of the main line proceeded fitfully; only after several postponements of the completion date did the railway finally reach Córdoba. Service was inaugurated on 18 May 1870, in the presence of the local bishop who blessed the locomotive *Wheelwright*.[44]

Meanwhile, in Buenos Aires, the early history of a number of smaller lines was even less auspicious. A brief enquiry into the affairs of the Buenos Ayres and San Fernando will illustrate some of the hazards which faced the railway pioneer. In 1860 the company applied to the London Stock Exchange for the quotation of its shares.[45] Hardly had approval been granted when dealings in the railway's scrip were suspended. It transpired that there had been a great deal of speculation and some of the dealers had oversold; the city editor of *The Times* was reputed to be supporting a plot to discredit the company.[46] Nevertheless, work on the line commenced on 25 February 1862; the company was reorganized and renamed the Buenos Ayres Northern (sometimes known as the Northern of Buenos Aires) in an attempt to minimize odium associated with the old Fernando concern; a new concession was obtained and the capital increased.[47] For a brief span all progressed smoothly. The line was inaugurated on 1

December 1862 by President Mitre, who travelled on a special train along the five miles of completed track from Buenos Aires to Alsina station.[48] The company's future appeared assured when, at the end of the first six months' working of the completed section, revenue was such that the railway was able to declare a dividend without recourse to the government guarantee.[49] Yet this was a false dawn. Soon the company found itself in serious financial difficulties which were attributed, by a shareholders' committee of investigation, to bad management and dubious financial operations on the part of the contractor. The committee called upon the shareholders to withdraw their support from the board of directors.[50] 'This once promising undertaking,' thundered the *Railway Times*, 'is in a condition as low and lamentable as may well be conceived . . .', a view which found support in other sections of the press.[51] The chairman was called a swindler, and company meetings began to receive the unwelcome attention of journalists who reported proceedings in depth.[52] Undoubtedly the financial basis of the entity was deplorable: the original capital of £60,000 had been 'watered' by the addition of some £150,000 new issues.[53] The directors were said to have falsified the accounts they were required to submit to the provincial government of Buenos Aires in order to obtain payment of the guarantee.[54] By the time the line had reached Tigre, 18 miles from Buenos Aires, the company was capitalized at a rate of £16,500 per mile.[55] In view of this outrageous behaviour the Buenos Aires provincial government withdrew its guarantee until such time as the company should be reduced to good order.[56]

The Early Investors
Given the rather hazardous nature of early railway development in Argentina, it is not surprising that foreign investors did not show an immediate interest in the scrip of these enterprises. During the initial period of their development the railway companies were financed largely by merchants and landowners (often British) who had already acquired an interest in the development of the region. Also, in most cases, as has been seen, there was a reliance upon a degree of state support, either in the shape of a guarantee or direct government investment. The *Oeste*, although nominally an Argentine enterprise, provides an interesting case study. The concession was awarded to several promi-

nent local merchants: Jaime Lavellol, Mariano Miro, Manuel de Guerrico, Bernardo Larroude, Norberto de la Riestra, Adolfo van Praet and Daniel Gowland.[57] Gowland was president of the local British chamber of commerce. The line itself was constructed by a British contractor, William Bragge, with 160 British navvies.[58] As has been related above, from the first the company depended heavily on substantial state investment, and was ultimately purchased by the province. A similar example is presented by the Central Argentine. Upon the issue of the initial capital — some £1,000,000 in 50,000 £20 shares — the Argentine government purchased 2,000 shares and General José de Urquiza, President of the Argentine Confederation, took an additional 1,000.[59] Ultimately, a further 10,000 shares were placed locally.[60] But direct government investment did not end here. By 1867 the proceeds of the first share flotation had been expended and a further scrip issue became necessary. Unfortunately such action was deemed inexpedient in view of the tightness prevailing on the London money market after the failure of Overend Gurney and Company the previous year.[61] This *impasse* was circumvented when the Argentine government and the railway contractors, Messrs Brassey, Wythes and Wheelwright, each agreed to take up £300,000 of the outstanding balance of the railway's authorized, original capital. Thus the initial capital of the line stood at £1,600,000 of which the Argentine government had subscribed to 17,000 shares.[62] The state was to effect the purchase of the 15,000 new shares by supplying the company with £200,000 6 per cent government bonds and delivering £150,000 cash in monthly instalments of £10,000 to be raised from customs receipts.[63] The contractors' subscription was later converted into £30,500 debenture stock.[64] Subsequently the government was able to utilize its extensive shareholding in the Central as collateral for short-term borrowing.[65]

Apart from a heavy reliance upon the state, the Central was also closely connected with Anglo-Argentine mercantile interests, as may be seen from an examination of the beneficiaries of the Central's extensive land grant. The schedule of railway land sales contains the name of virtually every prominent British family connected with the River Plate; Armstrong, Banfield, Barkley, Bell, Blyth, Brandt, Campbell, Dick, Gowland, Hall, Hope, Kingscate, Lafone, Laurie, Miller, Seward, Shaw, Talbot,

Thomas, Towers, Trotter and Tudor.[66] Gowland, as already mentioned, was a prominent member of the British merchant colony, and connected with the *Oeste*. Thomas Armstrong, who also held a quarter share in the original BAGS concession, was currently the Central's local agent in the Argentine. He had taken a large number of shares in the company, but was more interested in the development of his estates near Rosario which would be opened up with the coming of the railway: 'I am going to derive a great benefit by the Undertaking if carried out. Consequently I work with pleasure in the Affair without aspiring to any emolument.'[67] And, also representative of the nature of British involvement in Argentine railway promotion at this juncture, it should be observed that a member of the House of Barings had originally been nominated to serve as chairman of the Central Argentine's board of directors.[68] Indeed, Wheelwright himself realized that it was in this direction that he would have to turn to obtain backing for his scheme.

However, it is the Great Southern which provides the typical illustration of early British interest in Argentine railway affairs. The case of John Fair, the Southern's local agent, is particularly noteworthy as epitomizing this connection. At the time of the flotation of the company he was Buenos Aires' consul in London. His family possessed many and varied interests in land, sheep and cattle in the River Plate.[69] From the start he had a significant participation in the venture, owning some 500 Southern shares.[70] Later he would become engaged with other companies, besides rising to the London board of the BAGS. Fair's case was not unique. Like Fair, the group which came to the aid of the company during its early difficulties, and joined together to provide the sub-guarantee, had extensive, non-railway interests. All had much to gain from the stimulus to domestic economic activities associated with railway construction. Prominent Anglo-Argentine family names feature among the sub-guarantors: Thomas Armstrong, George Drabble, Frederick Elortando, John Fair, Henry Green, Henry Horratt, Gregorio Lezama, A.P. Lezica and Edward Lumb.[71] In the case of the Great Southern this point is further reinforced by an examination of the individuals who composed the company's London board.[72] By the mid-1860s shareholders who held 200 shares might stand for election to the board, yet most of the London directors were substantial shareholders in the company and, moreover, possessed extensive interests in Argentina.[73] The company's increasing prosperity was often attributed to this intimate connection between the directors and Buenos Aires, and their special knowledge of local affairs.

These, then, were the principal capitalists associated with Argentine railway development. Thomas Armstrong spoke not merely for himself, but also for his peers when he maintained that his motive in promoting railways was to benefit wider interests. The archetypal large-scale investor was a merchant or landowner, domestic or foreign, with extensive commitments in Argentina.[74] He tended not to limit his interests to any one particular company, but sought to encourage railway development in general. Armstrong, as we have seen, was connected with both the Central and the Great Southern. Similarly Daniel Gowland was associated with the Central Argentine and the *Oeste*. David Robertson, charter chairman of the BAGS, had been prepared to support the Central in its quest for British capital because it was an 'all important matter for Buenos Ayres (i.e. Argentina)'.[75]

Nothing characterizes more precisely the initial reasoning behind early Argentine railway development. Railway investment was seen not as an end in itself but rather as a means of stimulating the local economy and opening up markets — a process that would benefit investors' primary activities. It was only after this formative period, when the various railway companies had proved themselves viable, profitable concerns, that they became vehicles for large-scale 'foreign' investment; only subsequently would British savers look to Argentine railway stocks, especially debentures, as means of providing a secure and remunerative return on their own account. Due to the hazards of these years, when Indians still attacked the trains, when rumours of chicanery were rife, and zones underdeveloped, who can blame the foreign investor for demonstrating a lack of interest in railway companies so far from home? Indeed, these very facts explain the paramountcy of mercantile and land-holding interests, and the nature of railway financing. Such local interests had the ear of government which provided the partial financing and lines of credit so vital to all the early companies. It would be difficult to overestimate the significance of benevolent government intentions during the early 1860s; in addition to providing the essential guarantees (which might later serve to attract capital from a wider spectrum of investors) the state could also be relied upon to supply direct financing when other sources proved unwilling or unable to do so.

Initial Achievements
The immediate impact of the railway age upon Argentina was not necessarily that which had been anticipated. Undoubtedly the coming of the railways performed an important political function, serving to unify the country — considerations which, as we have seen, had from the first been advanced as sufficient justification for generous state aid to the companies.[76] Assumptions regarding politics and strategy had certainly played their part in the formation of the Central Argentine, and lay behind several extensions to the Southern network.[77] In 1874 railways facilitated the easy suppression of one of the periodic revolts to which the country was still subject: at a critical juncture some 2,600 troops and their supplies were transported from Rosario to Córdoba in a day, ensuring Colonel Roca's victory over rebel forces.[78] As travelling times were reduced, so centres of population were brought into closer contact with each other. Journeys which had previously taken months could be accomplished in as many days. Where it had required one month to journey from Rosario to Córdoba by bullock cart, only 15 hours were spent on the rail journey.[79] When the *Oeste* reached Moreno, 25 miles from the city of Buenos Aires, a diligence service was organized to join the capital with most major towns in the province.[80] The Buenos Ayres Northern inauguration express covered the 19 miles from the city of Buenos Aires to Tigre in 29½ minutes.[81] The regular service from Buenos Aires to Chascomús was accomplished by crack trains which covered the 70 miles in an unprecedented four hours.[82]

Freight rates, however, did not always register a correspondingly significant reduction. Passenger fares of £3 first class and 32 shillings second class for the trip from Rosario to Córdoba were thought to be 'high for the country', even allowing a 25 per cent reduction on return journeys.[83] At a time when the diligence service between Buenos Aires and San Fernando cost six shillings during the summer and ten shillings in the winter, the Buenos

Ayres and San Fernando considered that the market would bear a passenger tariff of three shillings for the trip between its termini. The company estimated that such a tariff would yield profits of between 12 and 15 per cent.[84] But, as we have seen, the San Fernando did not immediately achieve this ideal position of profitability. The *FCO* and the Great Southern levied charges of a similar order.[85] Although comparisons are difficult to establish, given changes in currency values and distinct fare structures based upon the differing traffic flows, it appears that the standard charge for second-class passengers ranged from approximately a penny halfpenny to twopence (current prices) per mile during the mid-1860s; second-class fares were normally two-thirds the first-class tarriff. Such rates were indeed 'high for the country', and compare unfavourably with charges levied by companies operating in Britain. The data is even more confused regarding goods freights. Although a recent work has stated that the coming of the railways permitted commodities to be moved for one-twelfth of the charges demanded by the carters,[86] contemporaries state that the cost of conveying merchandise by bullock cart was approximately 20 to 36 shillings per cart for a two to three month journey and that rail freights of one penny per ton/mile did not work out significantly cheaper over long distances, despite the saving in time.[87] At this stage, few companies were prepared to levy obviously developmental freights (though there were a limited number of exceptions), despite the interests of some shareholders. Cautious estimates of the traffic-generating capacity of the zones through which they passed, coupled with the need to service capital abroad, tended to encourage high freights. The nature of much of the traffic which, though bulky, did not necessarily require speedy transportation and the indexing of tariffs to the gold premium also explain the prevailing structure of rail freights. Early attempts by the BAGS to apply developmental rates provide an interesting case-study.

The Southern had been constructed in the most populous region of the province of Buenos Aires. In 1870 it had been estimated that approximately half a million inhabitants resided in the province. Of that number, 177,000 lived in the city of Buenos Aires itself, some 73,000 in the north of the province, and 105,000 in the west. Within the BAGS zone were to be found some 137,000 inhabitants. In addition, the company's extensions were being constructed to the larger towns of the region: established, thriving urban centres were a major feature of the Southern network — Carmen de las Flores, Dolores and Azul, each with over 7,000 inhabitants; Tandil, a community of almost 5,000.[88] It was anticipated that these urban areas would generate traffic and prosperity for the company. With great confidence the directors held before the shareholders the prospect of growing profits as the line became the main carrier in the southern region of the province. During the first six months of 1866 the railway shipped only 13 per cent of merchandise entering the southern market of the city of Buenos Aires: a year later the company's share had risen to 28.8 per cent for the same period. Forecasting the rapid demise of bullock cart competition, the company increased its rolling stock park.[89]

Table 1: Volume of produce entering the southern market of Buenos Aires

	Shipped on BAGS (%)	Shipped by bullock cart (%)
1866	26.54	73.46
1867	34.26	65.74
1868	44.00	56.00
1869	56.00	44.00

Source: Buenos Ayres Great Southern Railway Company Limited, Report of the Directors to the Shareholders and Statement of the Revenue and Capital accounts for the year ended December 31, 1869 (hereafter Annual Report . . .) (London 1870).

Gradually the railway's traffic increased until, in 1869, the line was carrying over half of the volume of produce entering the southern market of Buenos Aires. Yet, while the proportion of the traffic carried by the railway rose, the actual volume of goods shipped by cart did not fall. The expansion of economic activity in the province allowed the carts to hold their own, and maintain an effective competition with the railway. The major problem experienced by the Great Southern arose from the fact that much of the trade to and from the city of Buenos Aires originated south-west of the Río Salado. The company's railhead was situated on the opposite bank of the river. Having reached the river by cart, the tendency was for goods to proceed on to Buenos Aires in this fashion, rather than incur the additional costs involved in transferring from cart to railway wagon once the river had been forded. It was anticipated that when the railway bridged the river which, during the wet season, was impassable to carts for months on end, the Southern would be able to tap the rich districts of the south and west.

The long-projected bridge was opened in 1873, but despite this incentive, the company nevertheless felt it necessary further to encourage traffic by reducing tariffs.[90] This tactic was successful and the following year the company recorded a marked increase in the volume and revenue accruing from every item of traffic.[91] But despite the apparent advantages of rail transport, carters maintained an active competition with the line, particularly when exceptional circumstances prevailed. For instance, in 1877 the world trade depression severely strained the Argentine economy, causing the depreciation of the paper currency. In order to counter the effects of exchange losses arising from the fall in the value of the *peso*, and also to maintain revenue in the face of declining traffic, the Great Southern increased its tariffs.[92] This action was considered most ill-advised by Nicolas Bouwer, Baring Brothers' representative in Buenos Aires. He felt that the 10 per cent tariff surcharge was 'injudicious for the very reason that the competition of bullock carts is thereby likely to be successful'.[93] Even more instructive was another developmental exercise undertaken by the BAGS. The company had gone to considerable lengths, and no little expense, to encourage cattle traffic. Special padded wagons had been ordered to prevent animals suffering injury, and a corresponding loss of value, in transit. English *estancieros* were prevailed upon to ship their animals by rail. All the hopes of the company were vindicated; cattle arrived at the market in a much better condition than those making the journey on the hoof; their weight was heavier and they were generally fresher. Yet buyers refused to pay higher prices for these animals than those offered for cattle which had suffered an exhausting and debilitating trek to market. So long as animals continued to be slaughtered primarily for their hides, the condition in which they reached the yards was largely immaterial. The cost of shipping an animal by rail was $38 paper per head; by road the cost was only $9 a head, even after allowing for the loss of the services of the *peones* required to herd animals on route. Little wonder *estancieros* preferred to despatch cattle on the hoof.[94]

Cart competition was a hazard which tormented most of the

early British-owned companies. Not even the Central, with its long hauls, was immune.[95] It was a disagreeable experience which was not finally overcome until trade had increased, or was capable of an increase, sufficient to permit an off-setting rise in aggregate income consequent upon a reduction in tariffs. The *Oeste*, whose *raison d'être* differed from that of the foreign-owned lines, consistently levied more 'moderate' freights and had little to fear from the carts.[96] But it had failed to attract private capital: the nominally lower tariffs applied by the provincial *FCO* may be represented as a state subsidy to consumers. Bullock carts, however, were not so much a threat to railway development as an indication of the unsophisticated nature of the market. While trade was carried on at the old, slow, leisurely pace, while quality control remained rudimentary, and as long as the level of economic activity remained 'colonial', there was little gain for railway companies in the application of cheap rates. Until the local market had expanded, or Argentina had been more fully incorporated within the international economy, the railways could not be expected to perform a more developmental function, even if the companies were themselves part of that process. While Argentina remained a net exporter of bullion, the early lines were essentially small concerns serving limited, regional requirements. Not until exogenous changes liberated world demand for temperate-zone rural products would railway construction enable Argentina to become a major international supplier of arable and pastoral commodities, or the foreign-owned railways become powerful, prosperous entities. Only then were they able to rely upon the British capital market for financing and, by the example of proven profitability, able to call forth those vast sums of investment which would be employed in the further development of the country.

The hesitant beginnings of railway development notwithstanding, it would be wrong to infer that the first lines had *no* influence upon the pattern of commercial activity. As early as 1864 the construction of the Central Argentine exerted an impact upon the trade of Rosario, the starting point of the railway. During the course of that year some 29 foreign vessels entered the port, 17 carrying supplies for the railway. Buenos Aires also witnessed an increase in mercantile activities directly related to the importation of railway supplies.[97] Three years later 52 vessels arrived at

Rosario with material for the Central totalling 20,382 tons.[98] These were small beginnings associated with the actual building of the lines, but their significance ought not to be underestimated for the pace of construction often served to carry a regional economy through minor trade depressions. In the late 1870s, when the influences of the 'Great Depression' of 1873 reached the River Plate, railway building remained a buoyant element in the domestic economy: a counter-cyclical factor of some significance in the regional market. British merchants would have derived much comfort from Consul Joel's report upon trade conditions in 1874 which recorded that the volume of shipping entering Rosario was nearly double the level of the previous year, representing a 49 per cent increase in tonnage.

> This very large augmentation of British trade has been almost entirely confined to materials for the railway in construction from Cordova to Tucuman, and from Rio Cuarto to Villa Mercedes, the work on both lines being actively pushed forward.[99]

If importance may be attributed to the role of railway construction as a local economic regulator, the influence of the lines as operational concerns would also appear to be focussed predominantly towards the domestic sector. Although registered in London, most companies at this juncture placed as much stress upon the earning potential of the local market as upon the prospects of an expanding external trade. While there had been a steady increase in Argentine foreign commerce during the first decades of the railway age — the value of exports cleared through Buenos Aires had risen from £1,398,154 in 1853 to £4,238,968 in 1860, and to £7,858,938 ten years later[100] — it would be difficult to ascribe this growth directly or exclusively to the railways. Indeed, for the British-owned lines themselves, the diversification of traffic produced by endogenous expansion was more remarkable. In 1868, Great Southern shareholders were specifically informed that the company had stimulated locally-orientated developments; emphasis was laid upon qualitative changes in the revenue account far removed from the requirements of foreign commerce.[101] Slack trade in exportables contrasted markedly with the buoyancy of passenger traffic (encouraged by something of a building boom) and the recently- inaugurated shipments of grain consigned for domestic consumption. The Central was similarly anxious to promote agricultural activities and capitalize upon its extensive land grant. Colonies were established at Bernstadt, Carcañal and Cañada de Gomez. By 1874 these settlements were valued respectively at £84,000, £111,000 and £23,500, with populations of 1,684, 386 and 319.[102] All this while Argentina's export trade remained largely confined to pastoral commodities.

Table 2: *Principal Argentine exports: relative composition, by value*

	1853 (%)	1860 (%)	1870 (%)
Hides – Cow, salted	17.50	18.00	11.00
Cow, dried	25.00	35.00	23.00
Horse	2.50	3.50	0.50
Tallow	23.00	6.00	25.00
Wool	17.50	18.00	28.50
Fleeces	1.00	3.50	9.75
Jerked beef	1.50	1.00	0.50
Various	12.00	15.00	1.75
	100.00	100.00	100.00

Source: *The Brazil and River Plate Mail* (hereafter *B&RPM*) 22 March 1871, VIII, 6.

As Table 2 indicates, the bulk of Argentina's exports derived from animal products, yet the railways were most closely interested in the stimulation of newer, agricultural enterprises. At this early stage the companies were, as we have seen, unsuccessful in their efforts to penetrate the commercial infrastructure supporting the pastoral industry. The possible exception was wool, the 'new' pastoral commodity which was the main point of expansion during the period, and was developing in the Southern's zone.[103] As early as 1868 the BAGS was shipping quantities of wool which, along with 'animal hair', was the largest single category in the company's earning schedule.[104] But it would be wrong to infer that the company actively encouraged this new line of traffic: wool paid one of the highest tariffs. With regard to more traditional items, markets were small and producers had little to gain by speedier means of communication, or systems of transport capable of shipping goods in a manner that entailed little deterioration in quality: the market would not bear a premium.

The Second Wave: Direct State Participation
Following the establishment of the early railway companies, there occurred a period of consolidation that witnessed few new developments. If the principal difficulties associated with the initial phase of Argentine railway history may be characterized as essentially 'political' — concerning the negotiation of concessions and terms of operation that were mutually acceptable to the local elite and foreign interests, the subsequent era may be interpreted as a period of 'economic' problems — issues related to a capital famine, and the desire of local interests to see the rapid extension of the country's railway network as against the caution of foreign groups loath to commit further funds to this end and unable to attract capital from a broader base until the original lines had demonstrated a capacity to earn a reasonable return upon sums already invested. Yet, in spite of the prevailing situation, the several companies already manifested a variation in approach to these problems which was largely determined by the nature and soundness of initial financing and construction. There were indications of widely differing attitudes to fundamental questions of development, to diverse views concerning the most effective means of establishing companies as profitable enterprises, and, not least, to the capacity of the railways to forego dependence upon the government guarantee. And the most striking feature of the immediate, post-formative period was the extent to which the state continued to play an important part — both directly and indirectly — in the consolidation and expansion of the system.

During the 1860s the *Oeste* network grew until it became the most extensive system in Buenos Aires. The provincial government actively pursued an expansionist policy, pushing the line westward across the *pampas*. By September 1866 the railhead reached Chivilcoy. To commemorate the inauguration of a through service to the west, the authorities caused a medal to be struck bearing the inscription 'Western Railway to Chivilcoy, 100 miles, constructed entirely by native resources', a plausible sentiment (which has subsequently been elaborated by Argentine polemicists), if not strictly correct.[105] But although the provincial government was responsible for maintaining the pace of railway construction during the 1860s, the central government signalled the beginning of a new phase of expansion at the end of the decade.

In 1869 the national authorities came to the aid of the *Primero Entrerriano*. It was a small, locally-financed line which had been formed in 1864 to link the town of Gualeguay with its riverine port, Puerto Ruiz, some six miles away. Capitalized at £20,000, it was ineffectively financed and badly constructed.[106] Severe flooding destroyed the greater part of the permanent way in 1869 and since private capital was unable, or unwilling, to re-establish the company upon a sound basis, the federal government felt obliged to subsidize the line further. Of the company's original capital, the national government had subscribed £3,000 (or $15,000 *pesos fuertes*). It now undertook to supply a further $187,000 p/f, the estimated cost of making good damage occasioned by inundation. Thus total federal expenditure upon the line reached $202,000 p/f.[107]

This incident heralded the beginning of a period of substantial direct federal government participation in railway development. When the Central Argentine finally reached Córdoba in 1870, it determined to rest upon its laurels: there had been the problem of raising capital to complete the line, while the insistence of the national government that the concern be placed in better working order had left the shareholders in a truculent mood. They had often been informed that their line would be the most profitable in Argentina; before making further disbursements they desired to secure a return upon initial investments. The Central shareholders decided that if further railway construction was to take place in northern Argentina, it would not entail a direct charge upon themselves. By default, this burden fell upon the Argentine government. In November 1870 the national authorities commenced work on the Río Cuarto railway. This line, the first section of which was subsequently known as the Andean Railway, was expected to become an important feeder to the Central. Commencing at Villa Nueva (Villa María), situated roughly halfway along the Central route from Rosario to Córdoba, it was anticipated that the company would build on to Mendoza and San Juan.[108] The first section of the line was completed as far as Río Cuarto, 82 miles from Villa Nueva, and opened to traffic in 1873, reaching Mercedes, some 150 miles west of Villa Nueva, two years later.[109] The Central negotiated an agreement with the state which provided for the joining of track and interchange of traffic at Villa Nueva.[110] But the major national enterprise undertaken at this time was the railway to Tucumán. Running for some 340 miles north-westwards out of Córdoba, the line followed the colonial trade route to Peru and would connect the major cities of the interior with the developing littoral. Contemporary opinion held that this line would not only stimulate the trade of northern Argentina but would also penetrate southern Bolivia: it would be the Argentine equivalent of the great transcontinental routes of North America.[111] In practical terms, however, the tale was a sorry one.

The region from Córodoba to Tucumán was economically stagnant: the coming of the railway would serve only, in the first instance, to destroy the regional economy which survived the loss of colonial markets. With the exception of the terminal cities, the area was sparsely settled; population was already declining in the intermediate districts. Although not difficult, the terrain north of Córdoba was less amenable to railway construction than the *pampa*, gradually giving way to the Andean foothills. Consequently, it was proposed to build a metre-gauge line which would yield a 5 per cent saving on the estimate for constructing a railway to the same broad gauge as the Central. Unfortunately, the original contract provided for an unrealistic costing at £4,500 per mile, or a total capitalization of £1,515,974. In addition, the railway was to be completed within four years.[112] The latter was possibly the only condition complied with; the line was inaugurated in November 1876.[113] Although the zone served by the company was fertile, the trade of the area required several years' assiduous cultivation. But the controversy surrounding the line's gauge only served to inhibit rapid development. Justifiable upon grounds of immediate economy, the decision to construct a metre-gauge line proved a doubtful saving in the long term, especially as the original economy was so small. Generally, it was regarded as 'a most serious blunder'.[114] The additional shipment costs inherent in a break of gauge seriously hindered the development of the region. Also, despite the national government's desire to obtain a low-cost line, the Córdoba-Tucumán contract proved the epitome of unbridled graft and corruption. Indeed, the affair provides an interesting example of the more bizarre business methods employed at the time.[115] Within three years of its opening the line was in need of substantial repair and secret negotiations were entered into with the Central Argentine for the transfer of the Tucumán railway. These negotiations came to nothing.[116] Yet for some time the company remained a white elephant. Maintenance costs were high, and the main beneficiary of the national government's attempts to open up the north-west was the Central itself, which enjoyed the additional revenue yielded by the meagre traffic of the line while not contributing towards its exorbitant running costs.

Undoubtedly, the state's railway building programme was initiated at a most opportune moment for the Central Argentine. The effects of the 'Great Depression' upon the London capital market would have made it extremely difficult for the company to raise the means with which to finance the construction of extensions, even in the unlikely event that the shareholders would have sanctioned such a policy. Witnessing the Great Southern engaged upon an extensive building programme, the Central considered itself fortunate to be in the happy position whereby the national government assumed the entrepreneurial, risk-taking function, but allowed the Central to reap the benefits which accrued from these labours. Almost every extension undertaken by the state represented a bonus for the British shareholders of the Central Argentine. The government bore the cost of construction and the expense of developing new regions, traffic from which flowed inevitably on to the Central. Not for the CA the unpleasant task of subsidizing unremunerative extensions. Secure in its monopoly of communications between the interior and the coast, the Central creamed off the traffic and revenue stimulated by the construction of national railway lines beyond Córdoba. In short, the Central became, for a brief period, the 'San Paulo' of Argentina.[117] Soon the Central Argentine would pay the price of this complacency, but for the moment shareholders merely congratulated themselves on their good fortune.

The Private Response
During this period only two new London-registered entities were formed, the East Argentine Railway Company Limited and the Buenos Ayres and Campana Railway Company Limited. The

East Argentine concession dated from 1864, but effectively the history of the line commences with the transfer of the concession to one Pablo Montravel on 13 August 1869. It was Montravel who, in May 1871, made over the concession to the company, a move that was not officially sanctioned until two years later by the Executive Decree of 10 May 1873.[118] The original concession provided for a 181-mile railway running from Concordia in the province of Entre Rios to Mercedes in the adjoining province of Corrientes. The concession carried the by-now-obligatory guarantee of 7 per cent on a recognized capital of £10,000 per mile. In addition, the franchise stated that the line would be constructed in two sections; the first, some 96 miles from Concordia to Monte Caseros, and the second, a further 85 miles on to Mercedes itself. Three years were allowed for the construction of the first section, but the company could delay building the second until the first part of the line should yield a return of 3½ per cent. The state would provide all land necessary for the right of way, passing loops, stations, etc. The company was to be exempted from all taxes and customs duties for 40 years.[119] Construction commenced in 1872 and the first section to Monte Caseros was opened on 20 April 1875, by President Avellaneda.[120]

The BA & Campana was built in order to facilitate communications between Buenos Aires, Rosario, and the north — a route which the Northern had hoped to exploit. Campana was situated on the River Paraná, and the port was able to handle vessels of up to 40 feet draught. Again, the company obtained a guarantee of 7 per cent upon a capitalization of £8,000 per mile.[121] The earthworks began in October 1872 and public service was inaugurated on 22 Aptil 1876.[122] A year later the company applied for an extension of its concession to continue on to Rosario. In Buenos Aires it was considered that the extension would not be sanctioned. The construction of such a line would inevitably bring the company into conflict with the *FCO* which, although it did not wish to enter Rosario, intended to preserve for itself the rich zone through which a line connecting the cities of Rosario and Buenos Aires would have to pass.[123]

Unlike the Central, some of the established smaller British-owned companies were attempting to pursue an expansionist policy and secure the traffic of their respective zones. The Buenos Ayres and Ensenada Port Railway Company Limited was founded in 1872 to take over the Boca concession obtained earlier by William Wheelwright who had already constructed a fraction of the line.[124] The BA&EP wished to develop Ensenada as the main port of the city of Buenos Aires. Primitive landing facilities at Buenos Aires lent credibility to the project. Indeed, the railway was one of several schemes conceived during the 1870s to improve Buenos Aires' commercial infrastructure. At Ensenada, some 31 miles from the provincial capital, there was a natural harbour capable of taking vessels of up to ten feet draught, while the outer harbour was able to accommodate even larger ships. Approximately a year after the line was opened throughout, Ensenada was declared an official port of entry (*puerto habilitado*) and the prospects of the company improved considerably.[125] Unfortunately, the line did not carry a guarantee. Wheelwright had obtained the concession on the understanding that assistance would not be sought, and on this basis had been granted a revision of the original 1857 concession.[126] Consequently, although work on the line was commenced in 1863, construction was not completed for a further ten years and the contractor found it expedient to offer a private guarantee of 7 per cent until 1875, when it was assumed that operating profits would yield a similar return on investment.[127]

The Northern was less favoured than the Ensenada. The company was never able to shake off the spectre of its unfortunate beginnings. Prospects at least had appeared bright while it retained a monopoly of rail services running northwards out of Buenos Aires and the directors cherished dreams of developing Tigre as a staging post for riverine traffic plying on to Rosario. These illusions were shattered with the coming of the Campana which, running parallel with and to the west of the Northern, effectively circumscribed the latter's zone of influence. Yet the company possessed an extensive and remunerative local traffic serving a region which was to develop into the desirable residential suburban districts of Buenos Aires — Belgrano and San Isidro — and also the delta resorts out to Tigre itself.[128]

Of the private concerns, it was the Great Southern which exhibited the most dynamic and enterprising tendencies. With the abandonment of its guarantee, consideration was devoted to the best means of improving earning capacity. Having constructed to Chascomús, the company witnessed a steady augmentation of traffic during the following years. However, as related above, the threat of competition from bullock carts continued to exercise the BAGS. A policy of strategic construction was viewed as the most effective means of eradicating this menace. Such construction would serve not only as a means of dealing with competition from carters, but might also pre-empt possible future challenges from other railways. Unfortunately, this strategy brought the company into conflict with provincial government. In 1866 the Buenos Aires authorities had requested the railway to push the mainline on to Dolores, a natural prolongation that had been envisaged in the original concession.[129] Such an extension was in accordance with company policy, subsequently articulated at successive general meetings, of building only to established commercial centres, with demonstrable revenue-creating potential. Indeed, at the time when the company was being floated, interests connected with it had argued strongly in favour of such an extension, that 'would increase considerably the profits and value of the shares'.[130] By the end of the decade more complex factors were at work. Although the Great Southern wished to expand its network, and although it was no longer dependent upon the guarantee, the company yet wished to retain some official financial support for its future constructions. Above all, the English line desired to extend its network south-westwards, rather than southwards; the company favoured branch line construction west of Altamirano in place of main line prolongation south of Chascomús. The principal explanation for this situation lay in the general anxiety of Buenos Aires to promote railway construction: while the provincial government was attempting to persuade the Southern to build in the south, the *Oeste* was also being extended. At this juncture, it appeared that the provincially-owned line might engage in southward branch line construction from its main line at Merlo, an extension the BAGS regarded as prejudicial [131] (see Map 3).

The ensuing dispute between the Great Southern and the province gave rise to much acrimony. The company refused to embark upon main line extension, but initiated work on the branch line. The provincial authorities raised the spectre of expropriation and the issue was resolved only with great difficulty. A compromise settlement was achieved whereby the province agreed to sanction both main line prolongation and branch line construction, provided the projects were executed concurrently. In addition, as was ordained with respect to approved extensions, the province would provide a subvention of £500 per mile towards the cost of construction, and it was determined that (in case of such an eventuality) the extensions would be expropriated at the rate of £7,200 per mile.[132] The agreement appears to have met the requirements of both parties. The British company was granted a desirable concession and secured its zone from possible competition. The province obtained the general increase of railway mileage envisaged — in designated areas — and while it was called upon to make some contribution towards this expansion,[133] was able to determine construction costs as effectively as if the railway had still been in receipt of a guarantee; not least, the company acknowledged the province's right to expropriate on certain fixed terms. Building proceeded apace. Despite experiencing some difficulty in obtaining land for the Las Flores section, branch-line construction out of Altamirano progressed rapidly. Earthworks on the second, Azul, section of the branch commenced in 1870 and within two years the line was fully operational as far as Las Flores.[134] Work on the main line extension to Dolores was completed in a further two years, and service inaugurated on 10 November 1874.[135] In order to cope with the anticipated increase in traffic the company augmented its rolling stock park by purchasing a dozen locomotives and some 200 goods vehicles; by 1876 the Southern possessed 33 locomotives, over 100 passenger vehicles and approximately 1,000 goods wagons, cattle trucks, and other vehicles.[136] It was an indication of the financial strength of the company that, having embarked upon this programme of expansion, it was able to carry it to completion at a time when the prevailing international financial and commercial situation was far from favourable and the local economy was still recovering from the effects of the Paraguayan war.

The period to 1880 accordingly saw the onset of the railway age in Argentina, and a gradual but steadily increasing pace of railway development. The first line had been opened in 1857 and by the late 1870s there were ten railways operating, including the provincially-owned entity and the two nationally-constructed extensions of the Central. In 1857 the country possessed seven route miles of railway track, in 1882 there were 1,697. The major part of this increase occurred during and after the early 1870s when the state and some of the privately-owned companies embarked upon a programme of expansion.

Capitalization and the Economies of Scale
Several features emerge from this early phase of railway development concerning the nature of railway financing and geographic location. In spite of economic fluctuations most companies achieved a basic minimum rate of growth. All the lines did not necessarily embark upon expansionist programmes, but even the smaller companies were able to fulfil franchise specifications. Notwithstanding the tightness of the London money market during the mid-1860s, nor the depressing effect of the collapse of prices a decade later, original schemes were completed. Unfavourable local conditions — the unsophisticated nature of the domestic economy, and the repercussions of political instability — prevailing in Argentina hindered rather than discouraged the completion of railway projects initiated during the period prior to the 1880s. After the early phase of railway formation during the late 1850s and early 1860s there occurred a period of expansion and consolidation from the mid-1860s to the late 1870s.

It is difficult to determine a unified theme in railway affairs during the years immediately prior to the 'boom' of the 1880s. Yet the seeds of future development were already discernible, even if the expressions of that development were varied. The Great Southern and the *FCO* provide examples of expansion, though maintained at an uneven pace, throughout the period. Differences in detail apart, these railways displayed an early awareness of the 'zonal concept', that is the necessity of devoting special attention to the potential and requirements of the regions through which they passed. Both were fortunate that their locus of operation was situated in the littoral, particularly in that region which was already demonstrating the most dynamic growth potential — the area immediately adjacent to metropolitan Buenos Aires. As the bases of economic activity in Argentina gravitated towards the 'new' agricultural complex, the BAGS and provincial railway were well placed to participate in, and foster, those developmental impulses.[137] Similar remarks may be attached, though in a limited fashion, to other *bonarenses* concerns such as the Ensenada Port and Campana. The critical difference regarding the Southern and *FCO* was that these companies more perfectly comprehended the nature of the forces at work, and sought to harness them by extension-building. Indeed, notwithstanding the peculiarities of the situation, analogous factors are discernible in the region served by the Central, even if in the latter's case new construction had been undertaken by the national government rather than financed by shareholders. The distinguishing features which marked the BAGS, the *Oeste* and the rail network focussed on the Central was that they were comparatively large, fairly integrated systems situated in regions capable of responding as much to the dynamic potential of the local market as to the pull of the international economy. It was no coincidence that the agricultural colonies established in the province of Santa Fé did not begin to flourish until the coming of the railway when they were able to expand cereal output, displacing imports in the national market.[138] Given more diversified traffic schedules and broader sounder revenue accounts, these three concerns were less inconvenienced by adverse short-term cyclical trends. On the whole, larger companies were more viable than smaller ones. Major railways were also better placed to command the attention of the public treasury, often of vital importance. Perhaps, too, the course of early events implied that Buenos Aires was a more congenial commercial environment in which to operate than other regions of the republic.

Apart from the fortuitous circumstances of geographical situation, one other salient feature may be distinguished during the years of consolidation and expansion concerning the financing of railway construction. Costs of construction were inevitably influential in determining future prosperity, as British shareholders were well aware. Again the Great Southern provides a useful point of reference. Initially it was assumed that the railway could be constructed for £10,000 per mile, but, as we have seen, the total cost of the original concession finally reached £800,000 nominal, or approximately £11,430 per mile. However, as the chairman informed the extraordinary general meeting summoned to consider the question of spiralling costs, it was estimated that subsequent extensions could be constructed for only £6,000 per mile.[139] The main line had been built by professional contractors; the company determined henceforth to construct its own extensions and so maintain a closer control over costs. Equally, the Great Southern decided that future extensions should not be permitted to become a drag upon the profitability of the principal undertaking. Consequently, each extension was financed as a separate entity; new capital only being incorporated with that of the parent company after each branch line had proved its profitability, although it was usually the practice to extend a basic guaranteed income to holders of extension stocks. In the face of the prevailing mood of optimism, the BAGS board soon revised its estimates of the cost of new track; incredulous shareholders were told that such lines could be built for little more than £4,000 per mile. Ere long investors appeared to have written off the more inflated construction costs of the original main line as 'experience'.[140] Such a view was almost justified; the first branch line extension to Las Flores was actually constructed for slightly more than £5,000 per mile.[141] The prolongation of the main line to Dolores ultimately cost rather more than the estimated £450,000, reaching approximately £8,500 per mile.[142] Towards the end of the decade the paid-up capital of the BAGS stood at £2,250,623 and the railway network at 270 route miles, representing an average cost of £8,300 per mile.[143] In the Great Southern, Argentina possessed a railway company which had been soundly and efficiently constructed. It compared favourably with the best in the world.[144] Moreover, it had been built at little expense to the state, notwithstanding the sums advanced by way of the guarantee and subventions.

The Central Argentine's original capitalization, as we have seen, also proved unrealistic, and even the finally agreed £6,400 was barely sufficient to construct the permanent way. Further funds were required to place the line in proper working order. Due to the low figure allowed for construction, only £82,500 had been applied to the erection of station buildings and facilities.[145] The result was squalor and neglect, as may be seen from a contemporary account of the Rosario terminus.

> ... those accustomed to the imposing appearance of railway stations at home will hardly be impressed with the rough and ready wildness of the scene which presents itself here [Rosario]. A few disjointed wooden sheds in an open plain, one side bordering on the river, some carriages and covered

wagons on the rails, at this time constitutes the terminus of a line already carried 158 miles into the interior . . .[146]

Inevitably there were complaints from the national government. Steps were taken to suspend the guarantee, while a private member's bill was introduced into Congress calling for the expropriation of the line, though this course was firmly rejected by the government.[147]

It was only with great difficulty that the directors were able to persuade shareholders of the necessity for raising further capital. In the first instance shareholders agreed to an issue of some £100,000 of debenture stock to cover the cost of station improvements.[148] The figure proved insufficient. More was required and the directors proposed that an additional £300,000 should be raised — the sum required to place the line in proper working order.[149] The shareholders bitterly opposed such a move, fully realizing that should the Argentine government refuse to extend guarantee cover to this extra capital, the effective guarantee would be reduced from 7 to 5½ per cent.[150] It was only after a tremendous battle — and the presentation of an abusive report by a shareholders' committee — that the board ultimately obtained sanction for the issue of the required scrip which was accomplished by bland assurances that the Argentine government could not fail to increase the guarantee.[151] Thus, by the middle of the decade, the Central was capitalized at some £2 millions, a mileage cost of approximately £8,000, and a substantial inflation of the original £6,400. This writing up of capital was due to erroneous or unrealistic initial costing. Unlike the Great Southern, the Central was to prove a continued burden upon the state. Not only had the concern been awarded an extensive land grant, but it retained its guarantee until 1884. Perhaps this explains the less generous treatment which the Central received at the hands of the national government than had been the Southern's experiences with the Buenos Aires provincial authorities. When the Central negotiated the cancellation of its guarantee the company was forced to repay £500,000 on account of advances already received.[152]

An even more highly capitalized company was the East Argentine. Like the Southern it carried a 7 per cent guarantee on a mileage estimate of £10,000. But unlike the BAGS, the EA was constructed to the standard gauge. The original concession had ordained that the line should be constructed to the broad gauge of 5'6". However, due to the company's proximity to Uruguay, it was decided to reduce the gauge to 4'8½". Sanctioning this change in the Executive Decree of 20 September 1869, the state neglected to effect a corresponding reduction in the authorized capital of the company given the likely change in construction costs, an omission which tended to confirm suspicions already current regarding the veracity of interests connected with the company.[153] Thus the East Argentine was built a standard-gauge line, but obtained a guarantee on a par with that enjoyed by broad-gauge companies. In this way the state committed itself to supporting the company by payment of a guarantee not exceeding £67,200 per annum.[154] Despite this generous coverage, the company's original capital of £960,000 proved difficult to raise, though rapidly spent. The original stock was never fully paid up and had to be supplemented by an issue of debentures totalling £350,000, part of which was expended on the construction of a three-mile branch line and the balance on completing and equipping the main line.[155] The final, nominal cost of the railway was consequently in excess of £13,000 per mile.

The story of the Buenos Ayres Northern was not dissimilar. Mismanaged and inefficient, the capital account grew until it stood at almost three times the initial guaranteed capital of £160,000. At the end of the decade the company was not even earning sufficient to cover the interest upon guaranteed stock, let alone on the remainder of its capital.[156] The Buenos Ayres Campana was also a highly capitalized line. The state had advanced a guarantee of 7 per cent on £400,000, placed as debentures, but a further £500,000 of unguaranteed, ordinary shares were issued. On this basis the company was nominally capitalized at the rate of £18,000 per mile.[157] Finally, the Buenos Ayres and Ensenada Port — the only British company which at this juncture had not been awarded a state guarantee — was capitalized at much the same rate as the Campana.[158]

By the late 1870s the total nominal capitalization of the six British-owned Argentine railway companies was a little in excess of £7 millions, while the combined network stood at 720 miles.[159] Yet this figure represented one of the lowest average construction costs in the world. However, the significance of this average lies not in the fact that it is the mean of a widely disparate range of figures, but rather in its relationship with the real construction costs of a limited number of entities. The lines that most closely conformed to the average were the Great Southern and the provincially-owned *Oeste*. As has been related, the Southern's original concession provided for capitalization at the rate of £10,000 per mile. Although the figure proved unrealistic, the actual cost of main line construction was close to the estimate. At this juncture the *FCO* was also capitalized at approximately £10,000 per mile.[160] These were precisely the railways which had secured their base of operations in the 1860s. Given the sound construction of their original trunk routes, and adequate provision of rolling stock and facilities, they evolved as dynamic enterprises, yielding a reasonable return upon capital and providing a reliable service for consumers.

Watering apart, it is difficult to avoid the conclusion that the more generous the initial capitalization, the sooner a company became established as a profitable entity. Indeed, by the end of the 1860s this fact appears to have been recognized by the Argentine government, *vide* the original East Argentine concession. Moreover, a relatively high original capitalization did not preclude subsequent reductions in average costs by the construction of inexpensive extensions. The BAGS was a case in point, as was the *FC Oeste* which nicely illustrates the maxim. Its original concession provided for a cheap line; when privately-owned the company demonstrated many of the symptoms of undercapitalization. The permanent way had been poorly laid, the rolling stock was inadequate and traction underpowered[161] — hence the unfortunate accident in 1857 when *La Porteña* left the track. Inadequately financed the line had languished, unable to provide an efficient service and a disappointment to its promoters. Consequently, the early shareholders were unwilling to risk further funds, and the line became increasingly dependent upon the state. It was not until the late 1860s, after the company had been purchased by the province of Buenos Aires and recapitalized to make good earlier deficiencies, that the average capitalization of the *FCO* assumed the proportions of the original BAGS concession. From this position of strength the railway developed. Subsequently, the *Oeste* also reduced its average rate of capitalization by effecting a policy of careful branch line construction. By the end of the 1870s, the provincial railway was capitalized at a little over £8,000 a mile, a sum very similar to that of the Great Southern.[162]

In retrospect, the 1870s proved a decade of consolidation rather than a period of dramatic innovation or remarkable expansion. Progress was by no means uninterrupted or uniform — it could hardly be, given the heterogeneity of prevailing structures and diversity of circumstances within which the assorted companies functioned. Some entities, such as the East Argentine, established during these years rarely manifest vitality or viability. Nevertheless, a basis had been laid for subsequent expansion. If the Central's position argued against the false economy of undercapitalization, the BAGS was already an effective testament to the potential of Argentina as a field for investment. The course of events in the post-formative phase of the railway epoch served, in addition, to confirm the continuing commitment of the Argentine state to its strategy of fostering and promoting infrastructure modernization. Government assistance remained available for those firms experiencing difficulties. Respecting the federal authorities, there was as yet little conflict, at the operational level, between state-run lines and private concerns: the relationship was symbiotic. Further evidence of maturity had been provided by the ability of several companies to weather economic adversity and temporary political upheavals. While it would be fatuous to maintain that international economic dislocation at this juncture did not touch the railways, the repercussions of the 'Great Depression' were slow to reach Argentina and were rapidly surmounted by the more dynamic enterprises. At the annual general meeting in 1880, Frank Parish informed Great Southern shareholders that although the situation was tight there was every prospect of a return to more prosperous times. Optimistic noises at AGMs were soon reflected in rising share values on the London Stock Exchange.

In the 1850s and 1860s economic and political forces had coalesced to herald and encourage the initial development of the railways: the latter years of the 1870s witnessed a similar conjuncture. As the companies advanced to and beyond the frontier of settlement they had been menaced by the Indians. This danger was eradicated by the 1878–9 *Salidas* of General Roca whose campaigns not only secured the railways from further depredations, but pacified a vast area, the exploitation of which would contribute to the boom of the 1880s.[163] Of more immediate significance, 1880 saw the resolution of a perennial constitutional problem. The political events of that year, when the province of Buenos Aires once again stood against the force of the nation, are of interest here in that, as the result of this altercation, there occurred the final settlement which 'ended the conflict between the Province and the nation as a whole and prepared the way for the modern antithesis of Argentine political life'.[164] With few minor exceptions, the internal order of Argentina was established against serious disturbance until 1929. A stable political structure apparently assured, the country stood on the threshold of a boom in which the railway companies would be major participants.

II

NATIONAL CONSOLIDATION

The third quarter of the nineteenth century had seen the establishment of the Argentine railway system: a period of continuity and growth. Fundamental changes were taking place that would transform the economic structure of the country: the railways were part of the process of transformation. But it was an on-going process, and one that was bound in turn to influence the course of railway expansion itself. Nevertheless, by the 1870s several, individual companies had demonstrated the viability of rail transport in Argentina. In spite of constraints imposed by the domestic economy, the BAGS and *FC Oeste* had yielded substantial returns upon investment. By the end of the decade even the Central was beginning to declare acceptable dividends. The expectation was that the other lines would do likewise. Not only had previous projects demonstrated the feasibility of railway operations in Argentina, but the accelerating pace of economic change itself provided further justification for the belief that substantial demand existed for new and more adventurous railway projects. Above all, a continued application of the guarantee system served to remove any doubts which might have remained in the minds of prospective investors regarding the advisability of supporting Argentine railway schemes. In the past, with a few justifiable exceptions, the authorities had punctiliously honoured those guarantee obligations; there was little reason to suppose that this policy would change.

The Making of a Boom
So the railways came of age. After two decades of somewhat fitful growth there followed a phase of rapid expansion. It would be incorrect to describe the whole period between 1880 and 1889 as one of railway mania; the decade divides neatly into two halves, separated by a mild financial and commercial crisis. The earlier

period was one of substantial railway activity, the fruition of long years of gestation: the latter was the period of mania proper, inevitably culminating in a crisis. The first phase was introduced with the inauguration of General Julio Roca as President of the Republic in October 1880. It was an occasion that allowed the companies to demonstrate the degree of maturity already achieved. Roca's accession to the presidency, representing as he did the interests of the interior, was greeted with fierce opposition in the province of Buenos Aires, resulting in a brief civil war between the province and the remainder of the country. Yet in spite of these unfavourable conditions the Central experienced bumper earnings. Gross receipts in 1880 totalled £231,097; the previous year's figure was £175,857. In addition, working expenses registered a heartening decline.[1] The Great Southern, nearer the centre of hostilities, found its line occupied by the military, and service suspended for one month.[2] But the interruption of traffic was not serious, although the company submitted a claim for damages. Army intervention was speedily terminated when, as the result of a personal disagreement, the military commander administering the line assaulted the traffic manager. The officer was suspended from duty and the operation of the railway handed back to the company.[3]

As calm returned, the domestic economy revived rapidly: the gold premium fell and railway dividends rose. Great Southern shareholders were informed that during the early months of 1880 tariffs had been increased to compensate for the depreciation of the local paper currency, but so speedy was recovery that by the end of the year the directors recommended the abandonment of contingency increases. In several respects 1880 may be seen as a turning point, especially for the BAGS. Hitherto the board had been inclined to limit dividends, while building up a substantial reserve of £100,000. The magical figure was reached in 1880, and the prospect of an 8 per cent dividend on ordinary stock thereby virtually assured.[4] Despite the total suspension of commercial traffic for 33 days due to the revolution, the company was able to report that results were 'exceedingly satisfactory, since a greater net profit has been realized than in any previous year',[5] a factor which must have occasioned some difficulty in view of the railway's claim for compensation against the national government for loss of revenue. The episode served to indicate the

Table 3: *Central Argentine: operating data*

	Gross receipts £	Working expenses £	Net receipts £
1879	175,857	102,498	73,359
1880	231,097	101,761	129,336
1881	253,279	113,815	139,464
1882	322,087	126,448	195,639
1883	431,635	158,599	273,037
1884	539,025	213,549	325,476

Source: Central Argentine Railway Company Limited, *Report of the Directors and Statement of Accounts for year ended 21st December 1886* (hereafter *Annual Report* . . .) (London 1887).

resilience of the economy.

As the general situation improved, the position of the railway companies became increasingly secure and profitable. In 1879 the Central's earnings were some £38,000 short of the total, guaranteed interest; the following year net receipts were £16,000 in excess of the sum required to meet the guarantee. The company found itself in the unfortunate position of having to make repayments to the government on account of previous advances.[6] A year later it was required to pay £26,000; the time had obviously arrived when the company should follow the example set by the BAGS and consider the abandonment of its guarantee. However, given the drain on the state's resources which the company had constituted in the past, abrogation negotiations were far from smooth. After several years' protracted discussion agreement was finally achieved in 1884. The CA abandoned its guarantee and agreed to repay (as obliged by its concession) sums previously received from the national government under the guarantee arrangement, less claims against the authorities for unsettled debts. In all, the company reimbursed the Argentine government to the extent of approximately £500,000.[7] This apparently generous settlement was undoubtedly occasioned by the rapid rise in the railway's profits which had embarrassingly occurred as negotiations were pending, and the desire to declare a dividend in excess of the guaranteed 7 per cent — an impossibility until the abrogation of the guatantee.[8] Dividends rose accordingly. From 1880 to 1883 the company had declared 6 per cent upon its

Table 4: *BAGS: operating data and dividends declared upon ordinary stock*

	Gross receipts £	Working expenses £	Balance for dividend distribution £	Dividend %
1880	429,748	164,155	178,000	10
1881	463,528	192,046	216,807	10
1882*	262,475	133,431	130,159	6
1883	583,969	299,046	250,200	11
1884	697,629	371,761	290,555	11

* For the period 1 January–31 June 1882. Until 31 December 1881 the company's fiscal year ran concurrently with the calendar year. After 1882 the company's fiscal year ran from 1 July to 31 June.

Source: *Bradshaw's Railway Manual, Shareholders' Guide and Directory* (hereafter *Bradshaw's*) LXXV (1923) 438.

ordinary capital: the year the guarantee was abandoned 10 per cent was paid.[9] This was vindication, if the shareholders required it, of the wisdom of forgoing the security of the guarantee.

In the province of Buenos Aires, the BAGS went from strength to strength. Earnings and dividends increased, and in 1883 the reserve was raised to £250,000.[10] Increased profitability was not confined to the major companies. Official Argentine government statistics indicate that for the quinquennium 1880–84 investment in railways yielded a return of approximately 6 per cent per annum: during the previous quinquennium, 1875–79, the average yield was 4 per cent.[11] London Stock Exchange quotations of Argentine railway securities mirrored these developments.

Under the circumstances it is hardly surprising that there was a building boom. The gradual up-turn in the economy which was in part occasioned by the dynamic impact of railway construction, began to manifest itself during the late 1870s and was subsequently reflected in the traffic returns of the railway. Thus the companies were anxious to develop and expand their zones, fearful lest new entities were franchised in regions which the established companies envisaged as falling within their orbit. For its part the state wanted to foster the continued expansion of the railway network, and to consolidate its hold upon areas recently cleared of the Indian menace. Moreover, as had already been demonstrated, railway development was a means of both opening

Table 5: *Argentine Railways: London Stock Exchange quotations of select British-owned companies*

	BAGS				CA				EA	
	Ord. Stock		6% Debs.		Ord. Stock		6% Debs.		Ord. (£20) Shares	
	High £	Low £	High £	Low £	High £	Low £	High £	Low £	High £	Low £
1880	148	130	126	124	19	16½	—	—	15	10½
1881	170	148	126	115	23¼	19	—	—	22	15
1882	175	153	129*/110	123*/110	†122	115	127	119	21	14
1883	191	171	112	107	157	126	127	122	20¼	18¼
1884	187	165	113	109½	179	150	129	125	20	13

*BAGS 6% debentures were converted to 5% debentures in October 1882.
†CA £20 ordinary shares were converted to £100 ordinary stock in March 1882.

Source: Compiled from various issues of *The Times*.

up and increasing the value of land, and land there was aplenty — particularly after the Indian campaigns — much of it being distributed to clients of the regime. Always a prestigious commodity, conferring status upon its holder, land was also a valuable economic asset, the importance of which could only increase under the impact of railway development.

But Argentina was not an isolated community. As the companies prepared to enlarge their systems, external events also made an expansion of the railway network both desirable and feasible. The decade of the 1880s saw Argentina's incorporation within the modern world economy; it was the period when the country entered international markets as a major grain exporter.[12] These years also saw the hesitant development of Argentina's meat exporting industry. Experiments had already taken place in an attempt to discover acceptable means of preserving meat and thus permitting its transhipment from one continent to another. In 1876 the aptly named *Le Frigorifique* left Rouen for Buenos Aires, loaded with a cargo of frozen meat. This historic voyage demonstrated the possibility of shipping animal carcases to and from the South Atlantic. The following year this fact was confirmed by the voyage of the *Paraguay* which landed a cargo of Argentine beef in France. By 1882 the first *frigorifico*, the River

Plate Fresh Meat Company Limited, had been founded by George Drabble, a director of the Great Southern.[13]

If Argentina was on the threshold of becoming one of the world's major food producers, in Europe markets were ready to receive her commodities. With real wages increasing, the labouring classes and urban dwellers of British would prove avid consumers of cheap Argentine foodstuffs.[14] In Argentina itself increasing immigration during the 1880s provided the labour necessary to facilitate economic expansion. At the end of the decade net immigration would be running at the rate of 200,000 per annum.[15] By that time total railway investment would reach nearly £70 millions.[16] The railways played an integral role in this development, and in Argentina's incorporation within the world economy: they were at once a factor and a symptom of that process.

Provincial Pressure and the Great Southern
In 1880, however, these events were yet to take place, and the railways were content to rest upon their laurels. In that year the Great Southern opened its Ayacucho extension, thereby increasing route mileage to 350 miles,[17] and saw the new decade as a time when its position would be consolidated, its earnings improved, and its financial affairs brought to proper order. Following established pattern, the BAGS had little intention of embarking upon further extensions until the fruits of past labours had been harvested. But the provincial authorities of Buenos Aires were to shatter this mood of complacency. The short-lived tariff increases of 1880 had not passed unnoticed. In addition, there were minor grievances outstanding between the company and the provincial government. Above all, the province wished to see the companies already operating within its boundaries pursue active, expansionist construction programmes. It was the intention of the provincial government that Buenos Aires should be covered by a network of railways.[18] When the Great Southern gave little indication that it would conform to these plans the local congress raised once again the spectre of expropriation.[19]

While the provincial government publicly disavowed any desire to nationalize, rumours continued.[20] Yet it is difficult to assess the seriousness of the government's intentions. Probably expropriation was not really contemplated; the threat was used in order to make the company more tractable. By the middle of September 1881, the company had 'already adopted some reforms to suit the public convenience'.[21] Passenger and freight tariffs were reduced; the speed and frequency of trains increased.[22] The following month a telegram from Buenos Aires informed shareholders that all problems had been resolved and agreement reached with the provincial government.[23] The company undertook to construct extensions to Bahía Blanca and Tandil, completing the work within two and a half years. These extensions would carry neither a guarantee nor a subsidy. In addition the BAGS promised to reduce tariffs still further, according special reductions on long-distance hauls. For its part the provincial government abandoned its right to expropriate the line until the expiration of the original concession, some 23 years of which remained to run. This programme was approved by the shareholders at an extraordinary general meeting held early in 1882. The board was authorized to continue the Azul extension to Bahía Blanca and prolong the Ayacucho extension in the direction of Tandil. The capital of the company was to be increased by the issue of £1 million in £10 shares; the directors were also empowered to issue up to £2 millions in debentures.[24]

Thus the Great Southern embarked upon its period of most rapid expansion, with a not-too-gentle prod from the provincial government. It would be unfair to say that the company would not have constructed these extensions without government pressure; rather, it would not have constructed them at that particular time. The company already recognized the soundness of building cheap branches which by 1882 had reduced average capitalization to some £7,920 per mile.[25] Moreover the Southern had intended investigating the possibility of extending to Bahía Blanca as early as 1880; it was acknowledged by sources close to the company that while such an extension would prove beneficial to the province, it was unlikely to be remunerative.[26]

The opening of the Bahía Blanca line was an occasion for great celebrations, amidst which any remaining animosity towards the provincial government was finally laid to rest.[27] The company complied with another request from the provincial authorities to extend the network with merely perfunctory protests. Having agreed to construct to Bahía Blanca without a guarantee or subvention, the company could hardly decline smaller projects. As the directors informed the shareholders in 1884, the board had no desire to proceed with further extensions but, in the interests of self-preservation, the company had to comply with the wishes of the government. Two further extensions were contemplated — to Mar del Plata, some 57 miles from their existing line, and to Tres Arroyos via Juárez, some 81 miles. These two lines were completed by 1886 bringing the company's total network to 825 miles.[28]

Inter-regional Construction: Competition in the North and West
Notwithstanding the dynamism manifest by the BAGS, a more important development was undoubtedly the formation of the Buenos Ayres and Rosario Railway Company Limited which would soon challenge the Central's monopoly in the north. As its name suggests, the new company was formed to link the cities of Buenos Aires and Rosario. Hitherto railway developments in Argentina had centred around, or emanated from, either of these two cities, but there was no direct link between them. In the province of Buenos Aires, as we have seen, the provincial government had long patronized railway development. In the upper provinces, construction sprang from attempts by General Urquiza to hold together the assorted provinces which composed the Argentine Confederation and establish Rosario as a viable alternative to the port of Buenos Aires. It was to these latter designs that the Central owed its origins, and from the earliest of days the national government had built lines in the north. However, until the completion of the Rosario line these two networks developed independently.

Several schemes had been promoted in order to establish direct rail services between the two cities. While the Buenos Ayres and San Fernando concession provided for a line of but 20 miles, it was anticipated that a steamer service would ply up the Paraná from its railhead. Indeed, this expectation was explicitly stated when the Northern was formed to take over the San Fernando. Although, during the 1860s, the route northwards to Rosario was conceived of in terms of a rail and river link, the implicit assumption was that a direct rail service would ultimately emerge. With the failure of the Northern to construct beyond the delta, this task was transferred to the Campana. Several of the early versions of the Buenos Ayres and Campana concession were most precise in this respect: it was to be the railway to Rosario.[29] When work on the line began, there was much euphoria, despite reservations as to the financial viability of the company.[30] In fact flotation took place at an awkward moment: money was tight in London and it proved impossible to place all the scrip.[31] It was a struggle for the line to reach even Campana. The great link between the two systems was thus incomplete: a railway which should have united the two principal cities of Argentina had succeeded only in providing a somewhat inadequate service between the capital and a rather sleepy riverine port.

This state of affairs prevailed until the early 1880s, in spite of several attempts to revive the project during the late 1870s. The main difficulty was to raise capital in London. But there was also a hint of opposition from the provincially-owned *Oeste* which was said to be anxious to construct branch lines within the region likely to be traversed by the trunk line to Rosario.[32] Late in 1883 the original concession was reissued and a new consortium formed to reorganize the Campana which was renamed the Buenos Ayres and Rosario.[33] In order to complete the extension from Campana to Rosario a further £600,000 was to be raised by the issue of £10 7 per cent preference shares, which carried the option of conversion into ordinary stock.[34] The line, however, did not possess a government guarantee. The Campana was a guaranteed line, but the extension to Rosario was only authorized, and granted a subsidy of £500 per mile, on condition that the original guarantee was abandoned. In return the government also cancelled the debts owed it by the Campana on account of advances already made under the guarantee.[35] As Frank Parish explained at the annual general meeting of the Great Southern, so great was the need for a rail link between Buenos Aires and Rosario, there was little reason for the government to burden itself with fresh guarantee commitments.[36] The prospects for any such link were incentive enough. Work on the extension commenced in 1884 and was completed two years later.[37] From the first the company, under the direction of its new board, was profitable. Earnings during the years 1884 and 1885 were sufficient to allow the payment of a 5 per cent dividend on ordinary stock, scrip which had hitherto yielded no return to its holders. The following year a dividend of 6 per cent was declared on ordinary capital.[38]

The new route was expected to save ten hours' travelling time on the 190-mile journey between Rosario and Buenos Aires, and almost 24 hours on the trip from Buenos Aires to Córdoba. Prior to the opening of the BA&R, northbound passengers left Buenos Aires at 3.15 p.m. on the boat-train for Campana, proceeding up river by steamer to Rosario which was reached by 9.00 a.m. the following day. There was then a twelve-hour wait before the departure of the Central's night express for Córdoba. When the Rosario inaugurated its new, through service, passengers left the capital at midday and arrived in Rosario at 8.00 p.m., one hour before the departure of Córdoba connection, the land route affording more predictable running times.[39]

The Buenos Ayres and Pacific Railway Company Limited, destined to become another of the country's major lines, was also founded during this era. The original concession had been awarded in 1872 when the Argentine government entered into an agreement with John E. Clark for the construction of a metre-gauge railway from Buenos Aires to Chile. Five years later this concession was amended to allow the construction of a broad-gauge railway. Nothing happened, however, until 1882 when the BA&P was registered as a joint-stock company in London and empowered to take over the Clark concession.[40] The new company did not assume responsibility for the whole of the original concession, merely for the section that ran between Mercedes, in the province of Buenos Aires, and Villa Mercedes, in San Luis province. From Mercedes the company obtained its access to the city of Buenos Aires over *Oeste* track; at Villa Mercedes it connected with the line that ran on to Mendoza and San Juan.[41] The company's capital consisted of £1 million preference shares, £300,000 deferred shares and £1,312,240 7 per cent debentures.[42] The government guarantee of 7 per cent, calculated at a cost of £6,400 per mile, applied only to the preference and debenture scrip.[43] Equity provision was an indication of the unrealistic nature of officially-approved costing.

Work on the line was begun by Clark (who retained the contract for construction) in July 1882, five years being allowed for completion.[44] A delay occurred in 1883 when the company failed to reach an agreement with the *FC Oeste* in order to effect a junction of the two lines at Mercedes, but the matter was soon settled.[45] The line was then completed to Villa Mercedes and officially opened on 8 October 1886.[46] At this moment an interesting episode occurred which throws light on the motivation of some companies, and suggests that the charges laid at the door of the foreign-owned railway companies by economic nationalists are not without some foundation. The line to Villa Mercedes was completed in early 1886.[47] A special presidential express travelled between Mercedes and Villa Mercedes on 6 March of that year.[48] Yet the board delayed opening the line to public service for six months, not unnaturally occasioning much bitterness. Local merchants and producers petitioned the President of the Republic and the Minister of the Interior, requesting that they use their good offices to secure the speedy inauguration of services along the line.[49] It emerged that the delay in opening the line was due to a provision in the agreement with the contractor that he should pay the interest upon capital invested in the company until a specific date. Thus, the line was kept closed by the board so as to obtain the final instalment of that interest, which would be forfeited if the line was accepted and operated by the company. 'We are convinced,' reported the *South American Journal* with some justice, 'that it would be better to have exhibited a spirit less narrowly selfish in its motives and character.'[50] A sentiment that was undoubtedly echoed by the residents of San Luis.

The company's action was no doubt easily justifiable in the eyes of the shareholders. The middle years of the decade had seen a minor crisis develop. In September 1884 the *Banco Provincial de Buenos Aires* was forced to suspend specie payments. It was considered that the crisis had been 'precipitated by a conjunction of extraordinary circumstances'. September floods greatly dislocated commerce and the inundation of the railways paralysed exports. Meanwhile dull conditions in the markets of Europe slowed down the sales of Argentine produce. On the other hand, the application of higher import duties from 1 January 1885 occasioned inflated levels of imports towards the end of 1884 as traders attempted to beat the Customs House. Yet the major portion of the blame for the crisis was attributable to the national government which went on 'spending money on public works, etc., notwithstanding the fact that the loans destined to provide funds for these purposes are still unissued, and that daily greater difficulties are experienced in obtaining funds from English investors'.[51] Whatever the cause, Argentina's export earnings were falling at precisely the time that her import bill was increasing. Inevitably, the convertibility of the currency was suspended. On 9 January 1885, with the gold premium standing at 25, a decree ordering the issue of a paper currency, *curso forzoso*, was published and was to remain in force for two years.[52] Moreover, 1886 was the year of the presidential elections, always a time of uncertainty and unease.

Given these conditions the Pacific feared for its state guarantee, and doubted either the willingness or the ability of the Argentine government to honour its obligation. In this case, as was the usual practice, the state became liable for the guarantee only as each section of the line was accepted by the company from the hands of the contractor and placed in service. Presumably, during 1886, the Pacific considered that it was more likely to receive interest payments due from the contractor than from the national government. No doubt a querulous public did not appreciate the niceties of the situation.

Yet in spite of this unfortunate incident, the Pacific was aware of the realities of railway operations in Argentina and even before the completion of the original concession was determined to secure an independent access to Buenos Aires. This move was approved by the national government and the extension awarded a 7 per cent guarantee in the face of severe local opposition which, as voiced in the Buenos Aires press, was calling for a policy of government retrenchment.[53] It was estimated that the 66 miles of extension would cost some £486,500 to construct and equip: the government guarantee on a recognized capital of £6,400 per mile would yield £30,240. Therefore the company decided to issue £604,800 of 5 per cent debentures (which would thus be completely covered by the guarantee) to meet the cost of building the extension.[54] The line was opened on 20 March 1888.[55]

The Central, of course, engaged in no such expansionist programme; the state continued to oblige. Once the question of the abandonment of the guarantee was settled, and threats of expropriation — never taken seriously[56] — were removed, the company prepared to enjoy the fruits of others' labours. During the early years of the decade reports from British consuls at Rosario and Buenos Aires abound with references to the government railway programme in the north-west. The Andean was being prolonged on to Mendoza:[57] the line from Córdoba to

Tucumán, the Great Northern, was to be extended to Salta and Jujuy, where it would further stimulate the already flourishing Bolivian trade. 'Enterprise in Jujuy,' wrote Consul Egerton, 'will not have long to wait for returns, as the approach of the railway ... will revolutionize the country, as was the case of Tucumán, and awake it from its torpor.'[58] Mendoza and Salta were indeed incorporated within the national railway system in 1883, and the additional works were well in hand.[59]

Traffic along these lines expanded accordingly. Between 1880 and 1882 the gross receipts of the Andean, which was farmed out to a private operator who delivered a percentage of the profits to the state in lieu of rent, almost doubled; net receipts rose from £14,000 to £25,000, and further improvements were registered subsequently when in 1884 the net returns on investments reached 4 per cent.[60] On the Great Northern too, gross receipts increased, but inefficient management and rising working expenses negated much of the gain. However, by 1882 the value of trade between Argentina and Bolivia had reached the surprising figure of £1,400,000, most of which travelled over the railway at some stage of its journey.[61] Although only 247 miles in length, the Central was served by over 1,000 miles of state-owned rails whose traffic depended on the Central for access to the port of Rosario and markets abroad. The CA stood at the apex of a railway network which covered most of the populated regions of the north and west. While it obtained the benefits of the traffic which railway construction had stimulated, the company had borne none of the costs of encouraging that commerce.

Yet all was not as it appeared. The Central was being overtaken by other companies. Soon it would have to pay the price for its lethargy, and for devoting too much attention to dividends. As the Pacific was extended to Villa Mercedes — establishing a connection with the Andean railway — it would siphon off the trade of Mendoza and San Luis. The BA&P provided the provinces of *Cuyo* with a direct link to the federal capital in place of the circuitous route over Andean rails to Villa María, thence via the Central to Rosario, and finally by river steamer to Buenos Aires. The Buenos Ayres and Rosario was also forging ahead. At the 1886 annual general meeting, Central shareholders decided that their company ought to pursue a policy of harmony with the other British-owned railways. The chairman, Henry Brockett, sensing the mood replied that in the near future the company might have to consider seriously the advantage of amalgamating with the BA&R.[62] These were straws in the wind, but for the Central the meaning was plain enough.

The Smaller Companies
The lesser lines did not fare so well, even during this period when capital was relatively easy to acquire. Though their earnings might rise, they were still dependent upon a government guarantee: good times passed them by. Both the Northern and the East Argentine became embroiled in disputes with the government over refusal, or tardiness, in the honouring of guarantee obligations. At a time of general expansion these enterprises appeared as bottomless pits into which treasure was poured without cease, and with little prospect of return. Inevitably, the question arose, why during prosperous times were such companies unable to stand upon their own feet? The case against the EA was proclaimed in the halls of Congress by deputy Torcuato Gilbert who sponsored a bill to expropriate a line which had brought few benefits to the country, and which had cost the federal exchequer an aggregation of guarantee payments equal to one half its nominal capital.[63] But, when the East Argentine's guarantee was suspended, the company's riposte was to threaten raising the affair before the Committee of the London Stock Exchange, requesting the suspension of Argentine loan quotations.[64] Thoroughly effective as it might be, such a course hardly endeared this concern to the national government.

Almost alone among the smaller companies the Ensenada Port railway gradually strengthened its position, improving its earnings, and reducing its working ratio. Despite these improved conditions the highly capitalized nature of the company meant that its small income was devoted to the service of over £700,000 of assorted stocks and also provide for renewals.[65]

In general, the early years of the 1880s saw a substantial extension of the railway system. Two new companies had appeared which were to take their place amongst the country's major lines. Paradoxically, both represented a challenge to an established British-owned line, the Central. In addition, these companies, the Pacific and the Rosario, served to integrate the national network: each

Table 6: BA&EP: operating data

	Gross receipts £	Working expenses £	Ratio %	Net receipts £
1880	53,000	34,000	64	19,000
1881	59,000	36,000	61	23,000
1882	69,000	45,000	65	23,000
1883	100,000	62,000	61	38,000
1884	143,000	80,000	55	63,000
1885	155,000	84,000	54	71,000
1886	165,000	86,000	52	79,000

Columns do not necessarily agree due to rounding.

Source: Buenos Aires and Ensenada Port Railway Company Limited, *Report of the Directors to be presented to the Shareholders for the year ended 31 December 1886* (hereafter *Annual Report* . . .) (London 1887).

provided connections between the hitherto separate railway systems of Buenos Aires and the north. The BA&R linked the north directly to the central littoral; the BA&P fulfilled a similar function for the western provinces. Yet the railway map of Argentina remained fragmented. These new companies and the more established systems were still pushing their trunk lines through largely virgin territories. Although their construction programmes joined together various regions of the country, intra-zonal rail communications remained inadequate. Even the Great Southern, which may be portrayed as the most-developed single system, consisted of widely-separated trunk routes. In addition, the main force of railway development continued to emanate from the larger companies. Although the Rosario had demonstrated that a small line might transform itself into a dynamic, expansionist railway, the other minor companies failed to follow its example. The age of the small company was yet to dawn.

Nevertheless, the state maintained its desire for further railway development, and retained a policy of supporting railway construction. That support often bordered on coercion, so anxious was the state, in the shape of the Buenos Aires provincial authorities, to see the extension of the system. There was, moreover, the example of railway profitability. And at this juncture there was the perception that prosperity was not necessarily the preserve of the major networks alone. The highest dividends might still accrue to Southern and Central shareholders, but the smaller companies appeared poised to participate in the general prosperity. Notwithstanding the unfortunate examples of the EA and Northern, the growing receipts of the Ensenada Port, culminating in the 1885 ordinary dividend, and particularly the example of the Campana indicated that small lines were not inherently unprofitable. The Campana/Rosario effectively refuted the Central dictum that extension building was necessarily debilitating, at least in the short term.

Thus, events in the first half of the decade combined to encourage the flow of foreign funds into Argentine railway development. These years also vindicated the Argentine government's railway policy. The BAGS and even the Central were successful examples of the application of the guarantee system. State assistance had enabled both to attain a profitable status. The Rosario indicated that henceforth the guarantee policy might be more selectively applied; not all lines required state support. Even the Northern and East Argentine could have performed a useful function if their example had served to warn the authorities against a too liberal application of the guarantee. Unfortunately it did not.

The Railway Mania
In retrospect it is possible to view the mid-decadal crisis as a harbinger of the more serious dislocation that would occur at the end of the 1880s. Between 1883 and 1884 the Secretary of the British Legation in Buenos Aires, G. Jenner, estimated that Argentina's imports from Britain alone increased from $24 millions paper to $104 millions, while her exports to Britain rose by only $8 millions to $68 millions.[66] In view of this trend the mid-decade financial upheaval was predictable. Yet scant notice was taken of the portents, and even less done to eradicate the underlying causes of instability. The *Standard* of Buenos Aires campaigned against the profligacy of the administration, but little attention was paid to its editorials.[67] The government view was aptly expressed by the Minister of Finance. Dr Pacheco stated that the authorities considered current revenue sufficient to provide for ordinary expenditure; further loans were merely required to meet extraordinary occurrences.[68] Baring Brothers' agent in Buenos Aires did not take such a sanguine view.

I myself do not see how any other policy but one of economy and retrenchment can be adopted, for whatever is done to ease the situation, if it is not based on retrenchment, will prove useless in the end, as it will not place the Government in a better position to meet its obligations.[69]

Such strident warnings proved unpopular counsel. Economy might have been politically embarrassing for the government at this juncture. Presidential elections were due, and General Roca was committed to the continuance of an expansionist, if not inflationary, policy.[70] As the President had discovered on an earlier occasion, railways facilitated rapid troop movements, and were instrumental in maintaining the *Paz Roquista*. In addition, the whole process of the concessions game served as a most effective means of patronage, notwithstanding the long-term economic benefits that might accrue. A new loan was negotiated in Europe by Carlos Pellegrini to tide the government over its temporary difficulties and, after a brief hiatus, the flow of foreign capital to Argentina was resumed.[71] The day of reckoning was merely postponed.

Too much blame for this policy should not be laid upon the Argentine authorities. If the country desired foreign capital, and was prepared to mortgage public treasure to obtain it, foreign capitalists were ready to pander to that desire without too close an examination of the projects involved, or serious consideration of Argentina's medium-term ability to service a rapidly growing portfolio of external debts. The mood of complacency which permeated the thinking of the times is admirably conveyed by the chairman of the Great Southern. Describing the sad state of financial and monetary conditions in Buenos Aires at the half-yearly general meeting in 1885, he stated that the railway was unlikely to suffer from any depreciation of the paper currency as it could always increase its tariffs.[72] Equally illuminating is the response of the Central Argentine to the construction of the Buenos Ayres and Rosario.

The Rosario company reached that city and was opened to service on 1 February 1886.[73] But barely had the BA&R achieved this goal when it determined to embark upon further construction. In the first instance it was decided to build along the Salado valley up to Sunchales. This extension proved to be immediately profitable, and the company approached the government in order to obtain a concession for a line on to Santiago del Estero and Tucumán. At an extra-ordinary general meeting it was explained to the shareholders that in order to give substance to these grand designs it would be necessary to raise some £3 millions of new capital. As an indication of their confidence in the scheme, the board proposed that this extra capital should be raised by an issue of £2 millions of ordinary capital which would carry a 6 per cent guarantee for five years, and some £1 million in 5 per cent debentures. It was pointed out that the new line would connect at Tucumán with the state-owned narrow gauge railway being built to Salta and Jujui, ignoring the fact that the metre-gauge line ran on to connect with the Central at Córdoba. Nevertheless, the BA&R would provide the most direct route between the national capital and the north-west.[74]

Here in microcosm was the railway mania which took hold of Argentina in the late 1880s. In constructing to Tucumán, the Rosario was duplicating a service, admittedly less direct, which already existed. By the mid-1880s the north-west was connected to the federal capital by the state-owned line which ran down to Córdoba, the Central which continued to Rosario, and the Buenos Ayres and Rosario itself, which joined the two cities after which it was named. The line from Rosario to Tucumán constructed by the BA&R, although further east than that traversed by existing track, represented a saving of only 50 miles on the long way round via Córdoba.[75] In taking this route the BA&R was attempting to secure for itself the zone to the north and east of the Rio Dulce. Moreover, this vast sweep of Rosario rails would hem in the Central, which would thus be restricted to the western side of its main line, a region already subject to the attention of a multitude of smaller companies, and also of the Pacific as it pushed directly westwards through the central *pampa*.

Not unnaturally the national government welcomed this more direct link with the north-west which brought with it the prospect of competition between the British-owned lines. So did local traders who had long been subject to the exactions and inefficiencies of the Central. The new company, under the competent direction of Frank Parish, George Drabble *et al* was welcome indeed. By 1891 the line had reached Tucumán, and the average cost of construction from Buenos Aires stood at some £9,300 per

NATIONAL CONSOLIDATION

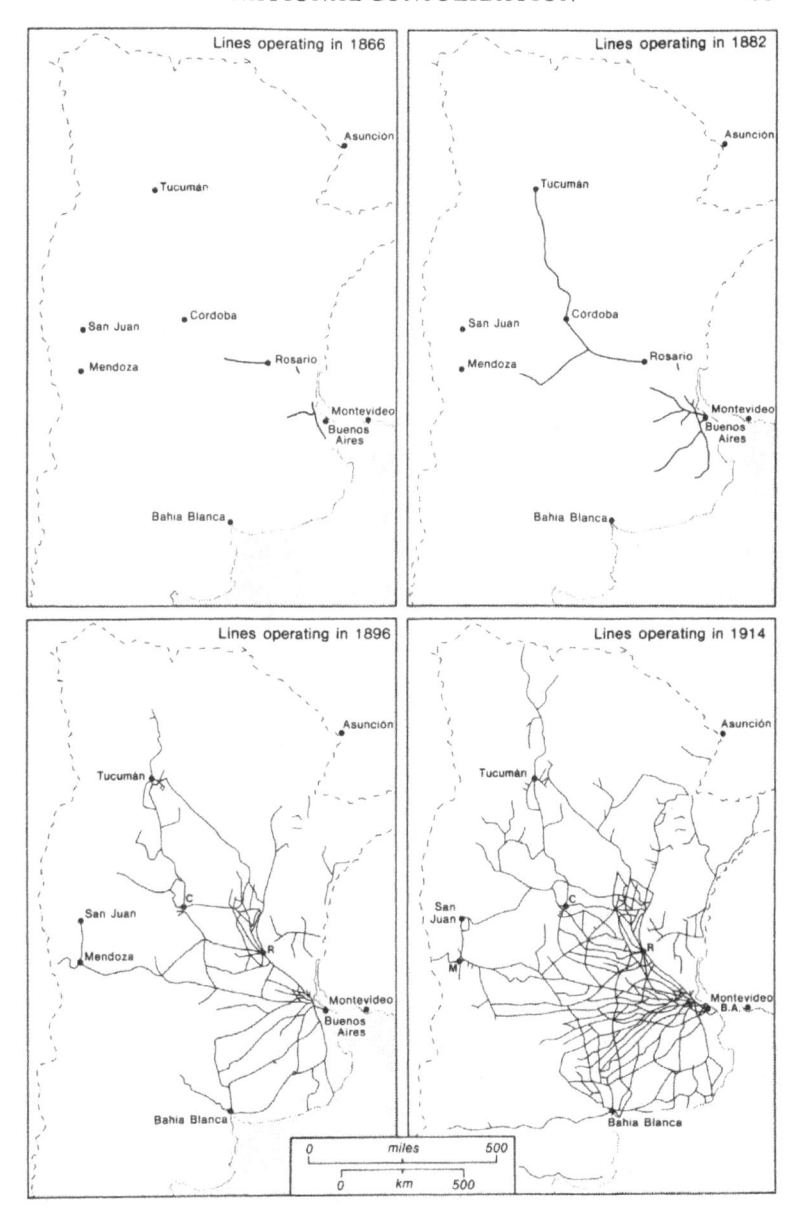

Map 2: Expansion of the Argentine Railway system

mile.[76] The Central's reaction to this threat was initially one of complacency. During 1886, when it appeared that the BA&R would terminate at Rosario, the Central Argentine cynically advocated a policy of harmony with the other British-owned companies. Others campaigned for a more forceful policy, and expressed the fear that the Central would be left far behind; its territories invaded, its revenues pirated, and its position usurped.[77]

When the intentions of the BA&R were finally revealed, the Central aroused itself with unaccustomed vigour. If the Rosario would build to Tucumán then the Central would build to Buenos Aires. The CA would thwart interlopers who poached in its territory, meeting extension with extension. Moves to effect an amicable amalgamation were scornfully dismissed by the Central's directors in a circular to the shareholders in 1892. A note of bitterness entered into the Central's dealings with the Rosario which, although understandable, was nevertheless unusual in the annals of British-owned Argentine railway circles in the extent to which it was voiced publicly. The scheme ultimately adopted by the Central was adventurous, but costly. The Buenos Ayres Northern was leased in order to obtain access to the federal capital. In proposing this course of action, the directors admitted that large sums would be required in order to place the BAN in good working order. Not only would the Northern's line require lengthy extensions in order to effect a junction with the Central, but some £80,000 had to be found to refurbish its stations, and £117,000 to augment rolling stock. And additional extensions totalling 243 miles were advocated. In all, the Central's answer to the Rosario's audacity would cost £3 millions.[78] The magnitude of these proposals may be comprehended only when it is remembered that for the previous twenty years the Central had refused to build a single mile of track. Its earlier policy had been based upon a retention of the monopoly on the link between hinterland and port. The Central had been content to let others construct the railway network of northern Argentina, so long as its position had been secure as the sole connection with the outside world, and so long as the commerce of the interior, stimulated by other railway lines, passed over its tracks.

Undertaken, as it was, on the eve of the Baring Crisis, this programme proved extremely difficult to fulfil when money became tight. Relations between the board of directors and the shareholders soured as the full implications of the company's past policies were realized. But both directors and shareholders were equally responsible for previous complacency, and a policy which had paid too narrow a regard to immediate profits. In the aftermath of the Crisis, when dividends disappeared, and the prospects of an amalgamation with the BA&R assumed a different complexion, an irate shareholder castigated the board in splendid metaphorical terms which must have struck a chord with fellow shareholders. Concerning the directors he wrote:

> They have piloted this once splendid property into the shoals and quicksands of disaster, and if left much longer in charge will run it onto the rocks of bankruptcy, and they ought to be court-martialled and dismissed for their ignorance and recklessness. If they had any pride or self-esteem left in them they would, before they are turned out, resign *en bloc*; but I presume they will stick like barnacles to the bottom of the wreck until it is cast high and dry, when, finding no longer any sustenance left, they will fall off of their own accord.[79]

In order to set these events into context, it bears repeating that for twenty years the Central had not constructed a single mile of track beyond the main line from Rosario to Córdoba. Spurred by the threat of competition from the BA&R, the refractory Central belatedly embarked upon a crash building programme commencing during the mid-1880s which continued through the crisis years, making heavy demands upon the London money market. Beginning with a call for approximately one-third of a million sterling in 1885,[80] succeeding years witnessed increasingly voracious sorties for funds. At the end of the decade, at the height of the Baring Crisis, the authorized capital of the CA reached £8,700,000 — a sum four times mid-decadal capitalization.[81] The greater part of this additional capital had been subscribed by existing shareholders, to whom it had been issued *pro rata*, the exception being a loan of £1 million obtained from Baring Brothers.[82] Fitfully at first, the company's network expanded, with growing momentum as the 1880s drew to a close. As late as 1884, the Central possessed but its 246-mile main line:[83] five years later only 27 miles had been added to the system, but approximately 200 miles of extensions were under construction.[84] By the early 1890s, when the programme was finally completed, the network ran to 720 miles.[85] The history of the Buenos Ayres & Rosario at this juncture followed a not dissimilar course. A creature of the 1880s, authorized capital stood at some £6 millions by the end of the decade, rising to more than £8,000,000 a few years later.[86] Mileage increased at a phenomenal rate: the scheme of expansion envisaged a network in excess of 900 miles and in 1889 alone approximately 400 miles of permanent way was under construction.[87]

Not all the British-owned railways, however, needed the threat of competition in order to pursue an expansionist policy. The Great Southern also increased its capital account and the scope of its network during the second half of the 1880s, although its record was not as spectacular as that of the more northerly lines. Its main contribution to railway development during the decade had already been achieved by the middle years, namely the extension to Bahía Blanca. This served to increase the Great Southern's mileage to almost 800 miles, and raise issued capital to £7.5 millions.[88] The company then slackened the pace of development. No further major works were undertaken. New concessions were obtained, and capital account was increased during the second half of the decade, but these additions did not represent pioneering efforts in new regions; they were not extensions of the company's zone of influence, but infillings within the existing network. For the Southern the second half of the 1880s was a time of consolidation, a period of steady, ordered growth. It did not seek to emulate its earlier record, nor to equal the extensions of other British-owned lines. Between 1885 and 1890 the network expanded by less than 200 miles. Only at the end of the period was this conservative policy modified, the company contemplating further extensions totalling something in excess of 1,000 miles.[89]

An explanation for this caution is not difficult to discern. Having only recently completed the line to Bahía Blanca, the crisis of 1885 placed the BAGS in a situation which could almost be described as 'difficult'. The company found itself with an increased capital requiring service, while its latest extension had not yet sufficient opportunity to realize the potential of the region it traversed. The company was taught the harsh lesson of over-expansion, or rather the realities of the situation were impressed upon it. New lines crossing virgin land required a period of gestation before they would yield a profitable return upon investment. In the past the Southern had been fortunate enough to traverse populous zones, superseding earlier methods of transport. This observation was of particular relevance in the Argentina of the 1880s, when the incentive to expand was keen, but the penalties imposed for premature construction were severe. Thus, during the mania of the late 1880s the Great Southern maintained an attitude of almost unbecoming calm. Two thousand miles of new track were opened in 1891; the Great Southern accounted for barely 100 miles.[90] In this way the company was better able to ride the storm.

The late 1880s was also a time of consolidation for the Buenos Ayres & Pacific, though induced by necessity rather than prudence. The main line was completed and the company obtained its own access to Buenos Aires, at least as far as Palermo, on the outskirts of the city. By the end of the decade authorized capital stood at £3,314,000, to which was added a floating debt of £150,000.[91] The line ran due west across the *pampa* from Buenos Aires to the Andes, but, as the shareholders were assured by Sir Gabriel Goldney, the chairman, the company would have nothing to do with the work of piercing the Andes themselves.[92] This at least was a questionable project at which concessionaires baulked even during the 'mania'.

New Companies and the Concessions 'Game'
But the experiences of established lines hardly explains the doubling of Argentina's railway mileage which occurred between 1886 and 1891, not even the ambitious extension-building policies pursued by the CA and BA&R. As the figures in Table 7 indicate, the period of most rapid growth during the decade as a whole, both in absolute and relative terms, occurred between 1890 and 1891 — years that are synonymous with the Baring Crisis and Revolution. This apparent contradiction is explained by the gestation period involved in railway development. Several years lapsed between the initiation and completion of extension programmes. Given the nature of contractual obligations, it is to be expected that a certain basic residue of construction will take place even at the height of a slump. Moreover, an unprecedented number of concessions had been awarded during 1889, the last

year of the boom; several of these projects were only beginning to take substance in 1891. The full impact of the crisis may be observed during the years between 1892 and 1896, when the completion of earlier projects, and the failure to initiate new schemes produced a record decline in the rate of expansion of the national railway network for the remainder of the century. But by far the greater part of mileage inaugurated between 1886 and 1891 was initiated by new companies; as has been stated, the major British-owned lines pursued relatively cautious construction policies during this period, or at least until the very end of the decade. Even the additional miles constructed by the Central and

Table 7: *Argentine Railways: expansion of the network*

	Operational mileage year end	Increase
1880	1563	—
1881	1563	0
1882	1636	73 (4.7%)
1883	1966	330 (20.2%)
1884	2261	295 (15.0%)
1885	2798	537 (23.8%)
1886	3627	829 (29.6%)
1887	4157	530 (14.6%)
1888	4705	549 (13.2%)
1889	5069	364 (7.7%)
1890	5861	792 (15.6%)
1891	7752	1891 (32.3%)
1892	8502	750 (9.7%)
1893	8607	105 (1.2%)
1894	8718	111 (1.3%)
1895	8772	54 (0.6%)
1896	8986	214 (2.4%)
1897	9169	183 (2.0%)
1898	9601	432 (4.7%)
1899	10199	598 (6.2%)
1900	10292	93 (0.9%)

Source: Compiled and calculated from República Argentina, Ministerio de Obras Públicas, Dirección General de Ferrocarriles *Estadística de los ferrocarriles en explotación durante el año 1913* (Bueons Aires 1916) pp. 396–98; A. E. Bunge *Ferrocarriles argentinos: contribucion al estudio del patrimonio nacional* (Buenos Aires 1918) pp. 120–21.

Rosario pale into insignificance when compared with the total weight of track commissioned at this time.

The quinquennium 1886–90 saw the issue of a plethora of concessions, and applications for many more. A flood of new companies inundated Argentina, either to acquire concessions or to purchase national and provincial railway interests. Symptomatic of the optimism engendered during the period were events in the province of Buenos Aires. During the difficult year of 1885 the provincial congress awarded a concession for some 775 miles of railway, carrying a 6 per cent provincial guarantee.[93] On this occasion reason prevailed; the governor vetoed the proposal on the grounds that it would be unwise for the province to assume further obligations at such a time.[94] The voice of moderation, however, was not heard for long. The following year the provincial assembly was approached by the governor himself, seeking authorization for a loan to extend the provincial railway. This scheme would have added a further charge of £28,000 per annum upon the provincial exchequer. In addition, a French company submitted proposals for a railway radiating from Trenque Lauquen, on the *FC Oeste*, entailing the construction of almost 1,000 miles of track linking such diverse points as Bahía Blanca (already joined to the city of Buenos Aires by the BAGS), Junin (on the BA&P), Nueve de Julio and Ferrari.

Other provinces followed where Buenos Aires led. Santa Fé planned major extensions as did the provinces of Córdoba and Tucumán. In the national Congress schemes were discussed concerning the construction of lines in the mesopotamian provinces of Corrientes and Missiones. Nor were the national territories neglected; the government considered the construction of some 1,000 miles of line in the Gran Chaco at a cost of £4 millions.[95]

In 1887 the national Chamber of Deputies awarded concessions totalling almost 8,000 miles, capitalized at some £55.5 millions, virtually all of which carried a 5 per cent guarantee. Although modified in the Senate, a total of 4,900 miles (capitalized at £24 millions) of these congressional projects passed into law carrying the ubiquitous guarantee.[96] Commenting on this course of events, especially the financial responsibilities assumed by the national government in the form of new guarantees, Bouwer stated:

These figures show clearly that unless the Govt. retrenches considerably and declines to incur much of the extraordinary expenditure voted, the [budget] deficit at the end of 1888 will be considerable and will oblige the Govt. to have recourse to another foreign loan ...[97]

The action of the Senate in refusing to sanction all the schemes sent up by the lower chamber did serve to check the headlong rush, at least momentarily. *La Prensa* thundered:

> The present year has been a most important one for the national interests connected with railways. The Congress of 1887 is suffering from railway delirium. It seems to be the victim of a wild passion for everybody who proposes the construction of guaranteed lines; and the ease with which concessions and guarantees are obtained astonishes and terrifies serious people.[98]

Indeed, many of the schemes presented during the course of 1887 made little sense. Often new concessions sought to duplicate existing services. One such example, and among those which the Senate refused to sanction, was a projected line that would parallel the Central Argentine all the way from Buenos Aires to Córdoba.[99] Perhaps the inhabitants of Córdoba did not view the matter as dispassionately. Nor was the local press alone in condemning the mood which had seized the country. Even that patron of railway projects, the *Railway Times*, was forced to sound a note of warning, and writing under the head of 'Railway Mania' advised its readers,

> It appears, however, from the Argentine journals recently to hand that the railway concessions game in that country is by no means played out yet, for the privileges asked for in the present session of Congress represent a fabulous amount of money and an extraordinary mileage.[100]

One of the 'fabulous' projects resuscitated in 1888, after being refused in 1886, was the Buenos Ayres and Talcahuano Great Inter-Oceanic Railway. This grandiose company was 'formed to construct railways in Argentina and Chile with the object of establishing, or facilitating railway communications between the Atlantic and Pacific Oceans'. All this could be achieved by the

NATIONAL CONSOLIDATION 71

issue of £5 millions in £10 shares.[101] Towards the end of 1888, the *Standard* of Buenos Aires was urging caution,

> The country is suffering from railways on the brain. Like measles and whooping cough, it is perhaps, an unavoidable complaint, and not very dangerous; but it requires treatment. Railway concessions are becoming dangerously popular, and it would be legislative wisdom to cut them short at least for a time.[102]

Sound advice, both at home and abroad, abounded like railway concessions themselves but was less popular, and calmer counsels did not prevail. During the 1888 session of Congress the national executive alone submitted a list of concessions totalling approximately 4,000 miles, charged with a guarantee of $7.5 millions gold. By 1889 the total number of guaranteed projects sanctioned and awarded by the government during the preceding years represented an annual claim upon the national treasury of almost three times that figure. A lone voice in Congress protested against this vast waste of public monies, 'la fabulosa suma de 21.000.000 de pesos nacionales ora'.[103] H.B.M. Consul Briggett estimated that during 1889 the length of new concessions actually under construction exceeded the existing mileage in operation.[104] Yet, in the course of that year a further 34 concessions were sanctioned.[105]

When the bubble finally burst many of these concessions lapsed or were cancelled. At the end of 1890 a dozen of the least feasible were the first to feel the impact of the Crisis.[106] Others fell by the way during 1891, but in 1892 it was still possible for the Argentine government to cancel a further 1,455 miles of concessions.[107]

In spite of the Crisis and ensuing dislocation, the events of the late 1880s provided the country with an extensive railway network. Most of Argentina's main trunk routes were initiated, or completed, during this period. If, in the immediate instance, the weight of railway mileage exceeded the country's requirement, further development would still take place about the system. Official government statistics show that by 1891 the country possessed 7,734 miles of track, capitalized at £75,350,108.[108] This expansion meant not only an increase or rails, but an extension of cultivable acreage. As a result of the railway boom, many previously inaccessible areas were brought within the pale of economic exploitation. The boom occasioned the joining together of scattered centres of population and the opening-up of new zones; it also effected an increase in railway density, providing a more efficient service in areas already incorporated within the skeletal railway network. By the early 1890s an embryonic 'national' network had emerged north of the Colorado.

Table 8: Argentine Railways: density of mileage in select provinces

Province	Surface area (square miles)	Square miles of area per route mile of railway track	
		1880	1889
Buenos Aires	63,000	84.62	19.60
Santa Fé	18,000	270.00	10.27
Córdoba	54,000	100.90	40.90
Entre Ríos	45,000	555.50	98.70
Corrientes	34,000	2,250.00	101.50

Source: *Railway Times* (hereafter *RT*) 12 July 1890, LVIII, 41.

A rather complicated calculation made at the time illustrates this point. As Table 8 shows, when expressed as a factor of the surface area of each province, the density of railway route mileage increased to such an extent during the decade that in every case, on average, the distance between an estate and its nearest railhead greatly diminished. Or, in other words, the margin of profitable cultivation was significantly extended.

III

CRISIS AND RECOVERY

The Baring Crisis had long-term consequences for railways in Argentina, but the immediate effects were also important for most enterprises. While the restructuring of the network was of more fundamental significance, in the short term the abandonment of the guarantees constituted a profound policy revision, and occasioned enduring changes. The movement towards amalgamation initially stimulated by the need for economy, was then brought to fruition as a result of regained prosperity. Nevertheless, while there were some general trends, sharp differences prevailed respecting the experiences of individual companies. Although every line was caught up in the events of these years, their particular circumstances and responses differed greatly. Above all, the Crisis reinforced the position already achieved by the larger networks. A consideration of the chronology of the Crisis and the course of recovery provides an explanation not only of the event itself, but also of the role played by the railways and the rejoinder which it invoked from various lines.

The Railways on the Eve of Crisis
In view of subsequent events, the complacency exhibited by railway companies during the late 1880s was hardly justified. The mid-decade upheaval should have served as a warning. Yet the mood of optimism which reigned at this time was understandable. It was a period of expansion and profitability for the established lines, large and small alike. Prosperity endured until the very eve of the Baring Crisis, and largely accounts for the willingness of shareholders to place increasingly greater sums in Argentine railway securities. But all lines were not established enterprises. A distinction has to be made between operating concerns, usually large integrated systems, and companies franchised during the boom. While the former were profitable entities, several

years had elapsed before the larger, consolidated networks acquired that status; despite the changing structure of the domestic economy, new railways were likely to experience a similar delay before they too achieved long-term profitability. Indeed, the successful record of the established companies at this juncture tended to mask weaknesses inherent in new lines. They were usually under-capitalized, located in backward areas, requiring even more time fully to develop. As a consequence, Argentine railway affairs during the late 1880s present a dual image: increasing difficulties were experienced by new lines, while operating concerns were apparently untroubled until overtaken by the crash.

The views of the major railways were appropriately expressed by Frank Parish of the Great Southern at the 1888 annual general meeting. Reviewing the overall situation in Argentina, he considered that there was little cause for alarm.

> No doubt the pace is rapid and no doubt the country's engagements and indebtedness are increasing to an enormous amount, but, on the other hand, recollect that you are dealing with a country possessed of enormous resources of national wealth ... So far we may say that the Argentine credit has stood the test in the London market, and although some of us older ones may question the practical utility of some of the projects in which money has been invested, still I may say this ... that any English investor exercising a proper amount of judgement and discretion, will find ample means in Argentina for investing his money to advantage.[1]

Parish's observations are of interest for they convey sentiments which are fundamental to an understanding of the boom mentality, even if those sentiments were appropriate within the narrower context of BAGS affairs. Although a trifle less sanguine, similar views were articulated at subsequent general meetings. And they were not confined to the Great Southern. Informing his shareholders of their company's answer to the Rosario challenge, the Central chairman maintained, on the very eve of the Crisis, that despite the magnitude of the project, it was well within their capabilities. He considered that the Central could easily afford the vast extensions envisaged, provided that 'there was no great commercial crisis on the other side'.[2] It was a prophetic remark.

BA&R investors were notified that there was little cause for alarm; continued progress could be anticipated.[3]

Table 9: BAGS: goods traffic (metric tons)

		Increase	
*1879	117,693	—	—
*1880	127,357	9,664	(8.2%)
†1881/2	202,338	74,981	(58.9%)
†1882/3	284,735	82,397	(40.7%)
†1883/4	382,224	97,489	(34.2%)
†1884/5	465,216	82,992	(21.7%)
†1885/6	372,189	−93,027	−(20.0%)
†1886/7	577,710	205,521	(55.2%)
†1887/8	676,151	98,441	(17.0%)
†1888/9	789,516	113,365	(16.8%)

*Financial year ending 21 December
†Financial year ending 30 June

Source: Compiled from BAGS Annual Reports.

Table 10: BAGS: earnings and expenditure

	Gross receipts £	Working expenses £
1884/5	921,976	566,984
1885/6	887,479	461,677
1886/7	1,012,919	471,224
1887/8	1,195,681	512,052
1888/9	1,320,458	642,255

Source: Bradshaw's LXXV (1923) 438.

These observations were firmly based upon the operating record of the larger lines. The Great Southern's prognostications, for example, derived from an expanding traffic account. Throughout the 1880s the company had experienced a marked increase in the volume of goods carried over its track, and although the rate of increase began to decline towards the end of the decade, in absolute terms the line was still handling an extra 100,000 metric tons each year. Part of this growth was occasioned by the inclusion of material used in the construction of the company's own extensions, which increased from 8,000 metric tons in 1881/82 to 65,000 tons in 1882/83 as the railway embarked upon its construction programme. Thereafter, however, this item remained fairly constant at approximately 60,000 tons per annum. The vast expansion in freight traffic indicates that the company's prosperity was based upon foundations more substantial than mere boom conditions. The Southern's earnings reflected the same tendency (see Table 10). A similar pattern emerges on examining the Central's operating returns. Gross receipts more than doubled between 1885 and 1889, increasing from £428,282 to £941,722.[4] And this prosperity was not confined to the larger networks. The Buenos Ayres & Ensenada Port exhibited equally promising increases in its traffic, while working ratio registered a healthy decline (see Table 11). These abstracts were translated into substantial dividends for ordinary shareholders.

Table 11: BA&EP: operating data

	Traffic		
	Passenger (numbers)	Freight (metric tons)	Working ratio %
1879	724,937	65,000	69
1880	774,626	73,000	64
1881	846,838	86,000	61
1882	934,807	99,000	65
1883	1,060,483	162,000	61
1884	1,073,740	237,000	55
1885	1,192,508	270,000	54
1886	1,312,644	260,000	52
1887	1,497,698	266,000	46
1888	1,851,718	358,000	48
1889	2,176,237	518,000	50

Financial year ending 31 December.

Source: BA&EP Annual Report . . . *1895* (London 1896).

Under these circumstances it is not surprising that foreign capital flowed into Argentina. There was a mood of optimism which, if it does not justify some of the more questionable enterprises undertaken during the late 1880s, explains why many of

Table 12: *Argentine Railways: dividends declared on ordinary stocks by select British-owned companies*

	BA&R %	BAGS %	CA %
*1880	—	10	6
*1881	—	10	6
1882	—	†6	6
1883	—	11	6
1884	5	11	10
1885	5	10	10
1886	6	8	12
1887	8½	10	12
1888	9	10	12
1889	9	10	10

*Financial year ending 31 December for all companies, thereafter BAGS's year terminated on 30 June.
†Dividend for period 1 January–30 June 1882.

Source: Compiled BA&R, BAGS, CA *Annual Reports* various dates; *Bradshaw's* LXXV (1923) 438.

the less viable projects were initiated. Repeatedly investors answered calls for further funds with an open hand. Firmly-established lines or newly-commissioned companies, unimpeachable securities or questionable scrip, all found ready takers. Argentine railway issues were the long-awaited *eldorado*. Despite calls for additional monies, Argentine railway securities became increasingly popular, as quotations on the London Stock Exchange rose to hitherto unimagined heights. Indeed, the course of the Crisis may be plotted from the movement of those quotations (as Table 13 demonstrates).

The danger was that this optimism became infectious. Prospective investors confused the record of the established, profitable lines with Argentine railway securities generally. Within the context of a boom mentality, new subscribers displayed an amazing ability for self-delusion. The BA&P was able to ignore the consequences of a depreciation in the local currency and the effects of flooding which occasioned the complete suspension of traffic between March and December 1889, merely because, during the first quarter of 1890, receipts registered a 100 per cent increase over the previous year.[5] The Cordoba Central Railway Company

Table 13: Argentine Railways: London Stock Exchange quotations of select British-owned railway securities

	BAGS				CA				BA&R				BA&P	
	Ords.		5% Debs.		Ords.		6% Debs.		Ords.		5% Debs.		7% Debs.	
	High	Low	High	Low	High	Low	High	Low	High	Low	High	Low	High	Low
1885	163	150	112½	109	177	158	130	126	—	—	110	102	115	104
1886	162	141	120	113	176	155	139	127	161	115	116	106½	129	116
1887	178	158	124	118	196	165	142	136	165	138	120	112	135	126
1888	209	180	131	124	213	173	154	142	176	152	130	121	145	135
1889	217	185	132	127	212	174	152	148	183	163	129	127	144	132
1890	186	159	132	125	181	88	151	150	169	135	104†	95	135	127
1891	163	114	103*	99	84	42	—	—	133	61	93	81	110	67
1892	132	108	104	99	72½	41	—	—	99½	62	94½	81	—	—
1893	119	98	—	—	69½	52	—	—	77	48	96	91	—	—
1894	105	91	113	107	70	57	147	144	68	51	100½	92	—	—

*Converted into 4% debentures on 1 July 1890.
†Converted into 4% debentures on 1 July 1889.

Source: Compiled from The Times, various dates.

Limited contrived to find 'satisfaction' in a situation that required the expenditure of at least £1 million in order to place the Córdoba-Tucumán line, which it had purchased from the national government, in proper working order.[6] The degree of optimism expressed by the newer companies bore an inverse relationship to their ability to weather the approaching storm.

The distinction between the established lines and the new companies is fundamental to an understanding of the railways' role in events leading to the Baring Crisis. It also explains the apparent suddenness with which the crash overtook the major lines. The fate of all companies was inexorably bound to that of the country in which they operated: all suffered from the adverse effects of cyclical fluctuations. The expansion of the system might also have been a function of the speculation in land which occurred at this time, and which was itself a supplementary factor in the Baring Crisis. But the railways played a more active role in the immediate cause of the Crisis — the growing suspicion that the Argentine government was unable to honour its obligations.

The Railways and the Baring Crisis
The Baring Crisis is usually characterized as a crisis of development, as distinct from a situation occasioned by maladministration and over-borrowing, though the latter were undoubtedly contributing factors.[7] That is to say, the problem lay in the structure of borrowing and the nature of investment projects. Most of the capital raised abroad at this time was tied up in schemes entailing a long gestation period. Until these projects — railway construction, land improvement, and others — came on stream and generated or facilitated the flow of exports necessary to service the funds involved, interest and amortization payments could in the short term be maintained from new borrowing. But the continued inflow of new funds was dependent upon the confidence of foreign investors in the ability of the government to honour the commitments it was assuming, and upon a perception of the utility of the projects for which their monies were being employed. This confidence was now eroded by two factors: the inability, or the unwillingness, of the Argentine government to apply a fiscal regime which, during a period of currency inconvertibility, would keep the gold premium within reasonable

bounds and also the unprecedented scale of guaranteed railway schemes authorized.

The rapid rise of the gold premium after 1884, when convertibility was suspended, indicated that all was not well, as did the fantastical nature of several of the more outrageous railway projects. The greater part of railway investment during this period was accounted for by the formation of new companies in receipt of government guarantees. The increasing unease with which these projects were regarded in the money market is reflected in the structure of the capital accounts of newly-projected lines. Notwithstanding their guarantee, many of these concerns felt it necessary to offer prospective subscribers the added illusion of security by issuing prior-charged, fixed-interest bearing scrip. This was especially so after 1888, when the flow of funds began to falter, and it was a process from which even the established companies were not immune. While the initial capital of the Central, for example, had consisted entirely of guaranteed equity stock, the first call for additional capital from the shareholders (to place the lines in good working order) had taken the form of a debenture issue.[8] Yet subsequent, limited calls for further funds had been met through the issue of ordinary stock during the 1880s. It was only at the end of the decade, when it became necessary to raise substantial sums, that the company had to resort to fixed-interest stock and debenture issues upon a large scale. In this respect, the Southern was less fortunate, and witnessed a marked change in the structure of its capital account during the decade.

As Graph 1 indicates, one of the favoured expedients employed by the Great Southern to finance new construction during the decade was the creation of a special category of 'extension' scrip. Between 1886 and 1890, while the absolute value of equity remained static, there was a marked increase in the volume of 'extension' capital, which rose from £1.4 millions in 1886 to £5.9 millions in 1889. However, such shares were allowed only a limited life; usually they were converted into equity stock after a specified period. Thus, for example, the Bahía Blanca and Tandil extension shares which had been issued in 1882 were partly converted into ordinary stock during the fiscal year ending in 1885, while further extension capital created that year was to be converted into equity scrip by 1890.[9] In addition, although such

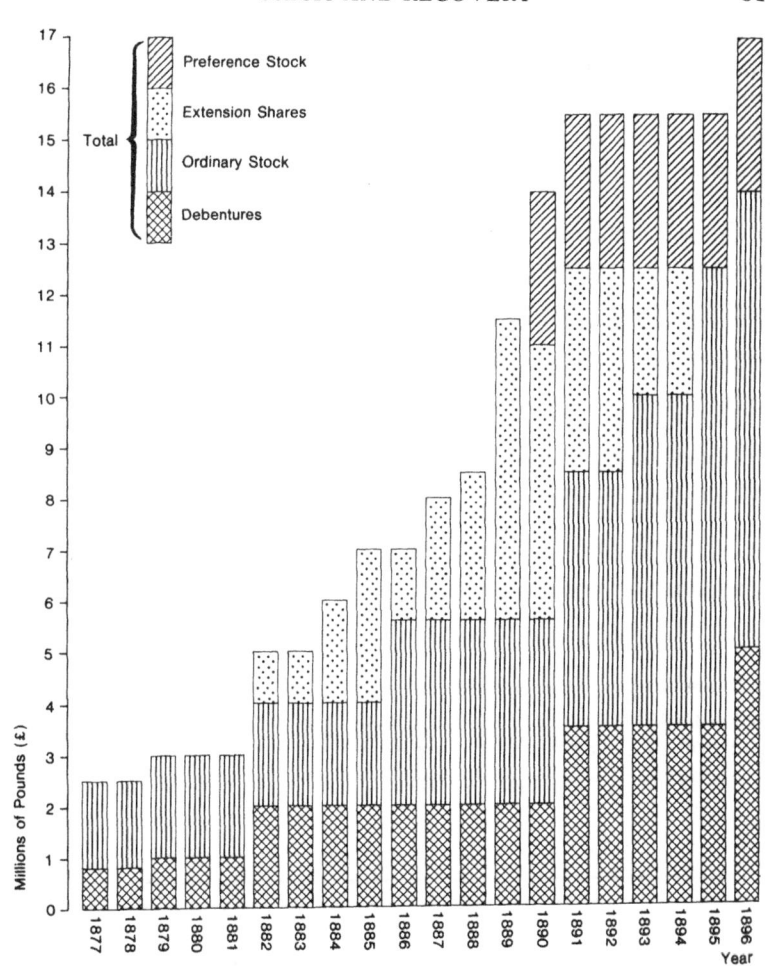

Graph 1: BAGS: capital account structure

capital often bore a fixed rate of interest, the charge was substantially lower than the prevailing dividend being declared on ordinary stock.[10] Preference and debenture issues were only resorted to in a sparing fashion. For the BAGS, the creation of special extension shares was as much a device to prevent the weight of new issues from overly reducing the rate of return upon equities as a means of promising a basic return upon new capital.

Newly floated entities were denied recourse to this device. For them the issue of preference shares or debentures was a necessity. When the Cordoba Central was formed in 1887 its initial capital consisted entirely of preference and debenture issues.[11] Several years later, when the original capital account had mushroomed from £600,000 to £5 millions, the mix of scrip was composed of assorted debentures, preference and deferred stocks and shares; not a hint of equities.[12] Founded the same year as the Cordoba Central, and almost as cautious in its issue of ordinary capital, was the Argentine North-Eastern Railway Company Limited. Some two and a half years after it had been established, the authorized capital of the company stood at £6.2 millions, of which £500,000 was to consist of ordinary shares. However, only £250,000 of equity capital had actually been created, but £3.3 millions had been raised in cumulative preference and mortgage debenture stocks.[13] Similarly, the Bahia Blanca and North Western Railway Company Limited, while making provision for some £650,000 ordinary shares in a total, initial authorized capital of £2 millions, had called up only the 6 per cent cumulative preference shares within a year of registration.[14] Such examples are legion. They indicate the nature of inducements necessary, as the market became tighter, to pursuade gullible investors to subscribe to questionable schemes — despite the apparent protection accorded by government guarantee.

Table 14: Argentine Railways: guarantee payments, total annual liability

	£
1883	60,000
1886	170,000
1888	440,000
1889	542,000
1890	620,000
1891	921,000
1892	1,369,000

Source: Compiled from *PP* 1890/1 LXXIV 9, 1892 LXXXI 67; *Economist* 28 November 1891 XLIX 1527; *Statis* 23 July 1892, XXX, 100.

Capitalized in this manner, newly-established companies faced bankruptcy when earnings proved insufficient to service their multiplicity of debenture stocks, and were thus doubly dependent upon the guarantee for their survival. It was the nature of the capitalization of these lines and the sheer magnitude of the guarantee liability which spelt disaster for guarantor and guaranteed. These were the railways responsible for the doubts entertained respecting Argentine credit. Notwithstanding reductions effected in the rate of return guaranteed, the volume of the obligations assumed by the national government rose alarmingly during the 1880s (see Table 14). While boom conditions prevailed, and the flow of capital into Argentina continued unabated, the state was able to meet these mounting commitments, although with increasing difficulty. The process could not continue indefinitely for the relative cost of servicing charges assumed by the Argentine national government consumed an ever-increasing proportion of the country's export earnings. Rising from 27 per cent at the middle of the decade, by the end of the eighties service charges absorbed 50 per cent of the foreign exchange generated by exports.[15] Within the context of these payments, disbursements to the guaranteed railways constituted the single largest item as the budget returns for 1892 indicate.

Table 15: *Service required by national government debt, 1892*

	£
Interest on 1886 loan	506,000
Interest on Funded bonds	270,000
Interest on Internal bonds	844,000
Interest on B.A. Water Works gold bonds	386,000
Interest on B.A. Harbour loan	82,000
Railway guarantees	921,000
Total	3,009,000
Interest and sinking fund due on scrip issued in lieu of previous service payments	1,440,000
Grand total	4,449,000

Source: *Statist* 23 July 1892, XXX, 100.

If the Crisis was caused by a belief that the Argentine government was, or would soon become, unable to honour its commitments, then the sheer scale of the guarantees, the principal liability assumed by government, was instrumental in creating this opinion. But the size of the railway guarantees was only part of the problem. Had the earnings of individual guaranteed companies been sufficient to service capital without recourse to state assistance there would have been little cause for concern. Undoubtedly, many of the railway projects embarked upon during the late 1880s had only a slight chance of yielding an adequate return in the short term. Indeed, it is questionable whether some of the schemes could ever earn an income commensurate with the sums invested. Several of the concessions awarded during the period are only comprehensible in terms of the prevailing, unbridled optimism. It was the speculative nature of this new railway investment which placed such a strain upon the finances of the national government. Unable to service their obligations, the newly-projected companies were dependent upon the guarantee. The reduced average return yielded by Argentine railway securities during the second half of the 1880s, which placed such a burden upon the resources of the Argentine government, was due to newly-commissioned lines, especially those railways inaugurated after 1888. The weight of this new construction served to depress average railway earnings for the remainder of the century, but the general reduction in the return upon railway investment was not mirrored in the affairs of the established networks. Until the crash actually occurred their financial record continued to lend support to the optimistic statements made at their respective annual general meetings.

As the data pertaining to the companies in Table 16 indicate, these railways do not provide evidence of a declining rate of profitability during the second half of the 1880s. On the contrary, they were only overtaken by events in 1889/90.[16] A decrease in the profits of these companies, although they were no longer guaranteed lines, might have occasioned an adverse reaction to Argentine railway investments generally. However, no such decrease took place. Their strength at a time of falling profits underlines their soundness and serves to reinforce the role of more speculative railway construction in the course of events preceding the Crisis.

The adverse role of the railways was thus determined by the weight of construction undertaken by guaranteed companies commissioned during the late 1880s — companies, directly

Table 16: Argentine Railways: net earnings and ordinary dividends of select British-owned companies and global yield

	BAGS		BA&R		CA		Argentine Railways
	Earnings £	Div. %	Earnings £	Div. %	Earnings £	Div. %	Yield on Capital %
1884	325,868	11	33,749	5	334,205	10	7.34
1885	354,992	10	64,872	5	281,340	10	4.63
1886	425,802	8	137,237	6	292,445	12	4.68
1887	541,695	10	247,766	8½	335,528	12	4.83
1888	683,639	10	332,983	9	396,084	12	5.05
1889	678,203	10	362,805	9	431,572	10	2.36
1890	587,663	10	232,999	7	289,222	2½	2.63
1891	580,283	8	196,660	nil	77,485	nil	1.74
1892	560,253	5	280,771	nil	183,532	nil	1.77
1893	595,309	5	280,266	nil	258,995	1	1.90
1894	635,727	5	294,984	1½	300,071	1½	2.04
1895	724,043	5	310,522	2	357,876	2½	2.59
1896	826,676	5¼	362,192	3	448,519	3½	3.05

Financial years ending 31 December, except for the BAGS, whose years terminated on 30 June. This factor explains the apparently healthier dividend declared by the BAGS in 1890. Given reduced net receipts for fiscal 1889/90, the maintenance of 10% dividend upon ordinary stock was accomplished only at the expense of various reserve and renewal funds which were not augmented in the usual manner.

Source: Compiled from respective Annual Reports; República Argentina, Ministerio de Obras Públicas, Dirección General de Ferrocarriles Estadística de los ferrocarriles en explotación, 1913 (Buenos Aires, 1916) pp. 396–98.

dependent upon the state, whose building programmes far outstripped that of established lines. As the principal official obligation, railway guarantees were undoubtedly a contributory factor to the financial difficulties experienced by the national government, and were largely responsible for the crisis of confidence which brought the whole fragile edifice of the Argentine economic miracle to ruin. These entities had always callously insisted that the failure of the government to meet the guarantees would reflect adversely upon the country's credit. The general acceptance of this view led precisely to their difficulties. Many of the companies formed during this period were committed to long-term dependence upon the guarantee. Indeed, as mentioned above, it might be argued that many were projected merely for the purpose of obtaining a guarantee. Railway construction, difficult to justify upon economic grounds alone, was often undertaken because concessionaires and promoters were able to obtain a substantial return given the willingness of investors to subscribe to virtually any project in receipt of a guarantee. Yet it would be wrong to level such a sweeping charge at all the companies incorporated during the hectic 1880s. In many cases the potential of newly-exploited regions did warrant such capital investment, and would in time yield a return sufficient to service the sums involved. When the Argentine government abandoned its guarantee policy, the chaff was separated from the grain. After the Crisis all companies were charged with over-expansion, and a too exclusive reliance upon the guarantee. The refutation of this charge lay in an ability — demonstrated by certain companies — to maintain a basic level of profitable operations, and the relative facility with which some lines were able to forgo the unilateral suspension of guarantee payments by government in the post-Crisis period. For others, liquidation or fusion with a larger entity was the only course.

Recovery
Economic recovery during the 1890s was accomplished with remarkable rapidity and lends weight to the view that the Crisis was one of development. The speed with which the country resumed servicing its foreign debts surprised even Argentina's creditors.[17] But the comparative ease with which the nation overcame the effects of the Crisis was particularly important for the

railway companies. The factors which occasioned recovery were also responsible for a radical transformation of Argentina's railway map. The apparent resilience of economic activity was primarily due to structural changes which had occurred during the 1880s. Buoyant export markets account for Argentina's resumption of debt service payments. Although the level of imports did not regain pre-Crisis peaks until the early twentieth century, export earnings recovered relatively rapidly, given a marked volume increase, and improvement in commodity prices after 1896.[18] However, if increased export earnings explain Argentina's financial recovery, it was the nature of those exports that accounted for the ability of the railways to regain earlier levels of prosperity. Economic restructuring during the final decades of the nineteenth century entailed the creation of a dynamic arable sector. Argentina ceased to be a net importer of grain, and became one of the world's major suppliers of cereals. Although the absolute value of more traditional commodities did not decline until the early twentieth century, new arable commodities had already achieved a paramount significance in the country's export schedule by the turn of the century.[19] Rapidly expanding bulk export commodities provided a ready traffic for the railway companies (see Table 17).

While the structure of staple exports was changing, Argentina

Table 17: Argentine exports: select arable products

	1884	1900	1910
Wheat and flour			
Volume (metric tons)	113,991	2,004,976	2,048,460
Value (£)	920,255	10,069,147	15,429,879
Maize			
Volume	113,710	713,248	2,660,225
Value	454,800	2,386,749	12,052,161
Linseed			
Volume	33,991	223,257	604,877
Value	339,916	2,134,802	8,920,879
Oats			
Volume	nil	7,619	370,948
Value	nil	25,449	1,628,515

Source: The Times, South American Supplement 31 December 1912 x.

was also increasing its human resources. Total population rose from 1,737,000 in 1869 to 3,955,000 in 1895 and by the time of the third national census in 1914 stood at nearly eight millions.[20] A large part of this increase was occasioned by the flow of migrants to Argentina, the greater proportion of whom, whatever else their intention might have been, settled in the urban areas. Population growth of this order, coupled with grain production, ensured a massive expansion of domestic urban consumer demand also tending to an increase in railway traffic.[21] Grain products became a major item of traffic on several lines, while the establishment of agricultural colonies in the rural areas stimulated a sizable return traffic from the ports.[22] In addition, diverse activities associated with the arable export industry ensured a relatively wide participation in the income flow generated, and served to further increase urban purchasing power. Although initially geared towards the consumption of imports, urban centres represented substantial markets for basic domestic products, the best example of which (after grain and pastoral products) was the wine and associated commodities of the *Cuyo* viniferous industry — a rapidly expanding sector following the region's effective incorporation within the national railway network.

Given these advantageous circumstances, railway companies were quick to discern signs of recovery. Bumper harvests of maize and wheat in 1892 and 1893 seemed to promise a speedy and painless return to former levels of prosperity. But political disturbances, together with more mundane matters, conspired to frustrate an early recovery. As the Great Southern informed its shareholders, they had to contend not only with revolutionary outbursts, low prices and a depreciated paper *peso*, but also with inclement weather.[23] Furthermore, even the established lines carried the burden of extensions which had little prospect of yielding an adequate return during the immediate post-Crisis period.

Although the pace of recovery was not as fast as many would have wished, by the mid-1890s there were indications of a general improvement. This theme was developed at annual general meetings where the mood became less strained and the atmosphere more cordial with the prospect of a return to prosperity. In April 1895 Central Argentine shareholders were notified that their company, in common with other Argentine railways, was making slow progress; there were better times ahead. The following year the chairman cautiously reiterated his claim that a 'gradual' recovery was under way. Finally, at the 34th ordinary general meeting, stockholders were advised of their company's 'satisfactory' results.[21] The Central was not alone. Its experience was typical of the larger, established lines, and not unrepresentative of some of the more recently commissioned railways. The Great Southern equalled, if not bettered, the Central's record, while even the Pacific had some cause for optimism. As the result of a financial reorganization, that company was able to resume servicing second debentures in 1895 and a year later rewarded the patience of first preference stockholders.[25] The smaller lines were not so fortunate. Better times were something of which the mesopotamian standard-gauge railways, the metre-gauge companies of the north, and a few of the small, broad-gauge pampean lines dreamt rather than experienced. Nevertheless, the traffic returns of the larger companies indicated that for them at least recovery was well advanced by mid-1890s. The chronology of improvement may be traced in Great Southern and Central operating statistics. As can be seen in Table 18, the BAGS and the Central earning schedules returned to pre-Crisis levels during the period 1894–96. Despite minor setbacks which might have occurred in any one year, gross receipts regained or exceeded the peaks of 1889 by the middle of the following decade, while a tight control was maintained over working expenses, thus allowing an even greater improvement in net earnings.

Although these companies were old established lines they had few features in common. Their early history and subsequent development were very different. Consequently, their collective experience of recovery has a more general significance, and may be held to be broadly representative of the major networks. Ultimately, and notwithstanding differences of degree, the earning schedules of entities incorporated during the late 1880s followed a similar trend, given a time lag. It was during this period that the impact of 'developmental' construction undertaken during the previous decade may be observed. New lines of traffic — reflecting the restructuring of the Argentine economy — assumed an increasing significance in the earning schedules of several companies. The BAGS provides an example: the growing diversification of its returns is a guide to the nature of the changes that were taking place. It is instructive to observe new methods of

Table 18: Argentine Railways: operating data, BAGS and CA

	‡BAGS		§CA	
	Gross receipts £	Working expenses £	Gross receipts £	Working expenses £
1887	1,012,919	471,224	619,604	284,076
1888	1,195,681	512,052	757,009	360,925
1889	1,320,458	642,255	*941,722	*510,150
1890	1,282,053	694,390	728,558	439,336
1891	1,098,446	518,163	†399,651	†322,166
1892	956,630	396,377	532,489	348,957
1893	1,054,077	462,181	623,612	364,617
1894	1,045,325	409,598	699,369	399,298
1895	1,123,797	399,754	774,416	416,529
1896	1,296,121	496,445	939,150	491,150
1897	1,400,677	534,078	743,539	445,788
1898	1,519,032	584,634	997,032	502,421
1899	1,995,725	867,954	1,286,655	611,354

‡ Financial year ending 30 June
§ Financial year ending 31 December
* Incorporating BAN section account
† Incorporating BAW section account

Source: Compiled from Annual Reports.

presenting statistical data in the Great Southern's *Annual Reports*; gradually the returns become more detailed as new elements of traffic are extracted from the 'catch-all' category, 'general goods', and itemized separately. Until the 1880s the company's freight had been dominated by 'traditional' commodities which had played a significant role in the economy of the River Plate since the latter part of the colonial period. Hitherto much space in the reports, and discussions at general meetings, had been devoted to items such as grease and tallow, hides and skins; 'colonial' lines which, amongst others, had been specifically disaggregated from tonnage totals. The major exceptions to these products were wool and hair. By the late 1870s the company gradually became aware of the possibilities for encouraging grain traffic, although this commodity was only regarded as of some significance when the frontier of cereal cultivation moved away from the immediate environs of Buenos Aires and the potentialities for a new line of

Table 19: BAGS: goods and animal traffic

	Wool & Hair (metric tons)	%	Hay & Grain (metric tons)	%	Stone (metric tons)	%	General goods (met. ts.)	Sub-total (metric tons)	Extension material (met. ts.)	Grand total (metric tons)	Animals (no.)
1881/2	43,147	22.2	17,394	9.0	—	—	133,424	193,965	8,373	202,238	208,394
1882/3	48,637	22.1	21,847	10.0	4,072	1.9	145,089	219,645	65,090	284,735	443,707
1883/4	58,545	18.1	29,811	9.2	20,548	6.4	214,883	323,823	58,511	382,334	525,344
1884/5	68,933	16.9	29,462	7.2	60,243	14.7	250,052	408,690	56,526	465,216	645,930
1885/6	72,125	19.4	23,528	6.3	77,723	20.9	198,813	372,189	47,779	419,968	668,802
1886/7	69,483	12.0	30,243	5.2	212,879	36.8	265,105	577,710	13,175	590,885	816,608
1887/8	71,560	10.6	61,668	9.1	231,491	34.2	311,432	676,151	21,791	697,942	1,168,000
1888/9	86,054	10.9	68,443	8.7	283,042	35.9	351,977	789,511	17,058	806,569	1,406,259
1889/90	71,113	7.9	98,341	10.9	309,890	34.2	426,192	905,536	70,677	976,213	1,469,419
1890/1	85,552	12.6	98,220	14.5	134,036	19.8	359,766	677,540	131,980	809,520	1,888,986
1891/2	85,552	15.6	148,007	27.0	62,126	11.3	252,308	547,993	119,632	667,625	1,463,359
1892/3	82,579	10.6	277,715	35.6	89,754	11.5	329,329	779,377	26,851	806,228	1,576,581
1893/4	90,115	13.4	203,817	30.4	90,783	13.5	286,041	670,756	74,502	745,258	2,111,083
1894/5	107,068	14.6	230,082	31.4	105,867	14.4	290,884	733,901	7,382	741,283	2,541,681
1895/6	113,763	12.2	346,382	37.0	121,189	12.9	354,526	935,860	44,299	980,159	2,589,389
1896/7	112,915	12.4	307,749	33.8	117,354	12.9	373,628	911,646	148,317	1,059,963	2,999,731
1897/8	119,221	14.1	184,479	21.8	140,113	16.5	403,673	847,486	258,162	1,105,648	3,323,758
1898/9	134,647	8.4	528,228	33.0	177,083	11.1	760,834	1,600,792	179,642	1,780,434	4,176,710

Source: BAGS Compiled and calculated from *Annual Reports*.

long-haul traffic were realized — particularly as the various sections of the Bahía Blanca extension were inaugurated.[26] Diversification continued apace during the nineties.

Table 19 shows there was also a dramatic rise in the volume of animal traffic. The annual average had been 288,000 head for the quinequennium 1880–84, 941,000 in 1885–89, 1,700,000 in 1890–94, and 3,126,000 during the second half of the 1890s. Paralleling the growth in animal traffic (mainly sheep, which accounted for something in excess of 90 per cent of the total), was the development of other new lines as substantial volume items. Hay and grain (especially the latter) also came into their own during the decade. Further evidence of diversification is provided by the separate itemization of different categories of grain in the *Annual Report* for 1892 and subsequent years. Another element in the transformation of the local economy may also be identified within the Great Southern's returns: the presentation of data pertaining to stone traffic was a function of urbanization.[27] The company was not slow to identify this process. The building of La Plata, and the beautification and expansion of Buenos Aires provided another volume item in operating data.[28] Although more volatile than other lines, this commodity generated revenue throughout the period. But the process of urbanization is not only reflected in the volume of stone traffic. Even more important was the growth in passenger receipts. The quinquennial annual average increased from a little over 50,000 for the period 1880–84 to 3.2 million people by 1895–99. In the last year of the decade passenger traffic exceeded five millions. There was a corresponding rise in passenger revenue, from £104,594 in 1880 to £518,759 in 1899.[29] Most of the increase in the volume of traffic was occasioned by the expansion of suburban passenger movements and journeys between Buenos Aires and the new provincial capital at La Plata.

Paralleling this development on the Great Southern, other networks witnessed the growing pre-eminence of new items of traffic. Cereals, wine, sugar, and finally livestock, assumed a dominant position in the traffic accounts of individual companies, depending upon the regions in which they operated, and carried the railways to recovery and prosperity. Like the Southern, the newly-incorporated Buenos Ayres Western Railway Company Limited developed as a cereal, and subsequently a livestock, line. Grains dominated the Central and Rosario, and some of the mesopotamian lines. Wine traffic was already the major item carried by the Argentine Great Western Railway Company Limited, and soon emerged as an important commodity on the Pacific. The metre-gauge lines of the north-west enjoyed a more diversified traffic schedule, but sugar or grain tended to predominate on individual sections. For other firms, recovery was also not based solely upon improved freight earnings. Passenger receipts had always been a major source of revenue for several of the companies. Indeed, during the immediate, post-Crisis period passenger earnings declined relatively less than other sources of income, and aided the railways during the worst years of the depression. Passenger revenue accounted for over 30 per cent of the Western's total earnings in the period 1890–92, while in 1891 (when the Central's gross receipts were nearly halved) passenger traffic represented one third of the company's revenue.[30]

The Consequences of Recovery
Buoyant aggregate traffic returns, although masking the changes which had occurred in the schedules of individual lines, explain the general improvement in railway affairs. But recovery was not an end in itself, and the combinations of factors which had occasioned recovery were also responsible for the creation of zonal railway networks. The zonal concept, however, had yet to be fully exploited. Climatic and geographical factors were already encouraging regional specialization, but before the railways could respond to those stimuli the confidence of shareholders had to be regained. Difficulties outstanding with the Argentine government had to be settled, especially the problem of the guaranteed railways, together with a general reappraisal of state railway policy — features which in turn depended upon the performance of the companies themselves. The solution to this chain of difficulties lay in the recovery of earnings in the mid-1890s and the effect which it had upon the private lines.

Due to the long gestation period involved in railway construction, the effects of the Baring Crisis upon the expansion of the railway network were not discernible until the mid-1890s. During the period 1890–94 the greater part of mileage commissioned represented the completion of schemes initiated at the end of the previous decade. The impetus imparted by pre-Crisis projects, however, began to fade between 1894 and 1896.[31] Yet it was precisely at this time that the major lines embarked upon a new programme of extension building. Although confined almost exclusively to the larger railways, and hardly comparable with the vast additions to the network which had occurred during the preceding period, this new construction was not without significance. It was important because it indicated a return of shareholders' confidence, and also because it began to give effect to the concept of regional railway development. The last years of the nineteenth century saw a steady extension of the Argentine railway network as various companies sought to establish their zones, and create regionally-based systems through amalgamation and consolidation.

In 1895 the BAGS responded to pressure from the central government to construct extensions in northern Patagonia. The company proposed to drive a line westward from its recently-established railhead at Bahía Blanca to the confluence of the rivers Limay and Neuquen. The Argentine authorities, conscious of the parlous state of relations with Chile, saw a strategic potential in this extension and awarded the company a bounty of £150,000. Notwithstanding its political significance, the estimated cost of the line was £1 million, and represented a return to the company's building programme of the *early* 1880s.[32] Despite the special circumstances surrounding the BAGS's extensions, a similar policy was pursued by most of the major British-owned lines. As Table 20 indicates, the increase in the total volume of investment in Argentine railways during these years was minimal, the annual average for the period 1894–1900 was 1.6 per cent. Limited aggregate growth, however, was the sum of substantial expansion for each of the small number of companies involved. The revival of investment represented not only the recovery of these railways from the effects of the Crisis but also the continued faith of British investors in those companies and the country in which they operated.

The reason for this return of confidence is not difficult to discern. In the case of the major lines improved earning potential was fairly quickly translated into dividends which, although well below earlier levels, nevertheless provided sufficient promise of better times. This slow improvement in dividends lent weight to

Table 20: *Argentine Railways: total nominal investment*

	Capitalization £	Increase £	%
1885	24,344,062	—	—
1886	29,442,641	5,098,579	(20.9)
1887	35,118,767	5,676,126	(19.3)
1888	39,001,970	3,883,203	(11.1)
1889	50,471,577	11,469,607	(29.4)
1890	63,742,811	13,271,234	(26.3)
1891	75,350,180	11,607,369	(18.2)
1892	87,573,072	12,222,892	(16.2)
1893	93,947,090	6,374,018	(7.3)
1894	95,694,521	1,747,431	(1.9)
1895	96,186,643	492,122	(0.5)
1896	98,660,170	2,473,527	(2.6)
1897	100,721,680	2,061,510	(2.1)
1898	103,757,594	3,035,914	(2.9)
1899	104,372,543	614,949	(0.6)
1900	105,321,364	948,821	(0.9)

Source: República Argentina, Ministerio de Obras Públicas, Dirección General de Ferrocarriles *Estadística de los ferrocarriles en explotactión durante el año 1913* (Buenos Aires 1916) pp. 369–98.

the arguments placed before shareholders at company meetings. They understood that there was little chance of ever again earning the 'fabulous' interest enjoyed during the hectic 1880s. Chastened by the depression, shareholders were content to receive a lower return on their capital provided they were allowed a measure of security. Table 21 proves that for Western and Southern shareholders this element of security had been obtained by the late 1890s. They were no longer earning over 10 per cent, but there was every prospect that they would continue to receive a steady 6 or 7 per cent. Rosario and Central shareholders were less fortunate, but the Central was able to pay 6 per cent by the end of the century, and early in the twentieth century the BA&R did likewise.

The recovery of railway earnings and profits during the second half of the decade, based as it was on structural changes in the Argentine economy, accounts for the continued interest of foreign investors in Argentine railway development. Railway earnings had proved more immediately susceptible to the crash than

Table 21: *Argentine Railways: ordinary dividends declared by select British-owned companies*

	BAGS %	BAW %	BA&R %	CA %
1889	10	—	9	10
1890	10	—	7	2½
1891	8	*4	nil	nil
1892	5	2½	nil	nil
1893	5	6	nil	1
1894	5	5½	1½	1½
1895	5	5½	2	2½
1896	5½	6	3	3½
1897	5¾	6	2	1¾
1898	6	4	2½	4½
1899	7	6	4	6

* Equal to a dividend of 4% on paid-up stock.

Source: Compiled from *Annual Reports*.

the process of railway investment, but the improvement of profits in the mid-1890s was critical. Revenue and profits recovered at precisely the moment when the influence of the time lag involved in long-term capital projects began to wane, and provided enough incentive to maintain the momentum of growth. In the early 1890s the weight of capital programmes helped carry the Argentine economy through the post-Crisis period; a circular process ensured that the companies themselves benefited from the dynamic effect of those projects. In 1894/5 capital account of the whole network grew by less than half a million pounds. Thereafter, the growing earning potential of the major lines ensured that a basic rate of expansion was maintained.

IV

THE RAILWAY GUARANTEES: A RETROSPECTIVE
REAPPRAISAL

The first casualty of the Baring Crisis was the guarantee system. This was perhaps inevitable. In the jaundiced climate prevailing during the early 1890s opinion began to turn against foreign-financed utilities. It was widely held that these companies had abused a privileged position, probably misappropriated public funds, and brought little benefit to the country.[1] In company circles it was considered that much of the odium associated with the guarantees was due to mishandling by the Argentine authorities, but British opinion too was ready for a reappraisal. The continued existence of guarantee legislation upon the statute books served to remind the state of a policy which had not fulfilled expectations. Unsettled guarantee claims, moreover, left a legacy of bitterness between aggrieved railway companies and the government, and created a climate of uncertainty among all lines. It was a short step from denouncing the opportunism of guarantee-hungry shareholders to questioning the whole principle of private railway exploitation, especially one based upon foreign financing.[2]

Unfortunately, circumstances surrounding the revocation of the guarantees during the early 1890s tended to foster many misconceptions, not least that the system was peculiar to Argentina. It was overlooked that guarantees had been applied in virtually every country at some stage of nineteenth-century railway development, with the possible exception of Great Britain. The vast sums needed for modernization of infrastructure invariably demanded some form of official participation, irrespective of whether the capital was to be raised at home or abroad, though the nature of state intervention might differ from country to country. When initially seeking to float the Central Argentine project, the government of the Argentine Confederation had sought to emulate the example of the United States, where land grants had been employed with success by both state and federal governments. But this device was not widely used, and direct financial participation was the norm. Often that participation took the form of 'joint-ventures', as in the case of the French railway system, where the state assumed responsibility for capital expenditure — the construction of the permanent way and so forth — while private enterprise was offered a franchise to operate railway services. Or the government might itself construct and operate railway enterprises, financed from revenue or borrowing. During the middle third of the nineteenth century, the guarantee system gained a measure of acceptance as the most appropriate mechanism. In India the system was applied upon a large scale. The Russian government experimented with profit guarantees, as did several Latin American states besides Argentina. Competing with other areas for foreign funds in order to establish a modern means of communication, Argentina was obliged to accept the 'rules of the game'. Railway guarantees were not peculiar to the Argentine Republic, nor a mechanism that was especially designed by foreign interests to serve their ends in the River Plate, as some Argentine authors appear to believe. The fact was that in Argentina during the 1880s a well-tried policy was ruined through over-use.

Guarantees: Original Intentions
Railway guarantees, as has been seen, arose from the belief of various mid-century interest groups in the political and economic significance of the railway concept.[3] Several attempts to stimulate railway construction had been hindered by, among other factors, an initial hesitance on the part of private capitalists. The guarantees were formulated as a means of attracting private investment by reducing the element of risk associated with early schemes. But equally important, the guarantee regularized state assistance to private companies. On the one hand the system granted shareholders a degree of security in terms of a fixed regular return upon investments, on the other it provided the state with a means of sponsoring railway development which did not entail an open-ended capital commitment. Perhaps these dual objectives were irreconcilable in the long term, but in the short period there was a substantial element of compatibility. Guarantee policy, conditioned by the early history of the *Oeste* and Central, was most

specific in its objectives and the duties and benefits which it ascribed to the contracting parties. In view of these antecedents and subsequent wide use, the guarantee clauses of the Great Southern concession are worth considering at some length. The precise definitions applied served as a model for virtually all future guaranteed railway contracts awarded by both national and provincial governments in Argentina.

III. The Government guarantees to the undertaking an interest of 7 per cent. per annum, upon the effective costs of the railway; that is to say, it engages to allow to the undertaking, annually, the amount which may be deficient, in its net profits, to make up the aforesaid 7 per cent. as interest upon the ascertained cost of the line; but in no case, is to be recognised a cost exceeding £10,000 sterling per mile, neither shall the Government, under any circumstance, pay a greater annual sum than £700 sterling per mile for the said guarantee. It being understood that the undertaking shall be bound to deliver to the Government the surplus which may be produced every year by the line, above the aforesaid 7 per cent. upon the recognised cost, until it has been reimbursed for the advance which may have been made under the same guarantee.

IV. In order to establish the cost which is to be recognised, there shall be taken into account, solely, the effective expense of the works and the materials employed, in addition, the value of the land expropriated, the legitimate and customary commissions, and the interest on the capital, at the rate of 6 per cent. per annum, while the line is being constructed, for the amount which may be paid in.

V. The said guarantee shall begin to take effect, in proportion as the line will be successively opened for public traffic, in the several sections (which will be specified at the time of the plan being approved) for the recognised cost of the same not to exceed the established limit of £10,000 sterling per mile.

Each section being finished, the Government will cause the works to be examined; and in case they should not be solid, or should not offer perfect security, it will not be liable for the guarantee, and will prevent the road being worked, until those defects shall be duly repaired.

VI. For the liquidation of the accorded guarantee, which will be effected at the end of each year, it is understood that there can be deducted from the gross proceeds of the Railway only the legitimate and indispensable expenses of management, wear and tear thereof, and in no case are any sums to be deducted for interest on large amounts, supplied to the undertaking, or taken on credit, to be employed, or for account of the said Railway, beyond the limit of cost, fixed in the 3rd and 4th Articles.

VII. The term of the guarantee shall be forty years, from the date when it shall commence running, at the expiration of which all obligations on the part of the Government will cease; the public lands assigned, remaining the perpetual property of the undertaking. The Government will not be bound to realise the guarantee during the periods in which the service of the Railway may be interrupted by the fault or neglect of the contractor.[4]

This style and form remained largely intact until the guarantees were abandoned. Only three changes occurred in subsequent years: provision was made for intervention in deciding tariffs, the rate of interest was reduced to 6 and 5 per cent in concessions awarded during the 1880s, and, in addition to the specification that only legitimate operating expenses could be charged against revenue, the government stipulated its right to one half of operating receipts. The latter was a further attempt to instil prudent management. In effect, the Argentine authorities chose to determine the working ratio of the guaranteed lines. It was an optimistic exercise. Even the established lines had found it difficult to maintain working ratios at this level for any length of time. During the first quinquennium following their inauguration the BAGS and Central Argentine averaged working ratios of 55.3 and 54.3 per cent respectively. Between the assumption of responsibility for working the line and the Baring Crisis, the ratios for both surprisingly averaged 51.3 per cent; the range for the Great Southern being from a low of 38.2 per cent to a high of 64 per cent, and for the CA from 37.8 per cent to 65.8 per cent. Very low ratios were the norm on the Southern during the period 1879–81, while the Central had kept the ratio below 40 per cent between 1882 and 1884.[5] But this was exceptional, even for these companies; other railways were much less able to maintain low working ratios. Between 1866 and 1880 the BAN ratio averaged 60.3 per cent, ranging from 42.6 to 87 per cent; only twice did the ratio fall below 50 per cent while for seven of these years it stood above 60 per cent.[6] The experience of the Ensenada Port was similar. Between 1876, when the line was taken over from the contractors, and the Crisis, the ratio averaged 60.6 per cent, ranging between 46.5 and 75 per cent: only on two occasions did the ratio fall below 50 per cent, while for eight years during this period the ratio exceeded 60 per cent, and on three occasions stood above 70 per cent.[7] Given prudent management, working ratios of 50 per cent and below were obtainable only after several years of careful operating.[8] It was highly unlikely that newly-commissioned lines would be capable of achieving such a degree of efficiency during their respective inaugural epochs, particularly in the 1880s.

It is clear, therefore, that it was not the intention of the state to supply guaranteed lines with a grant or an outright gift: the scheme provided for an interest-free loan, repayable as or when the financial position of a company permitted. Railway guarantees were a device to stimulate the flotation of railway companies; they constituted an undertaking to prospective subscribers that, until the railway was sufficiently established to obtain a reasonable income from its operation, their capital would nevertheless yield a regular return. Limiting the guarantee to recognize costs of construction enabled the government to determine (or at least indicate) what was considered an acceptable rate of capitalization, while scrutiny of operating expenses and the introduction of the 50 per cent working ratio rule was a further attempt to control capital expenditure (amongst other factors). These were mechanisms to safeguard the interests of the state against less scrupulous developers. Argentine authorities did not propose fostering unprofitable, or uneconomic, railway construction, or sanctioning unbridled exploitation. The state sought to encourage railway development, and was prepared to offer reasonable inducement to private interests — domestic or foreign — established upon a formal, regular basis that was designed to cater for the fair expectations of both parties.

Limitations and Difficulties

Despite the laudable intentions enshrined in guarantee legislation, the system was not easily administered. Its smooth operation depended upon the goodwill of both parties, a sentiment that was often dissipated by practical, technical problems. Justifiably stringent procedure for the examination of guarantee claims sometimes degenerated into procrastination, particularly when funds were insufficient to meet these obligations, though in many cases it was the difficulty of accurately budgeting for claims which hindered setttlement rather than a desire to renege upon agreements. But the existence of unsettled accounts, for whatever reason, did sour relations between the companies and the state, leading to imputations against Argentine credit and attempts to restrict Argentina's access to foreign money markets. Moreover, notwithstanding the rigorous investigations of claims and concessions, and despite the intentions of early legislators, schemes were sanctioned which occasioned charges of chicanery. Inevitably guarantees were accorded to lines that had little prospect of ever earning the specified interest, while other railways came to rely upon the government guarantee instead of using the system as a short-term measure in order to secure self-sufficiency.

Delays in the liquidation of guarantee claims formed one of the earliest sources of complaint against government, federal and provincial. Not that tardy settlement was confined to the railways: it was the general experience in Argentina.

> It takes a creditor of the Government months and months to get his claim acknowledged by the department whom it may concern. When acknowledged it takes perhaps an equal time to get it passed by the *Contaduria* and signed by the Finance Minister, and when in this stage he has all the trouble of getting the money from the *Tesoreria*.[9]

Frustration of this kind was felt by most lines, although the incidence of the occurrence was greatest in the case of struggling, less prosperous companies that were most dependent upon state aid. In spite of the relatively short period during which it was in receipt of a guarantee, the BAGS sometimes found the Buenos Aires provincial authorities less than punctual in honouring obligations.[10] The Central experienced a similar problem in 1872 with the national government, which was attributed to general prevarication.[11] By the end of the decade the company maintained that unsettled claims amounted to over £133,000, not all of which were acknowledged by the Argentine authorities.[12]

The most spectacular examples of non-payment and delayed settlement, however, were provided by the Buenos Ayres Northern and East Argentine, whose respective clashes with Buenos Aires provincial government and national authorities assumed almost epic proportions. More than once, doubts regarding the validity of the claims submitted by these companies provided an added inducement to equivocate. The Northern had not required assistance during its early years, but submitted a demand for the full guarantee of £10,500 in 1865. After examination, the provincial inspectors recommended a reduction of some 80 per cent, but the provincial government agreed to pay over half the company's original claim, settling £5,800 upon the line.[13] The following year, by which time the total guarantee cover stood at £11,200, the company sought £7,000 which was paid in full.[14] But the Northern still demanded the balance of the previous year's guarantee, which it had now reduced to £9,000, although the board lamented that the company's claim had probably been prejudiced by acceptance of the government's earlier offer of £5,800.[15] In 1867 the railway submitted a demand for £4,300 which was only partially satisfied.[16] Exasperated by the railway's continuing claims, the province ordered a survey of the company in 1868 and found that the line was not properly constructed. Consequently the guarantee was withdrawn by decree of 17 November 1868 and was not restored until 1871 when the company had spent some £20,000 on improvements, and the province considered the line to be in good order.[17] Neither party was pleased by this episode. The company felt that it had been the victim of unwarranted interference, while the province considered, with some justice, that as originally constructed and financed the BAN had little prospect of achieving self-sufficiency.

The East Argentine was an even more notorious example. As already stated, constructed as a standard-gauge line, the company enjoyed a guarantee commensurate with the broad-gauge companies, a feature that was said to owe more to bribery than oversight on the part of the national authorities.[18] As soon as the state became liable, the company submitted a claim for the full guarantee which was met in a dilatory fashion. The Argentine authorities quickly realized the mistake of according the EA such generous cover.

> ... the Government seems determined to escape to a certain extent the burden of the unconditional guarantee given, but will no doubt meet with great opposition as the only chance of a dividend lies in this guarantee. It will of course be said that investors bought their shares on good faith of the engagement taken by the Government, but on the other hand as the Exchequer is short of funds, the unprofitable concerns will have to be the first to suffer. Even a nation with a perfectly balanced budget would get into difficulties with such extra items of expenditure as $328,000 — for guarantee to a line some 91 miles long, and the prospects of which may be said to be nil.[19]

Even when it was disposed to pay the guarantee, the Argentine government did so only tardily, and found it increasingly difficult to keep up with the company's incessant demands. On 31 December 1875, the company's claim for unsettled guarantee debts stood at approximately £48,000. During the course of 1876 that sum was reduced by the remittance of £21,000, only to climb to £95,000 when the guarantee claim for that year was submitted. Further remittances from Argentina reduced the outstanding account to £75,000, but the 1877 submission almost doubled the debt, which then reached £131,139. Another settlement brought the company's claim down to less than £100,000, but again, when the annual accounts were submitted, the state found that it still owed the railway £153,833. This figure was subsequently reduced to £126,231, but by 31 Devember 1879 it had soared to £173,328 and a year later to £215,300. During the course of 1881 and 1882 a determined effort was made to settle the debt.[20]

Episodes such as these tended to bring the whole system into disrepute. Shareholders dependent upon the guarantee for their dividends were alarmed by delays, while the local authorities looked askance at mounting accounts presented by several of the less fortunate railways. Although provincial and national governments might question the validity of many claims, delays in payment were often occasioned by more mundane factors. An obvious difficulty, and one that emerged at an early date, was the irregular nature of demands made upon the exchequer. Claims were liable to change from year to year; sometimes the margin of fluctuation was substantial. In awarding a guarantee the state contracted to pay a sum which was regulated only in so far as a maximum disbursement was written into the concession. Within these limits the actual figure required could vary considerably.

The problem was exacerbated when the number of railway companies, and consequently guarantees, increased. Such a situation presented serious budgetary problems. For instance, in the case of the province of Buenos Aires, fluctuations in railway guarantee payments did not prove insurmountable when the sum of those obligations was small. The original Buenos Ayres & San Fernando concession had fixed the maximum annual guarantee at £10,500.[21] The BA&C's was £28,000.[22] The Great Southern absorbed £49,000.[23] These guarantees had been accorded to companies whose region of exploitation had been circumscribed, or was thought to be contained, by the pattern of population settlement and constraints placed upon expansion by the existence of the Indian frontier. The early lines did little more than supplement existing means of communication. The San Fernando was virtually a rural tramway running along the Plate, and although the Campana and the Southern boasted lines of 50 and 70 miles respectively, their spheres of operation were no less effectively curtailed by the existing state of the economy. The possible guarantee burdens imposed by these companies were supportable, and presented few difficulties for the provincial *Hacienda*. But should this liability grow due to the granting of new guaranteed concessions, or the sanctioning of guaranteed extension building by the existing companies, then the government would face complications. The need to provide indeterminate appropriations for a major item of expenditure made budgeting extremely difficult. These problems were compounded by the fact that the state was usually called upon to make more substantial payments during those periods when it was least in a position to raise additional revenue.[24] Moreover, during periods of economic dislocation, inability to meet extra-ordinary guarantee claims reflected adversely upon the government's credit, and thus endangered access to funds at precisely the time when they were most needed.

The Search for Remedies

Although these inconveniences were suffered by national and provincial authorities, it was the province of Buenos Aires which first attempted to remedy the situation. The provincial government sought to commute the fluctuating guarantee to a fixed annual charge, issuing a decree of the effect that,

> Whereas,
>
> Article 1. The system of according a guarantee on the capital invested in the construction of railways has been accepted by the public authorities of the Province, by reason, it seems, that it is an inducement, and at the same time a guarantee, for the introduction of capital into the country.
>
> Article 2. It is understood that a country like ours will not stop at certain sacrifices when these are made to endow it with railways built by foreign capital.
>
> Article 3. That in practice the system of guarantees offers serious difficulties in the liquidation of the accounts to which must be added that, in the present instance, the amount of the obligation is quite uncertain and variable.
>
> Article 4. It is believed that the Companies themselves would accept modification of their respective contracts, and in harmony with the ideas already expressed.
>
> Article 5. It would suit the Province that its obligations should be fixed and immutable, both for our Budget and for the interests of the shareholders, that the obligations of the government may be discharged with the same regularity for which we have ever been distinguished, and which has so much tended to enhance the credit of Buenos Aires in foreign markets.
>
> In consideration of the above the Government resolves that the delegate for the inspection of guaranteed railways, bearing in mind the laws of the concessions, and the sums received, may arrive at an arrangement with them upon the basis of the ideas contained in the decree, submitting it opportunely to the approbation of the Government, so that, in the event of the

latter authorizing the same, it may be laid before the Chambers.

signed Alsina

Dardo Rocha, Chief Secretary.[25]

While seeking to eradicate one disadvantage of the system, this provincial decree nevertheless provides an interesting justification of the concept, namely the balance of mutual advantage which the railway guarantee was presumed to confer upon the contracting parties. Yet, despite their avowed commitment to maintaining the system, the provincial authorities found it far from easy to effect the desired modification in the contracts of the various railway companies. Relief, however, was to come in another guise, no doubt hastened by the publication of this decree. Some five months after publication, the Great Southern negotiated the voluntary abandonment of its 7 per cent guarantee: the BAGS guarantee was the largest for which the Province was responsible. The San Fernando proved less obliging, and refused to contemplate any provisions other than the ones originally negotiated. Such intransigence survived the company's metamorphosis into the BA Northern. But this did not present too serious a problem, for despite the change in nomenclature, the line extended no further than Tigre, barely 20 miles from Buenos Aires, and consequently the total guarantee cover remained small. Moreover, any possible further expansion was unlikely with the appearance of the Campana, which had readily agreed to forgo its guarantee upon obtaining sanction to construct on to Rosario. Thus the provincial government was able to circumvent rather than solve the problem of fluctuating guarantee claims. The national government was less inclined to tackle this problem. Possibly it was discouraged by Buenos Aires' lack of success. Moreover, the national government was probably more conscious of its credit rating, and careful to avoid action which might reflect adversely upon its financial reputation.

Certainly both the Argentine national government and the Buenos Aires provincial authorities were aware of the need to preserve their financial credibility, which made them easy victims of less scrupulous railway promoters. The Northern and East Argentine again provide examples of the dangers consequent upon a lax application of guarantee policy. While both lines were badly conceived, the Northern was especially ill-managed. The line had been unsoundly constructed during its 'San Fernando' days, and remained under-equipped with inadequate provision for renewals. As the company failed to prosper there were frequent conflicts amongst the various groups of stock holders, and with the board. Charges of ineptitude and mismanagement were reported extensively in the press.[26] Such a state of affairs could not fail to come to the attention of the provincial authorities, who finally suspended the guarantee in order to encourage the company to place its affairs in order.[27] Although, by the late 1860s, the provincial government's suspension of the guarantee achieved some positive results, the line remained a burden upon the Buenos Aires treasury, especially during the period of crisis when substantial sums were required from the province to meet the guaranteed interest upon recognized capital; at times the company was unable even to service fixed interest scrip. The expenditure of some £100,000 on improvements between 1868 and 1873, while it was successful in persuading the province to reinstitute the guarantee, was unable to secure the line against adversity. The worsening economic situation in 1874 meant that the line once again became dependent upon the guarantee, and its position became even more difficult in 1876 with the inauguration of the Campana, which competed with the company along part of its route.

The national government, as has been related, experienced difficulties with the East Argentine, whose guarantee claims grew alarmingly during the late 1870s. Nevertheless, despite the undoubted sharp practices which had accompanied the formation of these railways, both possessed legitimate claims upon the governments concerned. When their guarantees remained unpaid they were able to obtain redress elsewhere. In 1879 the Buenos Aires government refused to meet the Northern's guarantee claim. Failing to obtain satisfaction from the provincial authorities, the company approached Baring Brothers, the London bankers and agent of Buenos Aires.[28] While Barings were initially inclined to ignore the approach, the company was not to be discouraged and threatened to raise the problem of unfulfilled guarantee obligations before the Committee of the London Stock Exchange unless satisfaction was obtained.[29] Barings thereupon became more conciliatory and their reply served only to encourage the railway's intransigence.[30]

The provincial authorities remained adamant in their refusal to honour what were regarded as false claims and the affair dragged on. Barings became more alarmed when informed by their Buenos Aires representative that the company consistently refused to allow the government to examine its accounts, as it was required to do by the original terms of the guarantee. Furthermore, the local manager of the line denied that the company was bound to reimburse the provincial authorities for advances previously received under the guarantee arrangement: an attitude which could only be calculated to harden the province's resolve to decline to send good money after bad. The railway's refusal to allow the public authorities to scrutinize its books was hardly surprising for the capital account, by the mid-1870s, stood at some £455,000, although the line should not have cost more than £150,000. As was stated at the time, 'It is clear that among concessionaires, promoters and the original Board of directors a very large amount of money has been squandered'. Fortunately, a way around the *impasse* was within sight. The original guarantee had been awarded in 1862 for a period of twenty years, and was soon about to expire.[31] No doubt this factor had not escaped the notice of the province, and probably explains its procrastination and, equally, the determination of the company. Ultimately a settlement was agreed, but not before the provincial authorities declared that the company had already abandoned the guarantee, and the company raised the matter before the Stock Exchange.[32]

The Northern's successful approach to the Committee of the Stock Exchange established a precedent, the significance of which was not lost on other companies. The Central was considering a similar course of action as its own claims on the national government met with little response during the late 1870s.[33] Indeed, the Central was prepared to go further and request unofficial diplomatic intervention in order to settle its outstanding guarantee payments.[34] However, the East Argentine was to employ this device to greatest effect. As the company's unsettled guarantee claims against the Argentine government increased, the EA turned to Baring Brothers. The company indicated that without some financial assistance its position would become untenable and it would be unable to honour obligations to creditors and debenture holders. This plea was successful, for not only did the good offices of Barings secure some remittances from the Argentine government, but the House was prepared to advance the company credit on account of the sums which it expected to receive from Argentina. Baring Brothers was particularly sensitive to the likely effect of 'hostile' publicity upon Argentine credit.

The government, however, was not prepared to meet the company's claim in full, merely making the minimum payment necessary to obtain respite from the EA's threats, as related above. But the railway would be content with nothing except complete satisfaction. The situation was made more difficult because the company pressed its claims at a time when the central government was least able to meet those demands. The impact of the 'Great Depression' reached Argentina during the late 1870s. Declining trade meant reduced customs receipts, falling foreign reserves, and a diminishing inflow of foreign capital, which increased the burden of guarantee payments. In the 1880s the federal government obliged the company to accept payment in depreciating paper; further difficulties ensued as the state maintained that it had liquidated its obligations, while the company considered that it ought to be compensated for exchange losses suffered from the fall in the external value of the paper *peso*.[35] The company seized every opportunity to press Baring Brothers and the Argentine government to meet its claims. When the railway discovered that the bank was about to float a loan for the province of Buenos Aires, the chairman of the company once again approached the House, and, while acknowledging that the company's claim was against the national authorities, threatened to take action to prevent the quotation of the provincial loan on the Stock Exchange because Buenos Aires was 'practically the whole life and body of the Confederation [and] it cannot be allowed to ignore its responsibilities to this Company'.[36]

Amazingly this threat secured Baring's intervention, and the partial settlement of its claims; although the guarantee for 1880 was paid, by the time the remittances reached London the claim for the following year was already outstanding.[37] The Argentine authorities despaired of the company, and were pressed to expropriate the line. After heated debates in Congress, the government established a special committee to negotiate the purchase of the railway.[38] In the final event, the euphoria of the 1880s railway mania appeared to provide a more acceptable solution. Additional railway projects for mesopotamia were sanctioned in the expectation that these lines, acting as feeders to the East Argentine, would generate extra traffic and revenue for the company, consequently reducing dependence upon the guarantee.[39]

So long as Argentina wished to obtain access to foreign credit, the guaranteed lines were provided with a useful counter to the government's refusal to settle their guarantee satisfactorily. Moreover, the East Argentine had made it plain that such action would not be confined to London; the company was prepared to raise the matter in Paris and elsewhere if need be.[40] In this situation even procrastination availed the aggrieved government little real benefit. In attempting to prevent the quotation of Argentine securities in the money markets of western Europe the railways resorted to the traditional means of redress employed by creditors who possessed a claim upon a recalcitrant foreign debtor.[41] The policy was successful because the debtor wished to obtain further accommodation in those money markets and because both parties believed that such transactions could only occur if the supplicant was seen to be credit-worthy. In retrospect the validity of this view may be doubted, but it was unquestionably held in Argentina during the 1870s and 1880s. In the case of railway guarantees an element of doubt did exist concerning their relative standing: whether or not they represented a direct claim upon the state in the same manner as loans raised by the Argentine authorities in foreign money markets. The railway companies themselves maintained that guarantee payments constituted a prime charge upon the revenues of the government, ranking *pari passu* with other services and amortization charges. This interpretation obtained a measure of acceptance before 1890.

Guarantee Inflation and Frustration
The Northern and East Argentine provide examples of the adverse characteristics and repercussions of the guarantee system. They were the early failures whose notoriety tended to discredit the concept generally. Yet the examples presented by

these companies may be countered with the successes of other lines. The BAGS was undoubtedly a railway which benefited from its guarantee, and employed the system to its own advantage and that of the guarantor. Notwithstanding other benefits which it enjoyed, the provision of a guarantee was the final incentive necessary to achieve the company's successful incorporation. It was held that the guarantee had been crucial during the early stages of the railway's development.[42] Thus protected from some of the risks associated with operating in new regions, the Great Southern had quickly obtained sufficient traffic and revenue to warrant the abandonment of its guarantee. In this instance guarantee payments had not fostered a mood of complacency nor engendered a spirit of indolence and lengthy reliance on the public exchequer. The Central may also be portrayed as one of the successes of the system. Although clinging to a 7 per cent prop longer than the Southern, it too served to demonstrate the possibilities of profitable railway development in Argentina. Moreover, the factors which had induced the Central to abandon its state guarantee (as related above) were in themselves a confirmation of the original intentions of the policy. Indeed, the vitality of the economy in the 1880s occasioned the belief that an even shorter gestation period was required before guaranteed lines might achieve a position of self-sufficiency, a situation that was confirmed by the Campana/Rosario.[43]

Thus, despite an unhappy experience with the BAN and East Argentine, the granting of further guarantees was not difficult to justify. Paradoxically, the Northern and EA were themselves partly responsible for the continuation of the system: their actions demonstrated to prospective investors in Argentine railway projects that the guarantees were not meaningless promises; they could be relied upon to provide a regular specified income. In the decade before 1890 the system developed apace. Within a short span of years there were 32 railway companies operating in Argentina. Five of these lines were owned by national or provincial governments; 12 were in receipt of a full or partial national government guarantee; seven held a full or partial provincial guarantee; the remainder did not possess, or had renounced their guarantees. Of the lines in receipt of a full, national guarantee, only three were completed before the Baring Crisis, one of which was the East Argentine.[44] In 1890 some 5,000 miles of track were under construction, over one half of which carried a guarantee.[45]

Yet it also became obvious that Argentina was not obtaining the benefits she had anticipated from guaranteed railway development. Moreover, it was becoming increasingly difficult, as we have seen, to service the weight of obligations assumed. Contrary to expectation, guaranteed companies sanctioned in the eighties displayed a marked reluctance to emulate the BAGS. Even the better lines appeared to be committed to a lengthy, Central-like dependence upon the guarantee, while less fortunate railways behaved suspiciously like the East Argentine and Northern. This realization, and government attempts during the late 1880s to circumvent guarantee charges, proved disturbing for all lines, not merely those in receipt of a guarantee. The difficulties experienced by the guaranteed companies in achieving a profitable level of operation, and their unfortunate relations with the authorities tended to reflect adversely upon all Argentine railways.

Opening Congress in 1888 President Juárez Celman maintained that some of the guaranteed lines were abusing their position. Reliance upon the state was due to bad management and not to the economics of operation. Lacking sufficient rolling stock these lines were unnaturally restricting the volume of traffic handled. This represented an inconvenience for Argentine producers, and also meant that the companies were not earning as much revenue as they ought. Consequently, dependence upon the guarantee was of their own making: equipped with an adequate rolling stock park, companies would provide a more efficient service, ship extra freight, increase earnings, and cease to be dependent upon the government for a guarantee.[46] Following the presidential lead, Congress determined to remedy this deplorable situation. A bill was passed empowering the national government to purchase additional rolling stock as required, deducting the cost of such purchases from the guarantee claims submitted by these railways.[47]

The East Argentine was the first company investigated in accordance with the new law. The government inspector reported that the railway possessed insufficient dilapidated rolling stock, most of which had been in service since the inauguration of the line: all the locomotives had also been commissioned at the opening of the railway and were in a sad state of repair, they were incapable of handling a train of more than 15 vehicles and were required to make constant stops in order to maintain a head of steam.[48] The company vehemently denied these and other charges, stating that rolling stock was sufficient to meet the requirements of the line.[49] Nevertheless, the national government decided to implement the inspector's recommendations and avail itself of the powers recently granted by Congress. Despite the threat that the company would attempt to prevent the quotation of Argentine securities on the London Stock Exchange and exhortations for caution from Baring Brothers, the state refused to provide an undertaking that it would respect the company's guarantee.[50] Universally condemned, the railway capitulated. The London board telegraphed to Buenos Aires, undertaking to place the line in proper working order and by implication admitted the justice of the government's charges.[51] This point gained, the guarantee was paid. Subsequently, as conditions in Argentina worsened and rising guarantee payment imposed an increasing burden on the national exchequer, the state perceived a means of extricating itself from the dilemma. The old charges against the East Argentine were resurrected, and a decree published suspending the company's guarantee on the grounds that the railway lacked sufficient rolling stock, and its accounts were improperly maintained.[52] But the decree had wider implications, as the last paragraph indicated.

> The National Railway Board shall inform the other railway companies enjoying the nation's guarantee that if they do not, within the terms prescribed, comply with the prescriptions of the General Railway Law, as already intimated to them, and with what is prescribed in their contracts, the payment of their guarantee shall likewise be suspended.[53]

At this point the affairs of the East Argentine became merely one item in the general holocaust which enveloped Argentina. Whatever had been the government's previous intentions with regard to railway guarantees, policies hitherto applied proved unable to cope with the magnitude of the problem. The administration now sought to effect a settlement of the whole guarantee question that would bring about some substantial, lasting reduction in the burden borne by the public treasury. In 1890 a new

General Railway Law was promulgated; *interventores* were appointed to examine the affairs of all guaranteed lines. They would examine the books of each company half-yearly in order to ensure that the guaranteed lines observed the terms of their concessions, applied the appropriate tariffs, and maintained their accounts in accordance with accepted practice. The new law formally charged the state with the obligation to purchase rolling stock on behalf of the companies should networks lack sufficient equipment to meet traffic requirements. The cost of such purchases would be charged against the various companies' guarantee claims. For its part, the state promised to deliver the guarantee promptly on 1 January and 1 July each calendar year. The total guarantee being awarded to the companies who were allowed to retain their gross receipts; readjustments in favour of the state would be mutually agreed subsequently.[54]

This was the last attempt to reach a solution of the problem based upon the assumption that the guarantee system was both viable and desirable. Under other circumstances it might have been a realistic scheme: appointment of *interventores* would provide a close degree of supervision and serve to inform the state of the realities of railway operations. The undertaking to pay the guarantee in full, twice yearly, without any previous deductions was a substantial concession to the private companies and resolved one of their major criticisms of the administration of the system. The delays associated with the annual submission and investigation of guarantee claims had generated a mood of acrimony and frustration which was as damaging to the development of good relations between the companies and the state as it was prejudicial to the railways' relationship with their own shareholders. Hitherto, as related above, the national government had demanded the surrender of one half of these companies' gross receipts before settling guarantee claims, an impracticable proposition implying as it did a working ratio of 50 per cent. As the percentages in Table 22 indicate, the most efficient concerns were not in receipt of a guarantee, and even they experienced some difficulty in achieving the desired working ratio. Although the Argentine authorities recognized the impracticability of demanding one half of the guaranteed lines' gross earnings at this time, they did not abandon this claim on the companies. The government merely waived its right to those earnings until such time as the companies ceased to depend upon the guarantee, when all unsettled claims could be liquidated. Subsequent negotiations would not be so reasonable. Future government action was directed towards ending the system rather than reforming it.

Table 22: *Argentine Railways: working ratios*

	1889 %	1890 %
Andean	51	58
Argentine Great Western	150	130
Buenos Ayres & Ensenada Port	49	54
Buenos Ayres & Pacific	131	87
Buenos Ayres & Rosario	51	58
Buenos Ayres & Great Southern	52	47
Buenos Ayres Northern	69	—
Buenos Ayres Western	67	57
Central Argentine	57	60
Chubut	71	63
Chumbicha	134	168
Cordoba & Santa Fe	—	82
Cordoba Central	75	49
East Argentine	92	99
Entre Rios	114	98
Great Northern	71	89
North West Argentine	84	100
Santa Fe Colonies	114	79
Santa Fe Western	120	99

Source: *PP* 1892 LXXXI 70.

The End of the Guarantee System
The true cost of guaranteed railway development was calculated after the crash. It was estimated that in some cases aggregate guarantee payments exceeded the total nominal capitalization of companies — a factor which occasioned much controversy at the time, and subsequently. In most cases the sums received from Argentine national and provincial governments were substantial,

while the lines in question had demonstrated little ability to forego reliance upon the guarantee (see Table 23).

Table 23: *Argentine Railways: aggregate guarantee payments*

	Total guarantee paid $		Capitalization £
Argentine Great Western	3,040,000 gold	(600,000)	2,050,000
Argentine North Eastern	225,000	(45,000)	1,430,000
Buenos Ayres & Pacific	4,515,000	(900,000)	2,740,000
Cordoba Central Central Northern sec.	2,310,000	(460,000)	4,170,000
East Argentine	5,010,000	(1,000,000)	970,000
Entre Rios	650,000	(150,000)	1,080,000
North West Argentine	56,000	(11,000)	380,000
Total	15,806,000 gold	(3,146,000)	12,820,000

Source: *South American Journal* (hereafter *SAJ*) 3 October 1891, XXXI, 390.

In October 1891 guarantee payments were finally suspended, never to be resumed in accordance with the terms of the original concessions. At the same time the government demanded the repayment of arrears of gross receipts which, for some years, the companies had not been required to surrender to the state on application for the guarantee. The railway companies found themselves in a precarious position. Assailed on the one side by the government, on the other they were unable to meet the claims of their debenture stockholders. Even the BA&P, relatively better placed than many of the other guaranteed companies, was forced to appoint a receiver, finding temporary relief from its financial difficulties by persuading debenture holders to accept payment of their interest in paper.[55] But financial affairs on the River Plate showed little sign of improvement, and despite the welcome given to the administration of Roque Sáenz Peña by mercantile interests in Buenos Aires, the new government maintained a firm line regarding railway guarantee, and remained committed to the policies inaugurated by the interim administration of Carlos Pellegrini which followed the revolution of 1890.[56]

The guaranteed lines were once again required to surrender

one half of their gross receipts to the exchequer, and also repay $7.75 millions gold to the government on account of other sums which the companies had been allowed to retain since 1888.[57] These demands appeared as little more than a prelude to an attack upon the whole concept of foreign ownership. There followed a general criticism of the methods and practices employed by the guaranteed lines: they were castigated for the manner in which their accounts were kept, and for siting their legal domiciles in London.[58] This questioning of hitherto accepted conventions tended to confirm suspicions that the Argentine government was about to mount an attack upon all British-owned railways. This was precisely the fear of the other, non-guaranteed companies. At a time when the quotation of Argentine railway securities on the London Stock Exchange was tumbling, irrespective of whether the company enjoyed a guarantee, there was a general unease in British-owned Argentine railway circles. A final settlement of the guarantee problem was in the interest of all companies. News of the establishment of the Rothschild Committee — set up to enquire into the scale of Argentine indebtedness and ability to honour obligations — stirred the guaranteed lines to action. They formed a Railway Committee, each firm nominating two representatives selected from 'men of the highest standing in this City [London] whose opinions should carry considerable weight'.[59] Apprising Lord Rothschild of their difficulties, they secured his intervention, resulting in an undertaking from the Argentine government to pay the guarantees in full.[60] Although this promise was broken, the knowledge that the Rothschild Committee was apparently prepared to act for the guaranteed railways caused the government to modify its previously hostile tone, and when in 1892 the companies argued that declining receipts would force them to suspend operations, the local authorities determined to make some conciliatory gestures.[61] The National Railway Board, responsible for carrying out government policy, resigned, and it was confidently expected that the newly-appointed body would be more receptive to the claims of the guaranteed lines.[62]

The Argentine government, however, was not disposed to deal with the companies collectively. It refused to recognize the joint approach maintained by the Railway Committee, but was prepared to negotiate with the lines individually. Tentative offers to the BA&P resulted in an agreement which other lines assumed would soon be applied universally. The government agreed to pay the Pacific guarantee without demanding 50 per cent of its gross receipts, and also promised to service the debts which the company had incurred as a result of the non-payment of the guarantee. In future, the national authorities undertook, yet again, to meet their obligations promptly. The Pacific bound itself to pay the government the net proceeds of working, but it was 'understood' that such sums would equal approximately 50 per cent of gross receipts.[63] Such a paper solution resolved nothing. It took no cognizance of the government's ability to meet the obligations which it had assumed in respect of the company, neither did it settle the vexed question of virtually computing the guarantee upon the basis of a 50 per cent working ratio. In reality this abortive settlement satisfied neither party and was unworkable. The Pacific did not receive its long-awaited guarantee, and the Argentine government was left with a growing account of onerous debts.

Unsatisfactory as it was, this settlement did indicate that the state was aware of the long-term problems associated with the guarantee. Unsettled guarantees and the near perpetual bickerings between the government and the companies did little to encourage a belief in Argentina's prospects. Already, early in 1893, the Argentine authorities had become alarmed at the dearth of new railway construction.[64] The reconstituted National Railway Board met on 24 July of that year, and one of its first actions was to recommend a resumption of guarantee payments to the Bahia Blanca North Western Railway Company Limited and the Argentine North Eastern Railway Company Limited, a recommendation which resulted in the provision of special financial assistance for these hard-pressed companies.[65] Later in the same year a committee was established to enquire into the whole guarantee question.[66] By this time, the problem of the weaker lines was becoming increasingly untenable, making them more receptive to the government's approaches.[67] The companies, moreover, had viewed with alarm the signing of the *Arreglo Romero* in July 1892. Ever since the Rothschild Committee had assumed responsibility for effecting a solution to the financial conundrum that beset Argentina, the guaranteed railway companies had been anxious that the Committee should recognize their claims against the Argentine government as principal obligations, on a par with direct state loans. Although the Rothschild Committee had been prepared to co-operate with the guaranteed Railway Committee, it would not go this far. The Rothschild Committee used its good offices in support of the railways' claims, but it had not been prepared to accord the guarantee claims the official recognition which the railway companies wished. While the Rothschild Committee had functioned, the guaranteed lines considered that they had a powerful ally at their disposal. Gradually their optimism on this account weakened as the Rothschild Committee sought to effect a short-term reduction in the direct obligations borne by the Argentine government, and also relate Argentina's desire for access to foreign credit with her ability to meet the consequent service payments. The *Arreglo* meant that the Rothschild Committee's work was completed, and the guaranteed railway companies could no longer expect further assistance from that quarter. Henceforth the settlement of their claims was purely a matter for themselves and the Argentine authorites.

Expediency had already forced the companies to accept a temporary measure whereby, as part of the general moratorium agreed between the Argentine government and its creditors, the railways accepted payment of the guarantee in Funding bonds. It was Dr Romero's policy to solve the guarantee problem by abrogating the guarantee clauses of the companies' concessions. He had intended to negotiate a settlement, individually, with each of the companies concerned. By promising to pay the arrears, he hoped to persuade the railways to abandon their guarantees. He was also prepared, in the interests of obtaining a just and equitable settlement, to waive the government's claim to the repayment of advances already made to the various companies in accordance with the terms of their original concessions.[68] Romero, however, did not long enjoy the fruits of office, but his successor at the Ministry of Finance was equally adamant in his desire to effect a final solution to the problem. In a press interview he expressed his intention of paying the arrears due to the railways — a sentiment warmly applauded by the companies.[69] Substance was given to these pious hopes when the government appropriated a sum of $2 millions gold to be distributed on a *pro rata* basis among the railways on account of the guarantee for

1894. Payments would be made quarterly, commencing on 31 March 1894.[70] The distribution of bonds certainly brought some relief for the weaker lines, but the companies did not consider this scheme over-generous.[71] According to its own estimates the government admitted that the companies were owed $8,444,660 gold.[72] Yet, it was a beginning, an indication of the authorities' good intentions. Moreover, the new scale of payments was realistic, and in keeping with the government's ability to honour its commitment.

However, for the hard pressed companies the promise of payments commencing in March 1894 did little to resolve their immediate financial problems. In an attempt to expedite matters they informed the Argentine government individually that any further delays in guarantee payments, which they emphasized were already occasioning serious hardship, would result in the suspension of traffic and might even lead to bankruptcy.[73] Nevertheless, by the antipodean autumn of 1894 gold gleamed on the horizon. The first company to receive its share of the promised $2 millions was the Cordoba Central.[74] Meanwhile, as these disbursements were being made, a scheme was under preparation to finalize the ultimate recession of the guarantee.

By this time too, the attitude of some of the companies towards the guarantee was beginning to change. Improved conditions during the mid-1890s and rising revenue allowed those lines least dependent upon the guarantee to view the prospect of a final abrogation with more equanimity than had previously been the case. These lines saw the prospect of being able to service capital from operating receipts, and were anxious to attract further investment in order to continue their development. Companies such as the Pacific were aware that if they were to obtain new funds it was first necessary to regularize relations with the Argentine government. Thus, as the resolve (to demand payment in full) of several railways weakened, the Argentine government approached the guaranteed lines individually. In exchange for a lump sum (to be paid in gold bonds) each company was asked to abandon its guarantee. In addition, the government promised to renounce its claim upon the company for repayment of advances already made under the terms of the guarantee and the company was to reciprocate by forfeiting its right to any unpaid guarantee. The same scheme was placed before all lines. The only difference lay in the sums which the state was prepared to offer each railway as the price for agreeing to the abrogation of its guarantee (see Table 24). These sums were additional to the $2 millions gold which were distributed amongst the guaranteed lines in quarterly *pro rata* payments in 1894, 1895 and 1896. The companies accepted: the last guarantee to be settled was that of the Cordoba Central, which was not agreed until 1898. In addition to these payments the government solved the 'guarantee problem' of two small companies by expropriation, purchasing the Cristobal and Tucuman, and the North West Argentine for $10,400,000 gold and $1,852,500 gold respectively. Thus, the guarantee question was effectively settled in 1896, by which time most of the lines had accepted commutation bonds.

Table 24: Argentine Railways: guarantee commutation payments

	$
Argentine Great Western	2,500,000 gold
Argentine North Eastern	11,500,000
Bahia Blanca & North Western	2,292,000
Buenos Ayres & Pacific	1,000,000
Buenos Ayres & Valparaiso Transandine	2,000,000
Cordoba Central	8,000,000
East Argentine	3,780,000
Villa Maria & Rufino	1,990,000

Source: Compiled from *RT* 21 December 1895, LXVIII, 800; *The Times* 31 December 1896, 12d, 18 June 1898, 17a, 9 December 1898, 15b.

One last delay occurred to disrupt the abrogation of the railway guarantees. Originally the intention was to issue special Railway Guarantee commutation bonds. But the government did not wish to incur the extra expense of printing an additional series of obligations, so it persuaded the companies to accept the new unified bonds which were to be issued as part of the external debt consolidation scheme. Asserting its independence at this point, Congress determined to discuss the debt consolidation programme fully, and temporarily withheld its approval for the printing of the new bonds, so postponing the final settlement.[75] It was perhaps a fitting conclusion to the affair that, had the special

Railway Guarantee bonds been issued, Baring Brothers would have enjoyed the commission for their service and amortization.[76]

Despite the controversy which surrounded the railway guarantees during the late 1880s it should not be forgotten that the application of this policy resulted in a vast increase of the Argentine railway network. Although, by the late 1870s, the policy might have been obsolete within the context of the economic expansion enjoyed by the province of Buenos Aires, it is doubtful if such large sums would have been invested in railway construction in other regions of the republic had it not been for the guarantee. The substance of the Argentine railway system was due to the projects embarked upon during the ten years or so before the Crisis, many of which benefited from a guarantee. Nevertheless, by the late 1880s the policy had outlived its usefulness. During the decade several companies demonstrated their ability to achieve a highly profitable status without government sponsorship. It was the Argentine's misfortune that this was not realized at the time.

The final settlement was long overdue, and necessary if the country was to continue to rely upon foreign funds to finance the construction of its railway system. As subsequent events demonstrated, the state was not in a position at this juncture to assume the burden of further development; on the contrary, it was inclined to withdraw from this activity. Abrogation in 1896, and the manner in which it was achieved, indicated that the Argentine government was anxious to maintain the momentum of foreign railway development. A mutual renunciation of previous grievances prepared the way for that development; it was one of the factors which enabled a second wave of expansion to take place during the early years of the twentieth century. Coupled with returned prosperity, this settlement between the state and the private, foreign-owned railways was a pre-condition of renewed growth.

V

DENATIONALIZATION AND REORGANIZATION

Crisis and recovery had a profound effect upon the railway network of Argentina. The boom, and ensuing scramble for concessions, introduced a period of competition which, in the aftermath of the crash, had a sobering influence upon the privately-owned lines. The experience induced a reorientation of railway strategy, which was further stimulated by structural changes already observed. In the private sector there emerged a spirit of co-operation leading towards amalgamation and the formation of zonal railway networks. Railway mania also occasioned a change within the public sector. The state re-examined past strategies: abandonment of the railway guarantees was only part of this process. Necessity, and a cognizance of the nature of modifications effected during the intervening period, encouraged national and provincial governments to pursue new policies. Apart from anything else, events had shown that a state subsidy was no longer a vital prerequisite of railway development. Economic reality served to develop this theme further.

Crisis and Privatization
The inducement of a 7 per cent return on capital offered to private investors constituted a compromise between the state's desire to foster infrastructural development and its ability to finance railway construction. As a successor to initial strategies of according loans, grants and subsidies to infant companies, profit guarantees had not always proved sufficient inducement to private initiative, and the state had still to enter the arena as a railway promoter. The abandonment of the guarantee principle permitted a different approach. If private capitalists were now prepared to support railway projects without demanding a government subsidy, might not the Argentine authorities be absolved from

the need to assume an entrepreneurial function? The prospect was appealing at a time of retrenchment, when the central government was committed to the maintenance of strict control over current expenditure and access to foreign borrowing was limited. Moreover, the very existence of these railways provided central and provincial governments with valuable properties at a time when negotiable assets were at a premium. So, while private companies turned to amalgamation, the state embarked upon a process of sale and withdrawal. Although denationalization was far from fully effected, the application of the concept marked a change in state policy that proved most beneficial for the foreign-owned railways. The importance of denationalization lay not only in the sales which actually occurred, but in the effect which those purchases had upon the private sector and resultant implications for the future growth of the system.

Though there is little evidence to support the view that in 1885 some 45 per cent of total Argentine railway investment had been provided by the state, a haphazard national system did emerge during the years after 1860.[1] By 1890 provincial and national lines accounted for some 23 per cent of total mileage.[2] Composed of various gauges and assorted companies, government railways were scattered about the country. In general, however, the state's approach to its own lines lacked co-ordination: while individual provinces possessed networks enjoying a substantial degree of cohesion, the central government holding was fragmented. Moreover, the national government, in contrast with the provincial authorities, usually adhered to *laissez-faire* principles, and where possible had avoided unnecessary involvement in commercial undertakings. As we have seen, this attitude could only be maintained given a willingness on the part of private interests to assume the burden of innovation. Where private capital, domestic or foreign, refused to venture, the state had assumed the role of entrepreneur, but the national government had normally allowed this function to devolve upon provincial governments which were more responsive to regional interests. Consequently, the central government's attitude was often hesitant and contradictory. Lines were surveyed by the government and then transferred to private interests: other railways were constructed and developed by the Argentine government only to be sold on achieving a profitable status. The formation of a consistent policy was also frustrated by changes in the political and economic environment; different administrations did not always agree on the benefits of non-intervention while economic fluctuations sometimes served to modify previously held views.[3]

Perhaps the major disadvantage suffered by the national system was the lack of an independent access to the city of Buenos Aires. As subsequently demonstrated, the foreign-owned railways considered such an outlet vital. Certainly, at a future date, the state system's acquisition of an entry into the federal capital was thought to be of great strategic significance. In view of this deficiency, and its equivocal approach to the matter, it is not surprising that the Argentine government was prepared to liquidate its railway holding in the aftermath of the Crisis. The lines were often a financial encumbrance, and due to the fragmentary nature of the system there was little prospect of some enterprises ever earning a substantial return upon capital or providing a reasonably efficient service. In 1895 when established foreign-owned railways were beginning to experience a rise in earnings and a return to prosperity, the nationally-owned lines yielded only 1.25 per cent.[4] Finally, the continued interest displayed by private investors indicated that there was less need for direct government involvement, despite the recent catastrophe.

Changing political attitudes lent support to these economic considerations. The collapse of the Júarez Celman administration, and the resultant exposure of corruption and malpractices following the revolution of 1890, served to reinforce underlying tendencies in favour of economic liberalism. If during the early 1880s Roca had judiciously applied a programme of railway concessions in order to consolidate his regime,[5] the device had been employed to even greater effect by his successor. But the granting of vast numbers of competitive concessions during the latter stages of the Júarez Celman administration not only provided opportunities for advancement to clients of the regime and a means of securing the interests of newly-established groups in Argentine society; it appeared to imply a substantially larger role for the state in economic affairs than hitherto. The scale of new concessions granted after 1888, the new banking legislation of 1887, the enhanced status of provincial state banks, and the conflict between the regime and some of the guaranteed lines seemed to signal a more interventionist role on the part of the state. Whether these policies were based upon a coherent development programme, or merely resulted from self-interested pragmatism on the part of a rising socio-economic sector, they were viewed with suspicion by foreign interests which regarded them as expressions of incipient economic nationalism — despite assurances to the contrary by the President himself. These policies were, in addition, witnessed with increasing alarm by more traditional elements in Argentina who, while they were not averse to the steady process of inflation that had occurred during the earlier years of the decade, would not tolerate the catastrophic rise of the gold premium at the turn of the decade nor the financial scandals associated with the regime and the course of debt repudiation upon which it appeared to be engaged.[6] Given the nature of the political interests constituting the post-1890 administration, it is not surprising there should be a resurgence of economic liberalism and a rejection of state participation in economic affairs, not least within the railway sector, in place of the rather confused oscillation between statism and non-intervention practised by the preceding regime.

Similar considerations persuaded provincial governments to divest themselves of railway holdings. Although provincially-owned lines were sometimes more profitable and generally constituted more coherent networks than those of the national government, the pressure to capitalize these assets was even greater. As a result of the crash the provinces lost much of their remaining fiscal autonomy. Economic considerations were probably paramount in accounting for the sale of provincial lines. Indeed, the very prosperity of some provincial railways meant that they were more marketable than central government lines, thereby increasing the inducement to sell. Those provinces which were not fortunate enough to possess profitable railways were probably equally anxious to unload their lines on to the market as the burden of financing operations increased during the early 1890s. Denationalization provided a ready source of cash, and the means of surmounting fiscal stringency at a time when liquidity was both desirable and necessary.

The Provincial Railways
The most important sale to occur at this period was that of the

128 DENATIONALIZATION AND REORGANIZATION

Buenos Aires provincial railway, the *FCO*. The transfer of this company to private ownership was of some historical significance. Initially financed by domestic private capital, the line was now to pass to a foreign consortium. The railway was not all that it had once been. During the 1880s the temptation to milk the line proved too strong, and inadequate provision for depreciation resulted in a marked reduction in operating efficiency. While contemporary (and subsequent) proponents of state railway construction continued to extol the virtues of the enterprise, the sadly reduced circumstances of the line were recounted at length by opponents of state intervention.[7] Nevertheless, the deterioration of the company was of relatively recent origin and it still compared favourably with those administered by the central government and other provinces. It remained a substantial asset.

Table 25: *BAGS and Oeste: gross yield on capital*

	BAGS %	Oeste %
1869	7.6	7.8
1870	7.9	9.8
1871	9.1	8.6
1872	6.7	7.0
1873	7.4	
1874	5.6	
1875	8.7	7.1
1876	6.6	8.6
1877	6.5	8.9
1878	8.1	7.1
1879	10.0	8.1
1880	9.8	7.9
1881	9.9	9.1
1882	8.9	9.3
1883	9.0	7.6
1884	9.5	7.6
1885	9.5	5.4
1886	7.0	
1887	7.5	6.6
1888	8.9	5.5

Source: Compiled and calculated from BAGS *Annual Reports 1869–1889* (London 1870–89); Raúl Scalabrini Ortiz, *Historia de los ferrocarriles argentinos* pp. 43, 46, 49, 50, 57, 76; Horacio Juan Cuccorese, *Historia de los ferrocarriles en la Argentina* p. 39.

Until the late 1880s the *Oeste* ranked as one of the most profitable, soundly administered and efficient railway companies in the country. Since it had been purchased by the province, the concern invariably earned a reasonable return upon the capital employed in its construction; the gross yield compared favourably with that of the Great Southern. Operating in the most prosperous province of the Argentine Confederation and located in similar areas, the two companies handled almost identical categories of traffic. It was hardly surprising that they yielded a substantial return. The data in Table 25 accurately reflects the differing perspectives of local and foreign investors: while a gross income of this order was sufficient to provide an acceptable dividend for foreign capitalists, native entrepreneurs were not content with so meagre a reward. Indeed, the operating profits of the *FCO* had once proved a ready source of income for the provincial administration, an asset pledged to the service of Buenos Aires' external obligations (many of which had been floated during the 1880s to expand the *Oeste* network). Unfortunately, although hitherto the revenue of the line had been enough to service and amortize that part of the provincial debt secured upon the company, inadequate renewals provision and the consequent increase in running costs served to reduce operating profits in the years following the mid-decadal panic. This process was exacerbated at this juncture by the *Oeste*'s tendency to levy lower tariffs than those applied by the BAGS.[8] But the provincial railway was not merely a convenient source of income for the government: the concern was a fund of expertise and information for the Buenos Aires administration. The *FC Oeste* was a bench mark against which the claims and pretensions of private companies might be checked. On more than one occasion the affairs of foreign-owned lines had been contrasted unfavourably with those of the provincial railway, and requests for tariff increases rejected on reference to the *FCO* regime.[9] Not least, several private lines obtained access to the port of Buenos Aires over *Oeste* rails, thus granting additional leverage to the provincial government in its negotiations with foreign concerns.

In spite of these benefits, events during the late 1880s conspired to encourage the province to part with the railway. No less than the national government, Buenos Aires experienced increasing difficulty obtaining domestic and foreign loans, while rising expenditure reduced the provincial exchequer to penury. In addition, the need to place the railway in proper working order and make good past deficiencies induced a mood of near despair at La Plata. The sale of the *Oeste* offered a simple solution to several of these mounting problems. Although the sale of the line had been mooted earlier in the decade, there was renewed speculation regarding the fate of the railway in 1888 when rumours of impending negotiations between the provincial authorities and foreign consortia began to circulate in Buenos Aires and La Plata.[10] Ironically it was initially thought that Baring Brothers, who had already been associated with raising capital for the line, would purchase the company in consort with several other financial houses. But Baring's offer was not sufficiently attractive.[11] In the event, the line was to fall into the hands of another group of British specialists connected with the River Plate.[12] In essence the line was sold for a substantial cash payment and the assumption by the successor company of a large volume of provincial paper, mainly loans secured upon the railway or bonds which had been issued to raise funds for its extension. The nominal purchase price was $41 millions gold (a little more than £8 millions) of which the Buenos Aires government received a cash payment of approximately $16 millions gold (some £3 millions): the new company also absorbed responsibility for the service and amortization of £4,955,380 of provincial bonds.[13] The private line was provided with a concession which was similar to those granted to most lines projected during the period: the provincial government waived its right to expropriate the railway for 40 years; the enterprise was to be free of all provincial and municipal taxes for 20 years; no competing line would be sanctioned within 20 kilometres of the company for 15 years; while the provincial authorities retained the right to intervene in the determination of the company's tariffs as soon as gross profits reached 10 per cent, the company was permitted to adjust tariffs in accordance with the depreciation of the local currency and the government could never compel it to accept tariffs lower than those prevailing on other railways operated within the province.[14] In retrospect the subject of severe controversy, at the time of the event the contract effecting the metamorphosis of the *FCO* into the Buenos Ayres Western Railway Company Limited was accomplished with little fundamental opposition; in the provincial senate the sale was approved by 12 votes to two.[15] Thus the provincial government obtained much needed cash and was also relieved of the burden of servicing a large volume of debt.

The example set by the administration at La Plata was not lost upon other provincial authorities. The Entre Ríos government was no less hard pressed by the Crisis than the Buenos Aires administration and, though lacking an investment of the calibre of the *Oeste*, was heartened by the possibility of reducing provincial obligations by means of liquidating railway holdings. The *entrerriano* authorities possessed a fairly extensive railway system of some 390 miles interlinking the more populous districts in the south and centre of the province. The Entre Ríos legislature had authorized the construction of the line in 1883 and capital was obtained by the issue of several special series of provincial bonds which were partially guaranteed by the national authorities. Work on the railway commenced in 1885; various sections of the network were inaugurated between 1887 and 1891.[16] Railway profits being insufficient for the task, the provincial government had experienced some difficulty in providing its share of successive loan coupons. Mounting financial pressure during 1889/90 and central government prohibitions upon further emissions of provincial bonds caused the Paraná government to dispose of the railway. It was proposed that the concern should be transferred to the bondholders in exchange for the cancellation those Entre Ríos obligations secured upon the line. The provincial assembly sanctioned this scheme in October 1890, but it was some time before the bondholders could be persuaded to accept such a solution to the province's pecuniary problems. Although a tentative settlement was reached in August 1891, it was not until January of the following year that the final arrangement was made between the province and its creditors, after the latter had been notified by the national government of its intention to terminate the partial federal guarantee accorded provincial paper.[17]

Thus was organized the Entre Rios Railway Company Limited, a London-registered concern with a capital of £3,276,400. Railway scrip was to be apportioned amongst the bondholders on a *pro rata* basis: £100 of Entre Rios Central bonds were to be exchanged for £65 preference and £35 ordinary railway shares; Entre Rios Central Extension bonds, the junior issue, were to be exchanged for £40 preference and £60 ordinary shares per £100 of bonds. As a final inducement to settle, the railway was to be endowed with £500,000 6 per cent national government bonds, and £300,000 5 per cent provincial bonds which were to be held as a source of revenue — a dubious reflection upon the earning potential of the line. In addition, the railway was to be free from all taxation, national, provincial and municipal, for 30 years, and was allowed to levy tariffs at the same rate as the BAGS. Several years later the company gained control over the whole of the railway system in the province when it purchased a short stretch of track, the *Primero Entrerriano*, from the national government.[19]

Although in national terms a minor system, within the mesopotamian context the Entre Rios network was relatively significant. The region's experience of private development, characterized by the East Argentine, had not been a happy one. Like the *FCO* in Buenos Aires, the provincial line had been amenable to local interests and pressures. So the sale of this railway was viewed with misgivings in some quarters, though the necessity of reducing the province's debt burden was generally recognized. Indeed, the province found it difficult enough to service the small allocation of bonds granted to the new railway company. After years of default the provincial obligations were finally exchanged for 4 per cent national bonds.[20]

A third province was to apply a similar remedy to its financial embarrassment. Sante Fé, the second most prosperous province in the Confederation, had sought in 1882 to further local economic expansion by improving the quality of transport services available to the growing agricultural colonies located within its borders, particularly those in the central, eastern and northern districts. Hitherto much of the railway construction that had been undertaken in the province was focussed upon the southern *partidos*: broad-gauge rails traversed the littoral in the region of Rosario. It was the intention of the local government to provide a rail link between other zones and the provincial capital: a contract to this effect was signed with Meiggs and Company at the end of 1884 for the construction of some 330 miles of metre-gauge track to be known as the *Ferrocarril Santafecino*, or Santa Fe and Colonies Railway, radiating from the city of Santa Fé to Rosario, San Cristóbal, La Sabana and Gálvez with subsequent extensions to Reconquista, Las Toscas and the frontier with Córdoba.[21] Capital for the original line was raised by the issue of 6 per cent gold bonds which were taken by the contractor at 85 while the extensions were financed by an emission of 5 per cent paper placed by Messrs Murrieta and Company in the European money markets.[22] As was the case with the sister province, the Santa Fé authorities found it increasingly difficult to service these obligations — especially the gold bonds — when railway revenue proved insufficient to cover interest charges. In 1889, capitalized at approximately £2 millions with 432 miles in service and a further 70 under construction, the railway operated at a loss, working expenses standing at 114 per cent of receipts.[23] Although economies were effected, the line remained a drain upon provincial finances when the Crisis struck. Thus the network passed into the hands of foreign capitalists; *La Compagné Française des Chemins de Fer de la Province de Santa Fé* was organized under the auspices of the *Banque Russe et Français*, which assumed responsibility for the provincial bonds issued to construct the railway.[24]

National Government Policy: Procrastination and Equivocation
As these events indicate, the national authorities did not assume a passive role in the denationalization of provincial railways. Buenos Aires' willingness to accord the Entre Rios railway an allocation of unified funding bonds demonstrates that the Argentine government was not averse to these transactions. It is doubtful if private interests would have been prepared to contemplate these transfers in the face of implacable opposition from central government. Indeed, schemes such as that proposed by the provinces of Entre Ríos and Santa Fé which entailed the cancellation of provincial debts found particular favour at this juncture. The national administration was pleased to see the retirement of obligations which could not be adequately serviced by the provinces concerned. Indeed, the federal government sought to prevent the provinces from raising further sums abroad. Yet the success of these provincial schemes undoubtedly encouraged the Argentine government to follow a similar course.

During the hectic 1880s the sale of individual government lines had often been considered, but the concept of a general liquidation had rarely passed beyond discussion stage.[25] Local opposition to the sale of national rails, the limited prospects of some of the lines, the deplorable conditions of others, breaks of gauge, and the tortuous pace of negotiations usually conspired to frustrate the transfer of national companies to private ownership. Conditions, however, had changed by the early 1890s. A general reorganization of national credit proved a more pressing incentive to liquidate the central government's railway holding than philosophical considerations regarding the role of the state. Official statistics (see Table 26) indicated that, immediately prior to the Crisis, the national government's railway holding was not insubstantial, if under-capitalized in comparison with British-owned concerns.

Table 26: *Argentine Railways: national government lines, 1889*

Enterprise	Mileage	Capitalization Total (£)	Per mile (£)
FC Andino	157.8	866,269	5,490
FC Primer Entrerriano	5.5	30,357	5,519
FC Central Norte	549.3	4,166,667	7,585
FC Central Norte (extensions)	140.4	1,188,492	8,465
FC Chumbicha-Catamarca	41.0	297,619	7,259
Proportion of total network	14.6%	13.2%	

Source: *PP* 1890/91 LXXXIV 7&8; *RT* 28 November 1891, LX, 553.

The burden placed upon the resources of the state by these railways was conveyed some years later when official operating data for the fiscal year 1895, a time when most lines were beginning to exhibit some signs of recovery, indicated that national networks were earning an average gross return of 1.25 per cent upon investment; 'guaranteed' lines yielded 4.20 per cent and unguaranteed lines an average of 7.79 per cent on recognized capital.[26] Statistics such as these lent further support to those advocating the disposal of all publicly-owned enterprises. As has been seen, the small standard-gauge Entre Ríos line was soon transferred to private hands, but of greater significance was the fate of the metre-gauge Central Northern and broad-gauge Andean railways. Both were relatively important lines and the latter was of some strategic significance, straddling the territory of several privately-owned companies. The metre-gauge line linked Tucumán to the rails of the Central at Córdoba, and its several branches connected many of the more important centres of population located in the Argentine north-west. It had long been viewed by the Central as a natural extension of its own system and the English company had made repeated offers to purchase the line, particularly during the late 1880s when the latter had found its monopoly of communications with the north challenged by the Rosario. Indeed, negotiations regarding the proposed sale of the Central Northern in 1887 and 1888 had occasioned a degree of friction between the state and the Central Argentine when the company's offer had been refused by the national authorities, although it was reputedly the highest bid tendered; it was claimed that there had been a breach of confidence on the part of the tender office.[27]

The Central Argentine was also engaged in further negotiations with the national authorities concerning the Andean line. Undoubtedly, the Andean represented a much better prospect than the Central Northern. The region which it served was much more developed; it was generally well administered and operated. Also its management had co-operated closely with contiguous British-owned lines. Moreover, the Andean was of the same gauge as neighbouring railways. It was the rump of a formerly extensive state holding of broad-gauge lines which had constituted part of the route between Buenos Aires and the Chilean frontier. During the 1880s when a previous scheme for the general liquidation of government railway holdings had reached a degree of fruition, the Andean represented the sum of that policy's successes. The acceptance of applications to purchase the entire Central Northern and Andean systems resulted only in the disposal of approximately 300 miles of the latter's network.

The immediate cause of renewed government interest in railway sales was the condition of national finances. In addition to the general problems of the early 1890s, and the schemes mooted to resolve them, the Argentine government experienced a pressing need for ready cash in order to implement its consolidation projects. Although the sums required were small, they could not be raised in the usual way due to the depths to which Argentine credit had sunk. Moreover, orders which had been placed in Europe for stores and equipment — especially for military supplies — had to be met. Given the parlous state of relations with

Chile, the Argentine government considered it inexpedient to cancel these orders.[28] Finally, the Central Argentine was at this juncture making substantial calls upon its shareholders, of which the Argentine government was one of the more important, for funds to finance its new extension building programme occasioned by competition with the Rosario. Accordingly it was once again determined to request tenders for the purchase of all federal government railways. Given the deplorable condition of the company, it was considered unlikely that a buyer would be found for the Central Northern, but the Entre Rios was known to be anxious to acquire the short standard-gauge section of national track; the Andean was thought to be sufficiently well placed to commend itself to prospective investors. The Argentine government's special representative in London was instructed to proceed with arrangements for either the sale or leasing of the Andean. Optimism reigned in Buenos Aires and the government was prodigal with its promises of the ends to which the proceeds of the sale would be devoted. In the event, however, the scheme fell through. Undoubtedly, the Argentine government took too sanguine a view of the prospects of the Andean and its marketability. At $8 millions gold (£1.6 millions) the line was substantially overpriced in 1891. Also, for reasons of his own, the Argentine minister in London opposed the scheme and did not proceed with the alacrity that his instructions enjoined.[29] Consequently, the project was abandoned, and with the establishment of the Rothschild Committee the need to effect a sale became less pressing. Nevertheless, schemes for a general sale of the state railways continued to exercise exchequer officials during the remainder of the decade, though with decreasing conviction as the overall financial situation improved.[30]

Ultimately the broad-gauge Andean was sold to private enterprise. Set 'in a sea of private companies' the track was divided amongst neighbouring British-owned railways and secured the remarkable price of £2.3 millions.[31] Contrary to all expectations, the Central Northern was sold before any of the other lines. Despite the adverse state of the railway it was purchased by the Cordoba Central, not the Central Argentine, which by this stage was engaged elsewhere and less occupied in the north now that the Rosario had driven a broad-gauge route through to Tucumán. Nevertheless, it is difficult at first sight to understand the

CC's interest in this enterprise; a report compiled in 1892 easily explained the Argentine government's supposition that it would not be easy to find a buyer for the Central Northern. Investigation revealed that the line's administration conformed to few of the normal standards of railway management. Regular accounts were not kept, although 'rough' running, day-to-day balances indicated inevitable discrepancies. Due to the dearth of revenue, the employees of the line rarely obtained a money wage but instead found themselves in receipt of promissory notes listing the number of days worked and tasks performed. These certificates circulated as money in the railway's zone. Structurally the company was in no better condition. There were virtually no stores, sections of the permanent way were disintegrating, little provision had been made for drainage along the track and embankments did not conform to legal specifications laid down in the original concession. The whole system was worked by only 38 locomotives, while the rolling stock was 'greatly neglected'. Finally, the company was indebted to the extent of $324,367 which was owed to its employees, the Railway Clearing House and the Cordoba Central.[32] Little wonder that the national authorities wished to divest themselves of all responsibility for the railway.

Yet, in spite of these adverse features, the line represented an important acquisition for the Cordoba Central which already operated a metre-gauge railway. The Central Northern's 550 miles were a substantial addition to the CC's existing network of 128 miles, and provided valuable, strategic access to the north. Initially, the Central Northern was transferred to the bondholders who held the national paper which had been raised to construct the line, or had been secured upon it. The bondholders thereupon registered the Central Northern Railway Company Limited which immediately leased itself to the Cordoba Central.[33] Thus the national government emulated the provinces, ridding itself of an encumbrance, and reducing the burden of debt service.

Consequences of Denationalization
The impact of denationalization was far-reaching. First, in terms of mileage, the networks acquired by private interests represented substantial, often strategic, additions for individual companies, or resulted in the creation of new groupings. Secondly,

the withdrawal of the state from railway operations, although far from complete, signalled a new official approach to Argentine railway development.

The demise of the *FCO* was the most startling event, for the successor line bore little resemblance to the provincial system. The sale of the Buenos Aires railway involved more than a transfer of ownership: the BAW network differed from that which had been liquidated by the provincial government in several important respects. The British-owned company was merely a truncated version of the *Oeste* as the new board leased or sold large portions of track to neighbouring lines. In the late 1880s the provincially-owned concern was one of the most extensive railway systems operating in Argentina. No less than the leading British companies, the provincial line assiduously developed its region and pushed its main line westwards besides constructing a number of lucrative branches.

Table 27: *Argentine Railways: major systems, 1889*

	Capital (£ millions)	Mileage
Argentine Great Western	3.5	319
Buenos Ayres & Pacific	3.3	425
Buenos Ayres & Rosario	8.3	344
Buenos Ayres Great Southern	8.5	839
Central Argentine	5.4	273
*Oeste	6.7	752

*including projected extensions, 90 miles.

Source: *PP* 1890/91 LXXXI 7–8.
These figures are based on official Argentine government statistics, and are slighly different from those presented by the various companies.

In Table 27 the marked differences in capital costs are occasioned by the various extension building programmes currently undertaken by individual lines. In some cases capital accounts have been augmented by the addition of extension issues, but (as the extensions had not been formally inaugurated) mileage figures have not been adjusted accordingly. Nevertheless, whether the calculation is made in terms of capitalization or operational mileage, the *FCO* ranked amongst the largest systems (even when allowance is made for inclusion in the data of *projected* extensions). Whatever criteria are adopted, the provincial railway was the second, or third, most important Argentine railway system on the eve of the Crisis. However, the *FC Oeste* lost this status when denationalized. The BA Western transferred all branch lines — which accounted for approximately one half of the company's total mileage — to other enterprises, retaining merely the main lines (see Table 28). These branches were leased in perpetuity (although the Southern ultimately purchased its acquisition outright) at a rate of £450 per mile per annum, representing a return of 4½ per cent upon a capitalization of £10,000 per mile.[34] In this way the new company obtained a guaranteed annual income more than sufficient to service and amortize the provincial obligations which it had assumed, while the leases obtained cheap, developed branch lines that would yield a remunerative return over and above the cost of the lease. In addition, the BAW undertook to revise the *Oeste* extension programme. Several concessions were transferred to the leasees and other abandoned.

Table 28: *BAW: distribution of Oeste track*

	Mileage
Main Lines	
Buenos Aires – Trenque Lauquen	
Buenos Aires – La Plata	338
Branch Lines	
Purchases by CA	
Lujan – Pergamino	
San Nicolas – Junin	202
Purchased by BAGS	
Merlo – Saladillo	94
Purchased by BA&EP	
Ringuelet – Ferrari	24
Grand Total	660

Source: Buenos Ayres Western Railway Company Limited. *Report of the directors to the proprietors and statement of the revenue and capital accounts for the half-year ended 31 December, 1890* (hereafter *Half-yearly report* . . . (London 1891); *BOI* 1891 IX 581; *Statist* 25 June 1892, XXIX, 720; *PP* 1914 LXXXIX 513; Scalabrini Ortiz *Historia* pp. 66–7. Although all originate from the same source, there is a slight disagreement amongst these texts concerning the exact mileage leased.

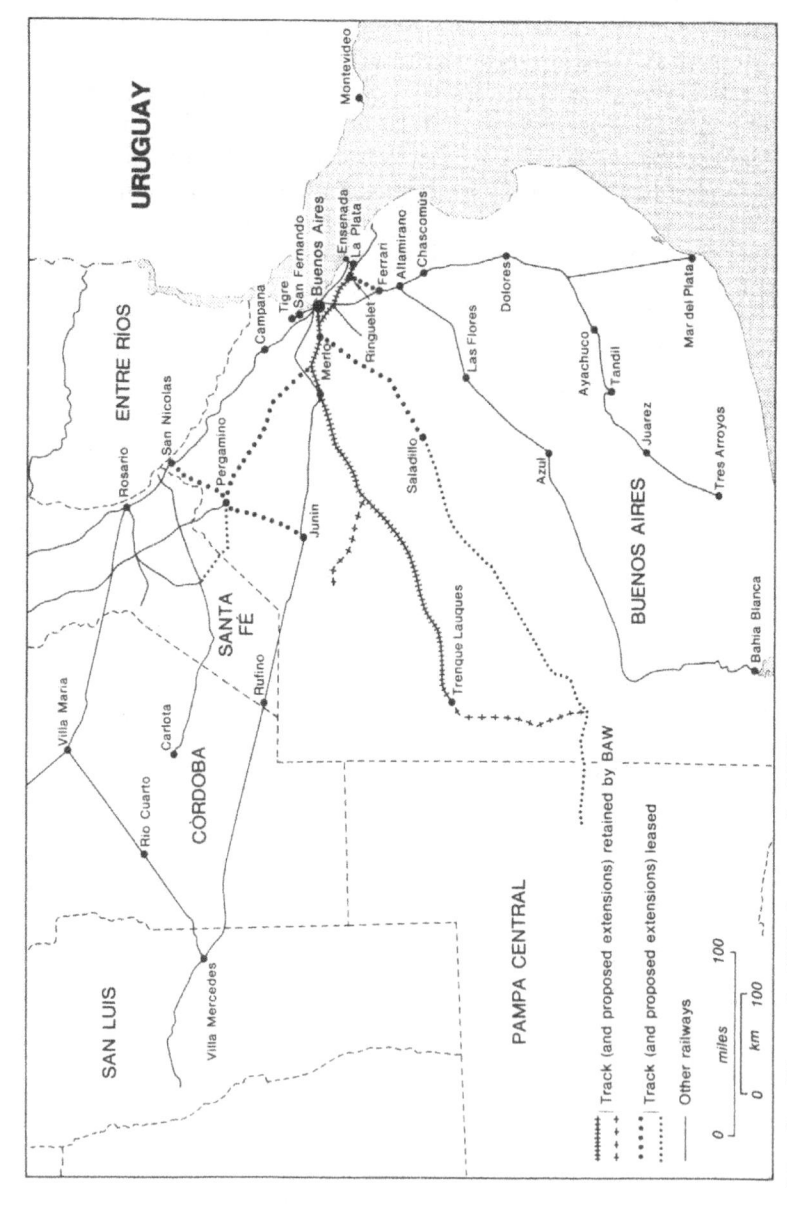

Map 3: Disposal of *FC Oeste* track, 1890

Thus the sale of the *FCO* resulted in the reorganization of the railway map of Buenos Aires. It was a restructuring decidedly to the advantage of the British-owned companies; a dangerous rival had been removed, and replaced by a compliant ally. The expansion of the provincial line during the late 1880s had attracted the attention of neighbouring British lines who had become increasingly alarmed as the railway's expansionist designs unfolded. In 1889 the *FC Oeste* was in the process of constructing, or had obtained concessions to build, an additional six miles of extensions for every seven route miles of track currently in operation. No other railway could equal this record. The BA&R which was also heavily engaged in new construction works during 1889 was overshadowed by the provincial line. Although the Rosario intended to build almost as many miles of track as the *Oeste*, its completed network would be no greater than the latter's pre-extension system. The programmes of the other British lines could not be compared with that of the Buenos Aires railway; the Central was only increasing its network by 50 per cent, while the BA&P and the BAGS were not then engaged in extension building.[35] Denationalization meant the break-up of a large and strategically placed railway system, the significance of which was not underestimated in British Argentine railway circles. As a result of the arrangements entered into with the Western, neighbouring lines enjoyed substantial accessions to their respective networks. The Great Southern system was increased by approximately 11 per cent, while it also gained a further 200 miles of concessions. The track leased by the Central was equal to almost one half of the existing network, and the BA&EP's agreement with the BAW resulted in a 74 per cent increase in route mileage.[36]

In relative terms, the Cordoba Central's acquisition was even more spectacular; the concessions and operational mileage of the Central Northern represented a fourfold increase in the company's network. Yet, as was stated, the condition of the formerly national line necessitated substantial capital expenditure in order to place the track and equipment in good working order. But the new, integrated system that emerged was well placed to foster the development of the north-west. Subsequent additions led to the formation of an extensive metre-gauge network, offering a through service to the ports, that eradicated earlier inconveniences and inefficiencies occasioned by breaks of gauge. Paradoxically, the sale of the Andean, on the eve of the First World War, had little impact on the course of Argentine railway development. Divided amongst the Argentine Great Western, the Pacific and Central, it represented a trifling addition to the respective companies' networks.[37]

Of the new, private, foreign-owned companies established in this manner, the BAW was the most powerful and profitable. It fulfilled the early promise of the *Oeste* and subsequently became one of the 'big four' British-owned railways. Closely allied with the BAGS, the enterprise enjoyed many of the latter's advantages; it served a prosperous, fertile zone and was endowed with a capable management, well-connected in Argentina, familiar with the local situation. The ER was less fortunate. Situated in an underdeveloped area, it also emulated its predecessor. The struggling company did not prosper until the twentieth century, when its region was more fully integrated into the national economy and amalgamation with the other railways of mesopotamia led to the formation of a more viable entity. Much the same could be said of the French company. The first decade following reorganization was one of difficulty and caution: little attempt was made to expand the concern. With the completion of its outstanding extension works during the early post-Crisis years, the newly-established enterprise pursued a policy of retrenchment until the beginning of the twentieth century when it too engaged upon a substantial programme of branch line construction.[38] However, for Argentina, direct French participation in railway operations constituted a breach of the near monopoly held by British capital (a situation later evolved as official strategy).

Denationalization was a multifaceted process. At the time much significance was attached to the withdrawal, or partial withdrawal, of the state from the railway sector. Although government, in the guise of the national authorities and provincial administrations, did not totally leave the field to private enterprise and was to reappear as a railway promoter at a later date, abandonment of the entrepreneurial function at this juncture served to reassure the private companies about official attitudes towards their role as the principal force in Argentine railway development. By the end of the century the private sector had

DENATIONALIZATION AND REORGANIZATION 143

gained a paramountcy which it never before enjoyed, or was subsequently to achieve. In 1899 the private companies accounted for approximately 88 and 90 per cent respectively of total railway mileage and capital but they handled 92 per cent of all goods traffic and carried 98 per cent of passengers.[39] The effective retreat of government from the process of railway management and construction, after a period when the private lines had experience much criticism from various quarters, restored the confidence of private capitalists in Argentina. When the economy again required external funds for further infrastructural development, private foreign capitalists honoured their commitment to provide the rail services demanded by dominant sectors of the Argentine state. In addition, the appearance of these new private companies, and the re-allocation of track which accompanied the process provided an early fillip to the concept of zonal railway systems.

The withdrawal of government from a major sector of the economy did not meet with unanimous approval. Both within and without Congress opposition was expressed. Argentine policy appeared to run counter to a general trend towards increased state participation in the economy throughout Latin America.[40] Nevertheless, the volume of criticism voiced at the time of denationalization was small compared to that which arose in later periods. A substantial *corpus* of literature has emerged which, while generally antagonistic to the dominant position gained by foreign interests in the Argentine economy, is particularly scathing of the events which took place during these years in the railway sector. Indeed, much of this writing is cast within the mould of conspiracy theory, viewing the Baring Crisis and subsequent settlement with foreign capitalists (especially the abandonment of the role of the state in social overhead capital creation) as a mechanism engineered with precisely this objective in mind.[41]

While the significance of the state's withdrawal from railway management must not be understated, this analysis is based upon a number of misconceptions, if not fallacies. It tends to ignore the fact that, as has been indicated, much of the finance employed in the construction of these lines was raised abroad. This was the case with the federal government line from Córdoba to Tucumán and the provincial networks created in Entre Ríos and Santa Fé; it was less true of the *Oeste*, though the vast expansion of the Buenos Aires provincial railway during the 1880s was dependent upon access to foreign money markets. In this respect, denationalization cannot be presented as the substitution of foreign for domestic capital; it was rather that external interests assumed a larger function in branches of railway administration. Nor should it be forgotten that some state lines had been leased to private interests before the crash. Moreover, abandonment by the state of the day-to-day chore of management in the case of some above-mentioned enterprises must not be interpreted as conferring total freedom of operation upon private lines. Concurrent with the liquidation of government railway holdings there occurred a greater degree, and increased efficiency, of official control through the codification of railway legislation and the expansion of the regulatory administrative bureaucracy. It was recognized that public utilities might constitute local or regional monopolies and, therefore, had to be regulated. Private companies had always been subject to some form of official control under the terms of their respective individual concessions, but the system lacked uniformity — particularly during the first three decades of the railway age. Then, despite the evolution of an *ad hoc* system of national regulations, most lines had been located within the confines of a single province and accordingly governed by local, in place of central, legislation. In 1891, however, a new general law of the national railways was promulgated which represented a substantial improvement upon the original federal legislation of 1872.[42] While this was far from perfect, and individual companies were still subject to the differing terms of their respective concessions, the new law was more coherent and comprehensive. In addition, it had a wider impact, for by the time it was inscribed on the statute books, most companies operated in more than one province and thus fell within the scope of national, and no longer provincial, jurisdiction. The 1891 legislation made specific provision for the inspection of private (and publicly-owned) railways and granted extensive powers to the General Railway Board, the commission charged with the implementation and policing of railway regulations. Besides being responsible for the compilation and publication of data (which became the basis for subsequent intervention in the affairs of private companies) the Board provided the government with information upon the minutiae of private railway operations, and served as a mechanism for the evolution of general policy, sometimes functioning as a channel of communication between government and companies.[43]

Denationalization, therefore, should not be confused with a general surrender of the interests of the state in railway affairs. Paradoxically, the demise of government railway holdings was associated with an increase in the scope and effectiveness of official scrutiny of the private sector. Such a scrutiny the companies recognized to be a perfectly legitimate role of the state. What had alarmed the foreign-owned lines had been the expansion of state-owned networks and the threat of 'unfair' competition, a fear that appeared to be justified in the increasing hostility engendered by the guaranteed lines during the late 1880s (which seemed to encompass all foreign-owned private lines, without distinction), and the spirit of economic nationalism which was exhibited during the post-Crisis era.[44] The sale of state railways confounded these apprehensions.[45] Denationalization, the commutation of railway guarantees, and the re-establishment of Argentine credit, all restored the confidence of foreign investors and permitted the ultimate inauguration of a 'golden age' of private railway expansion.

VI

ZONAL AMALGAMATION — 1

Around the turn of the century a change in the pace of Argentine railway expansion signalled the beginning of a new phase of development. As the momentum of expansion increased, full effect was given to earlier, tentative moves to create zonal railway networks. Although in many instances the structural reorganization of the Argentine railway system was not finally implemented until the period immediately before the First World War, these years witnessed the application of policies that had been formulated as a result of the previous 15 years' experience. The steady increase in railway capitalization and mileage which evidenced recovery from the effects of the Crisis, and which was observable during the period 1895–97, differed from earlier expansion not only in terms of the rate of growth, but also in its form: expression was now being given to the regional concept. The fundamental features of the railway system were, as we have seen, largely established during the 1880s. Most of the major trunk routes had been built by, or were initiated during, that decade. Subsequent expansion was of an intensive nature; providing more effective intra-regional means of communication, joining the respective areas of the country more effectively to the centre, and in some cases supplying inter-regional linkages. Thus in 1914 Argentina's railway system was characterized by zonal networks dominated by the major British-owned companies — basically half a dozen systems, the largest of which were the 'big four' pampean lines. The Great Southern and the Western covered most of the province of Buenos Aires with their rails: their trunk routes ran through to the Andean foothills of northern Patagonia and the national territory of *Pampa Central*. The Pacific group dominated *Cuyo* and administered the international service between Buenos Aires and Chile. The Rosario/Central operated the broad-gauge system of the north-west and also the main route between Rosario and Buenos Aires. In addition, there was the Cordoba Central metre-gauge network, essentially based in the provinces of Córdoba and Santa Fé, but with trunk lines stretching northwards to Tucumán and southwards to Buenos Aires. Finally, the smallest of the British-owned systems was the standard-gauge grouping of mesopotamia.

These zonal networks were formed by the merger of existing railways, not by the foundation of new companies. Much of the construction undertaken after the turn of the century was designed to effect zonal fusions, typical of railways at this stage of development elsewhere in the world. Mergers were created in a variety of ways, in some cases by means of simple amalgamations, or the successful takeover of one line by another; others were effected by more complicated working arrangements whereby a company obtained the use of another's track, or undertook to service another line's capital. The process owed much to the spirit of co-operation that developed after the 1880s. Indeed, the agreements which marked the break-up of the *FCO* indicate the real beginnings of limited collaboration amongst British-owned lines. Earlier stages of railway expansion had been rather haphazard and fragmentary. A national system did not finally appear until the previously separate northern and southern lines were joined together in the 1880s. However, as the country's network expanded, the need for co-ordination, if not co-operation, also increased. The position prevailing in the 1890s was not that which had existed during the previous thirty years. The system was now integrated; railway lines were no longer unconnected, serving purely local requirements. During the 1880s some companies chose to ignore the realities of this situation, and were more concerned with individual expansion than national consolidation. By the last decade of the nineteenth century they could not avoid the limitations and obligations consequent upon the emergence of a national network. One of the effects of the Crisis was to remind the companies of their interdependence; by this time no railway could afford to operate in total independence or without due consideration for others. As the Central discovered, an integrated national network meant competition. The construction of new lines offered alternative routes and new services to shippers. With the expansion and integration of a national railway system the possibilities for friction or co-operation increased.

Economic changes in Argentina also served to emphasize the need for railway rationalization. Although the type of railway network required by pastoral and arable interests differed, the developing agricultural sector, irrespective of its sectional characteristics, demanded a uniform service from the railways — an ability to move bulk cargoes cheaply and efficiently to market. Renewed prosperity and the conciliatory attitude of the state explain the return of shareholders' confidence. The basic needs of agriculture dictated the form of development fostered by renewed optimism. Rationalization demanded co-operation, and it was in this sense that the events which preceded the formation of the BAW were important. They point to an awareness in Anglo-Argentine railway circles of the nature of the problems facing the country, and to the means of effecting a solution to those problems. The way in which the Western disposed of its leases indicates a remarkable degree of unanimity amongst its neighbours, and a desire to contain competition. Born out of adversity this was a mood that would bear fruit with the passage of time.

The Central and the Rosario: Friction and Fusion
The consequences of unbridled expansion and rivalry were seen in north-west Argentina during the 1880s. The events, already related, concerning the construction embarked upon by the BA&R, and its 'push' to Tucumán, underline the lack of co-operation hitherto experienced. The competition of the Rosario and the Central for the limited traffic of this far-from-prosperous region created severe difficulties for both lines in the post-Baring Crisis period. While there were other factors bearing upon the problem, the unsettled conditions prevailing were partly explained by wasteful construction contracted by both entities. Each experienced the adverse consequences of over-expansion, the effects of which were further compounded by the crash. Subsequently, *rapprochement* offered the only practical solution to their difficulties. The Central and Rosario came together at a time of exhaustion after a period of bitter rivalry occasioning much recrimination on both sides. Amalgamation was not easily accomplished; early approaches were not based upon a new-found amity but were a function of the problems facing both

lines. Indeed, the slow progress of moves to integrate the companies was due to the depth of their original mutual antipathy which compounded the individualism prevalent in Anglo-Argentine railway circles. The Central in particular found it difficult to muster the degree of cordiality necessary to enable negotiations with its erstwhile rival to progress without recurrent disagreement. However, force of circumstances ultimately triumphed and modified initial recalcitrance.

The concept of amalgamation was not new. As early as 1886, when the BA&R was building out of Campana, the Central had contemplated the advisability of such a course.[1] Even then the gains were apparent and both companies had been informed that the national government would favour such a development.[2] In addition, the Rosario had shown itself amenable to a merger; the company's chairman, Frank Parish, who was also a Central director, actively sponsored the scheme.[3] The juxtaposition of the two lines, the obvious advantage of amalgamation and the attitude of the Argentine government encouraged Parish to pursue this policy. In reality conditions were not so conducive. The Central, conservatively administered, was little interested in the project except upon its own terms. In the past other companies had developed the interior, constructing lines that served as feeders to its trunk route between Rosario and Córdoba. Dominating the main artery of communications between the port and its hinterland, the CA profited without having to bear the cost of development.[4] The initial success of this complacent policy, and the spirit of aloofness which it fostered, hardly prepared the Central for the negotiations and compromises necessary to effect an amalgamation. The Rosario envisaged a merger of equals. Such a view did not prevail in Central circles. Confident of their position in the north-west, CA shareholders were unsympathetic to the Rosario's request for equitable consideration. The advantages presented by an efficient link with Buenos Aires were scorned by the Central when the price of that connection was the Rosario's participation in its monopoly profits. The BA&R's reply to this rebuff was to build on to the north, beyond Rosario, obliging the Central to obtain its own access to Buenos Aires and look to the defence of a shattered monopoly. Ensuing rivalry dashed any prospect of further co-operation. Amidst general recriminations, Parish resigned from the CA board of directors. After ten years' faithful service to the company his resignation was met with scant courtesy by the Central's chairman.[5]

The following years saw much construction as both railways completed their extension programmes; these were schemes which, although initiated in the 1880s, did not reach completion until the early years of the following decade. The intervention of the Baring Crisis, and the strains imposed upon each concern by the maintenance of ambitious policies in the face of adversity, tended to modify previous attitudes. Moreover, during the intervening period the rapid development of the Rosario had elevated that company to a position of first-ranking importance. Indeed, by the mid-1890s the Rosario was the second largest British-owned railway in Argentina, with a weight of capital and length of track significantly greater than the Central's.[6] The Rosario had challenged and despoiled the Central's monopoly, transforming the lethargic, 50-mile Campana into a network of approximately 1,000 miles, linking the principal cities of the north-west with Buenos Aires and Rosario. In comparison, the Central had vegetated for several decades and had done little to extend its main line or effect a link with Buenos Aires. When finally the CA rushed headlong into a series of costly acquisitions and extensions, they had to be sustained at a time of financial stringency and were effected in such a manner as to inflate the mileage capitalization of the company. The Central had to carry one of the highest rates of capital in Argentina, thereby placing a severe constraint upon ordinary dividend payments and thus confirming the worst fears held by shareholders regarding the inadvisability of extension building.

Inevitably, the wisdom of earlier policy was questioned and the sagacity of the board doubted. Irate communications from disillusioned shareholders appeared in the British press, and from 1890 a lively discussion ensued during which the more unfortunate experiences of the Central received a thorough examination.[7] It was a sad story when the once-proud Central could be described as the 'Cinderella of the South American celebrities'.[8] The directors warranted the abuse heaped upon them. Many had only a peripheral interest in the company, and were unfamiliar with Argentine conditions, in contrast to the BAGS board.[9] Perhaps this explains why the CA so often misjudged the situation in the republic. The board had encouraged shareholders to adopt a complacent attitude. For too long the Central depended upon its guarantee, refusing to construct extensions at the most opportune moment.[10] Subsequently, a costly, ill-conceived and ill-timed expansion programme was responsible for most of the difficulties experienced by the line in the early 1890s.[11] In its assessment of the earning potential of the extended network, and the likely effects of competition, the board had been unduly optimistic. An example of the contradictory prognoses presented to shareholders may be found in the board's views on the possible effects of competition upon the revenue received from the Tucumán traffic, and its contribution to the prosperity of the enterprise:[12]

Central Argentine Circular, March 1892
The Rosario Company, by their extension to Tucuman, have, no doubt, tapped a source of traffic in which hitherto the Central Company has participated, and the real competition with which the Rosario Company will have to contend is that between Rosario and Tucuman, in which the Central Company has now little interest, but the burden of which they would have to share if the two railways were amalgamated. There are already two rival routes open to Tucuman, one broad and the other narrow gauge, and a third also narrow gauge, is well advanced towards completion. Of the first two, one is the broad gauge of the Rosario Company, the other the narrow gauge system of the Cordoba and Rosario, Cordoba Central, and Central Northern lines. The rivalry between these two systems cannot fail to be severe, as the Central Northern (which has the advantage of a government guarantee) depends mainly on the traffic to and from the Tucuman district, and this rivalry will be intensified when the third is open.

Chairman's speech, AGM, May 1893
It was a very severe blow to the Central Argentine Railway when the Buenos Ayres and Rosario Company prolonged their line to Tucuman. That at once cut off one-half of the valuable traffic from the province of Tucuman and the more northern provinces. When the narrow gauge railway, the Central Northern, was prolonged first to join the Rosario, we lost

nearly the whole of the traffic; but during the current year we have made a connection between our own line and a narrow gauge line belonging to a French company which goes to Tucuman. Of course it is obvious that the French company and ourselves cannot possibly have any adverse interests, and we shall have every possible reason for helping one another to get as much as we can of the valuable Tucuman traffic, and that I hope may make some difference in the returns of the current year.

As these statements indicate, the Central board either had little grasp of events, or sought to mislead shareholders over the real implication of developments taking place in the north-west. The company had done little to placate local interests or strengthen its monopoly by constructing branches. Consequently, when a plethora of rival concessions were awarded during the 1880s the CA was ill-placed to retain its stranglehold upon the region.[13]

The Emergence of a Consensus
It was in this new atmosphere that the prospect of an amalgamation was broached once more. Early in 1892 the proponents of accommodation again began to air their views. The likely advantages and possible financial savings to be obtained from a fusion of the lines were invoked to emphasize the past failings of the Central's management. Not unnaturally, the board would have little truck with these schemes; an acceptance of amalgamation was seen by the Central board as an admission that many of the charges which had been made against them were well founded. On 18 March 1892 the board circulated a detailed memorandum among the shareholders (an extract from which appears above) emphasizing the favourable prospects of the company, the general uncertainties of the situation in Argentina, and the dubious advantages to be obtained from integration with the Rosario.[14] The board's interpretations were once again accepted by a majority of shareholders. Having already committed themselves to one reversal of policy, the bulk of investors were not prepared to effect another *volte face*. Moreover, many shareholders still retained a basically antagonistic attitude to the offending Rosario, at whose door they laid the blame for many of the Central's difficulties: they were sceptical of the Rosario's future intentions.

The directors easily survived this challenge and frustrated attempts to elect a pro-amalgamation director on to the board.[15]

Nevertheless, once they had secured their position, and sounded the true strength of the amalgamation lobby, Central officers and officials followed a more conciliatory policy with regard to the BA&R. While continuing to reject fusion, the Central looked for an understanding with its rival. Although the London board was able to maintain a solid indifference to the Rosario — in May 1893 the chairman firmly informed the shareholders that there had been no communications with the Rosario about amalgamation during the preceding 12 months[16] — there were undoubtedly contacts at the local level in Argentina. Despite the unequivocal claims of the Central's chairman it was reported a few months later from Buenos Aires that the local managers of the two companies had settled their outstanding difficulties.[17] And so matters remained for the next few years; both companies pursuing independent policies, but cognizant of the other's position. The Rosario constructed in the north and the Central obtained its access to Buenos Aires. The constraints imposed upon both lines by the general situation ensured a degree of harmony if not cordiality. It was little more than an uneasy truce, a fragile relationship which could not be expected to continue indefinitely unless a more formal arrangement might be concluded. Moreover, it was a limited agreement which had been encouraged by the hard years of the early 1890s when the prospects for further rapid development were not great and foreign-owned railways had been encouraged to settle their differences in the face of a government which sought to channel some of the blame for its own misdeeds on to others.

As the situation began to improve, and prospects brightened, it appeared that the Rosario and Central were once again set upon a collision course. During the financial year 1895/96 the Rosario considered that the newly-commissioned Central line to Buenos Aires was responsible for the possible loss of some passenger revenue, although given buoyant conditions the company had carried an increased number of passengers.[18] Both railways possessed parallel lines between Rosario and the federal capital; there was a substantial degree of overlapping in many areas of the north-west which were served directly or indirectly by their respective branches and the rails of allied or associated companies.

In view of this situation it was perhaps inevitable that the railways should find themselves locked in competition unless a solution could be evolved. At their respective annual general meetings in 1899 both chairmen informed shareholders that amalgamation negotiations were under way — the first occasion when the London directors had engaged in direct discussions. More explicitly, Frank Parish of the Rosario spelt out what his company expected to derive from a merger. There would be a saving in running costs, a more efficient service would be offered to members of the public, tariff reductions could be implemented (producing increased traffic), economies upon capital account could also be initiated, and, finally, a general improvement in the efficiency of both lines could be expected. The Central's chairman was more circumspect. He emphasized that an amalgamation would only be contemplated by the Central if the terms were fair and equitable.[19]

Gradually during succeeding months the two companies moved together, and while negotiations may have been less than smooth, there were indications that much of the earlier hostility had faded. In September 1899, it was reported, with a symbolism which was not lost upon their respective shareholders, that the two lines were to effect a junction near the Madero port at Buenos Aires, and would erect a joint station at Retiro.[20] But in spite of these portents there were still substantial differences between the companies. The very year that witnessed these agreements also revealed the fragile nature of the *rapprochement*. It was a good season for both companies, but the Central experienced a spectacular increase in grain traffic (see Table 29). During the fiscal year 1899 the Central carried almost twice as much grainstuffs as the Rosario.[21] Not unnaturally, the Central utilized this differential in amalgamation discussions. It determined that fusion should take the form of a profit-sharing arrangement in which it would be accorded a 50 per cent advantage over the Rosario upon the grain revenue account. Equally, the Rosario was not prepared to allow its future profits to be prejudiced by an exceptional year. As both lines were major grain carriers, neither was prepared to give way upon this point, and negotiations were terminated once again.[22] On this occasion the breakdown was of short duration, and discussions were revived the following year because the Retiro station project suffered a setback in Congress and necessitated further joint consultation. Congressional amendments to the original agreement proved unacceptable and the project was suspended.[23] The two companies then prepared to co-operate in an application for grain elevator concessions at Buenos Aires.[24]

Table 29: *Central Argentine: grain traffic*

	Total	Wheat	Maize (metric tons)	Linseed	Others
1894	1,324,935	554,823	32,348	20,725	717,037
1895	1,492,673	392,843	302,797	58,558	748,475
1896	1,727,287	303,444	520,597	71,180	832,066
1897	1,098,040	151,874	105,537	49,440	791,189
1898	1,293,052	278,759	242,087	25,761	746,445
1899	2,010,636	589,367	446,828	49,054	1,025,507
Annual Average	1,491,103	378,518	275,032	45,786	810,120

Source: *Statist* 26 February 1898, XLI, 339, 16 April 1898, XLI, 641, 14 April 1900, XLV, 575.

Despite these vicissitudes, the years around the turn of the century proved a crucial time for amalgamation. While conducting dilatory negotiations both companies had actively pursued their individual interests. In particular they assiduously expanded their networks, acquiring a number of strategically-placed lines in the important province of Santa Fé. The Rosario had proved a little more astute than the Central, and although the costs of expansion had been heavy for both lines, they weighed heavier upon the Central. Towards the end of 1900 the Central gained control of the Western of Santa Fe (*Oeste Santafecino*) at a cost of some £950,000 in 3 per cent debentures.[25] Financial interests close to the WSF had considered as early as 1891 that the future of the line lay in seeking an accommodation with the Central, and proposed contacting the latter regarding a leasing arrangement.[26] However, negotiations between the two companies proceeded fitfully, complicated by the financial structure of the *santafecino* line; while debenture capital was held in Britain, equity stock had been placed in Argentina. At first sight, it would appear that there was little of interest in this line for the Central.

It was a metre-gauge company, there had been difficulties with the right of way and it had been in receivership since 1894.[27] But the enterprise was located in a critical zone between the Central and Rosario, and the WSF held what could be regarded as equally strategic extensions.[28] During the six years before the Central absorbed the company it had yielded an average net revenue of approximately £31,000, an insignificant sum hardly enough to service the additional capital the Central had to raise in order to gain control of the line, let alone provide an income for other stockholders.[29]

Consequently, the Central became more tractable when renewed approaches were made by the Rosario. The heavy cost of yet another programme of expansion, coupled with unfavourable returns for 1900 made the company more responsive to the amalgamation issue. Perhaps for the very first time during 1901 the directorate and shareholders of the Central considered their relations with the BA&R in a realistic fashion. The Retiro project and joint elevator scheme indicated that co-operation between the companies was possible. The next stage would be more fundamental, involving full-scale amalgamation which would thoroughly integrate both companies, their operations and administrations. In one sense this raised even greater difficulties than negotiations concerned with income sharing. Any amalgamation entailing a unified capital account would require stock exchange or conversions. Had both lines been capitalized in a similar manner this would not have presented serious difficulties. Unfortunately they were not. Total capital accounts were not separated by a wide gulf in 1899, but the structure of those accounts was less easily reconciled.

As Table 30 indicates, approximately 47 per cent of the Rosario's capital was made up of ordinary stock; in the Central's case the figure was almost twice as much, standing at 87 per cent. This meant that under normal circumstances the greater part of revenue was expended upon the service of prior-charged capital (debentures and preference stock) while the converse applied for the Central. But during prosperous years, Rosario ordinary stockholders were liable to enjoy a much higher participation in their company's earnings as their holding was comparatively small, given the fixed rates applied to debentures and most preference stocks. In good years there was a tendency for Rosario

Table 30: *BA&R and CA: capital accounts, 1899*

Central	£ millions	Rosario	£ millions
4% Debentures	0.7	4% Debentures	3.5
6% Debentures	0.4	7% Preference stock	0.3
Ordinary Stock	7.4	7% Extension preference shares	1.2
TOTAL	8.5	Ordinary stock	4.5
		TOTAL	9.5

Source: *Statist* 7 October 1899, XLIV, 561, 24 February 1900, XLV, 288.

ordinary shareholders to enjoy a high yield upon their investment, but during poor years they were likely to suffer lower dividends as prior charges consumed a set amount of earnings, irrespective of the company's performance. The opposite applied to Central ordinary shareholders. They had little prospect of ever gaining spectacular returns except in especially prosperous years. On the other hand, during poor years there was little chance that prior commitments would consume all earnings as the proportion of prior-charged capital was relatively insignificant. Consequently, as the CA capital account stood in 1899, earnings above the £52,000 required to service debenture and preference stocks could be distributed amongst ordinary stockholders. The Rosario needed £245,000 before it could distribute a dividend to ordinary shareholders. Earnings above these levels would have to be distributed respectively amongst £7.4 millions of ordinary Central stock, but only £4.5 millions of Rosario equities. Capital account structure was undoubtedly responsible for the attitude adopted by the various shareholders to the several arrangements proposed. In this manner the final amalgamation negotiations centred upon the net earning potential of the two companies, and the method by which earnings were distributed amongst groups of stockholders. During the period immediately prior to amalgamation, the net receipts of the two companies were as shown in Graph 2.

The graph indicates the income remaining to each company for distribution to ordinary stockholders after interest and dividends had been paid upon debenture and preference capital.

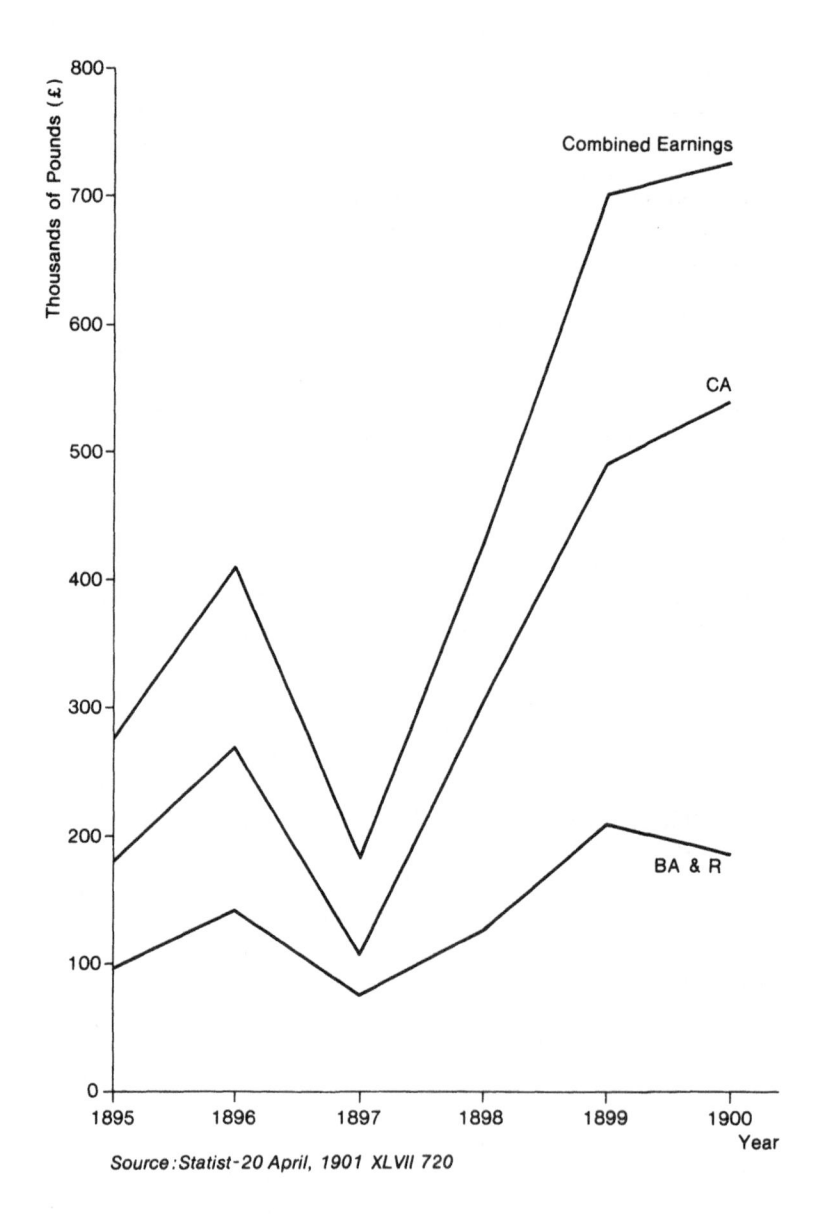

Graph 2: CA and BA&R: net earnings

Several factors emerge; there was a steady general recovery in earnings during the second half of the decade, but despite the substantial increases which occurred in Rosario earnings, the Central would have provided a growing proportion of combined revenue had the two lines been amalgamated in 1895. Herein lay the major difficulty. If the companies had already been united, the Central would have generated the lion's share of the common fund, which would have been enjoyed by Rosario ordinary stockholders. CA ordinary shareholders were adamant that no amalgamation would be contemplated unless it took cognizance of this fact. Rosario shareholders, on the other hand, wished to ensure that their prospects of earning higher dividends should not be sacrificed indefinitely in a general reorganization. At issue was the formulation of an acceptable ratio for stock transfers. It required a nice calculation as to the amount that Central Argentine ordinary scrip holders should be offered above the nominal value of their capital, and the extent to which Rosario scrip was to be written down. The lines determined to effect an exchange of stock upon the basis of the past yield of respective categories of securities. A provisional agreement was reached by the boards on 19 December 1901. CA ordinary shareholders were to be granted £30 of 7 per cent preference and £115 of ordinary stocks in the new, consolidated company in exchange for every £100 of Central scrip. Rosario shareholders, on the other hand, would receive a straight exchange of £100 consolidated ordinary stock for every £100 of Rosario ordinary capital, plus £15 of new consolidated deferred stock. The amalgamated concern would be named the Buenos Ayres and Rosario Company Limited.[30] The scheme was submitted to shareholders for approval.

At the BA&R extraordinary general meeting the mood was euphoric. Frank Parish, still chairman, spoke for the majority when he portrayed amalgamation as a significant development in the annals of Anglo-Argentine railway affairs. The merger could not be represented as the absorption of a weak line by a more powerful neighbour. Rather it was the fusion of two strong entities, pre-empting future clashes of interest which would have entailed useless expenditure. Indeed, had the amalgamation taken place at an earlier date, unnecessary expense would already have been avoided. Nevertheless, fusion should benefit not only the shareholders but also the government and public in Argentina. The Rosario shareholders accorded the amalgamation their unanimous approval.[31] The CA extra-ordinary meeting was more subdued. The chairman considered that the conditions of amalgamation were fair to both companies; they were terms that had been worth waiting for and could not have been obtained in 1890. Almost apologetically Central shareholders were informed that the name of their company would be suppressed, though, as a sop to wounded pride, he stated that a change of name was being considered.[32] Nonetheless, the scheme was approved.

The Results of Amalgamation
A life's work completed, Frank Parish retired from his position at the head of the Rosario board. His withdrawal made it easier for ex-Central directors, some of whom had hounded Parish from their company in the 1880s, to sit upon the amalgamated board. Also, it allowed Walter Morrison, ex-CA chairman, to head the company. The new board itself was composed of the ex-directors of both railways, minus retiring members, plus one new appointee to ensure an equitable balance of interests.[33]

Having received the sanction of the shareholders the railway now faced the equally delicate task of obtaining the Argentine government's approval. Not least among the difficulties in achieving this most necessary objective was the means by which the union of the two railways had been effected. As has been recounted, each shareholder in the new company had received an assortment of stocks calculated to yield, all other things being equal, the same income as had been obtained upon Rosario or Central scrip. Due to the difference which had existed in the structure of their capital accounts, the application of this rubric meant that the nominal capitalization of the amalgamated line did not bear a very close resemblance to the sum of the capital accounts of the deceased companies. Based upon earning potential, the London Stock Exchange valuation of the combined capital account reflected accurately the aggregate of the previous values accorded to the new defunct scrips. The nominal value of the new scrip, however, was considerably in excess of the old. Thus, though ex-Rosario ordinary shareholders were issued with a like amount of ordinary stock in the new company, their receipt of an additional, newly created deferred stock represented a writing-up of that company's capital by some £812,000. An even greater augmentation occurred in the case of former CA paper. Though the market value of old and new scrip held by ex-Central ordinary stockholders was much the same, their nominal holding was inflated by approximately 50 per cent, representing an increase of £3,748,000 upon the old company's capitalization.[34] The capital account of the new company exceeded the sum of the capital accounts of the amalgamated lines by £4,560,000. This device, a perfectly legitimate fusion procedure in London, appeared in Buenos Aires as a rather sordid attempt to introduce a substantial amount of water into the Rosario capital account.[35]

Provisional recognition was accorded to the amalgamation by a presidential decree of 29 August 1902, subject to certain limitations. The Argentine government only sanctioned the transfer of Central Argentine property to the newly constituted railway on condition that the lines were worked independently, and that the obligations laid down in the original Central and Rosario concessions were fulfilled.[36] This objective achieved, the new BA&R prepared a scheme for the consolidation of its contracts and concessions which, it was hoped, would obtain the necessary congressional approval. In this the company was a little premature; the government was adamant that both lines should be worked separately and would not tolerate a fusion of their services. It was another six years before the company obtained permission to integrate thoroughly and effectively the two networks. Part of the price paid for congressional sanction was a further change of name. Because of its historical connotations, Congress wished to resurrect the defunct title, Central Argentine Railway Company Limited.[37] Thus the long-desired amalgamation was finally, and formally, achieved. The re-named company anticipated a greater efficiency and economy of working than had ever been associated with the old Central.

The complicated, often tortuous, negotiations that preceded Central/Rosario amalgamation did not disguise the significance of the event. If the break-up of the *Oeste* system marked the beginnings of co-operation amongst British-owned lines, the fusion of these companies signalled the arrival of rationalization. The formation of the new company was important for the two lines immediately concerned, for the region in which they operated, and for railway affairs in general.

In the first instance, the new company became the major

British-owned Argentine railway (both in terms of capitalization and route mileage), and quickly demonstrated the advantages of an integrated network. After a bad harvest and generally poor conditions during the first post-amalgamation year, the situation improved dramatically in 1903 and the company was able to boast:

> Two features stand out pre-eminently in the past half year's [January-June 1903] results of the [amalgamated] Buenos Ayres and Rosario Railway. The one is the enormous growth in earnings, and the other is the marked success which has attended the efforts of the company to handle the increased traffic with skill and economy.[38]

Amalgamation brought a degree of order to the situation prevailing in the north-west. During the years immediately before the merger both Rosario and Central, as described above, pursued policies of acquiring control over, or seeking working agreements with, tributary lines. The latter leased the BAN, part of the *FC Oeste* network, and purchased the Western of Santa Fe;[39] the Rosario absorbed the Santa Fe and Cordoba Great Southern Railway Company Limited. In addition both had constructed extensive branch lines and feeders to their respective trunk routes. Consolidation of this nature eradicated many of the anomalies and circuitous routings that had previously disrupted traffic movements in the north-west. The removal of separate railway administrations, the standardization of rolling stock, and conformity of service made for more efficient shipment. Extension building meant the creation of direct routes and the easing of bottlenecks. In this sense the amalgamation of the Central and Rosario represented merely the final stage of broad-gauge railway rationalization in the area.

In general terms, however, the influence of this merger was more far-reaching. The example of a successful amalgamation served to encourage other lines. All the railways had suffered the adverse effects of the depression of the early 1890s, none more than the Central. Indeed, the Central epitomized — on a larger scale — the problems experienced by several British-owned companies. Consequently, this achievement was all the more startling. It had occurred despite the bitterness and recriminations which had previously divided the Rosario and Central, and the equivocal attitude of the Argentine government. Moreover, the new company was the first truly regional railway. It was an integrated concern geared to the requirements of its zone, and, notwithstanding competition from narrow-gauge lines, was able to yield a return upon capital sufficient to guarantee the sustained inflow of infrastructural investment necessary to push back the 'internal frontier' — the expanding margin of profitable cultivation that provided a dynamic element in Argentine economic growth until the inter-war period.[40]

The new company adopted both the Rosario's name and past policies. It pursued an active programme of extension building upon which much of the country's prosperity was based. The downward trend in cereal prices, already observable by the early twentieth century, necessitated a continuous expansion of output if earnings and income were to be maintained in the face of declining prices. Increased output was dependent upon the expansion of the railway network and the provision of an efficient service that would allow the area of cultivation to be profitably extended. Railway expansion in turn was consequent upon the prosperity of the existing networks. Prosperity arose from cheap, efficient, integrated railway operations. The problem was circular; amalgamation provided a ready solution.

VII

ZONAL AMALGAMATION — 2

Many companies desired to emulate the Central and Rosario, but regionalization was only accomplished in other areas after struggles similar to that which preceded the formation of the new BA&R. Although several concerns acknowledged the benefits to be derived from zonal railway development, co-operation was rarely readily achieved.

The Emergence of the Pacific Group
Early moves to construct a railway between Argentina and Chile had gradually dissolved into a number of less spectacular, and possibly more feasible, projects. As was stated above, the original concession drawn up in 1864 envisaged a line running from Buenos Aires to San Filipe in Chile via the Argentine cities of Junin, Villa Mercedes, Mendoza and San Juan; the actual transandine link to be constructed from either of the two latter provincial capitals. This scheme was approved by both governments and was promised financial support.[1] But the concession was never fully implemented; by the turn of the century some three companies functioned as successors of the original scheme.[2] The BA&P operated the eastern section of the international link. It had obtained the concession for the stretch of track between Mercedes and Villa Mercedes, and built an alternative approach to Buenos Aires, virtually duplicating that part of the original concession effected by the *Oeste*. The middle sector, westwards out of Villa Mercedes into the foothills of the Andes, had been purchased from the Argentine government by the Great Western while the last section, from Mendoza to Chile, was owned by the Buenos Ayres and Valparaiso Transandine Railway Company Limited, although the connection with the Chilean railway system was not finally completed until 1910.[3]

Moves to unify the administration of the international system (which was not only managed by three separate companies, but also constructed to two different gauges) were initially stimulated by the projected sale of the *FC Andino*. At the time rumour linked together the names of all the private companies upon which the state-owned railway impinged. It was maintained that, under the pretext of submitting a joint tender for the federal entity, the BA&R, BA&P and AGW were contemplating amalgamation.[4] While the Rosario had little in common with other lines, except a desire to obtain possession of the *Andino*, the Pacific and Argentine Great Western were bound by stronger influences. Despite the train of historical accidents which led to the formation of successor companies, the essential unity of the transandine railway route to Chile was based upon sound economic reasoning. The main line of each of the three companies formed part of the same trunk route, and no matter how they might subsequently develop, or from which sources seek a more diversified traffic, the *raison d'être* for their existence lay in the original desire to effect a means of communication between the two countries. As such, it was inevitable that the profitability of any one company depended to a degree upon through traffic originating upon, or destined for, another line. This observation was less pertinent for the Pacific, and most applicable to the Transandine railway company, but all the lines were conscious of their interdependence.

Aware of the limited nature of the Chilean trade, and the factors inhibiting a rapid expansion of inter-republic commerce, the Pacific had availed itself of a central pampean location to foster alternative sources of revenue. It had forged close links with the Villa Maria and Rufino Railway Company Limited, another British-owned, broad-gauge concern strategically situated in the developing grain zone which lay between the Central and BA&P. This firm connected the two towns after which it was named, situated respectively on the Pacific and CA main lines: it ran for approximately 140 miles from south to north via Villa Nueva and Carlota. It was a valuable feeder for the Pacific. Until the Central leased the BA Northern, the BA&P route afforded agriculturalists situated along the VM&R with their only direct access to the port and market of the federal capital. Also the line provided the BA&P with a useful entry into another region which implied that lessening of dependence upon the Chile trade. Thus, although the two lines were independent and separate companies, their respective boards reflected this close community of interest: they were identical, even the chairman and vice-chairman holding exactly the same position upon both boards.[5] It was hardly surprising that as a result of the Baring Crisis these two companies formalized their relationship. Guarantee negotiations in the aftermath of the crash provided a forum for all companies, and focussed attention upon the interdependent nature of some types of traffic. When, during the course of the negotiations, it became obvious that the Argentine government was disposed neither to honour its obligations nor to reach a speedy settlement, the VM&R cast about for a substitute guarantor. Accommodation with the BA&P appeared the only alternative.[6] Indeed, the necessity of acquiring a substitute for the government guarantee was an overriding consideration as the Villa Maria had been forced into temporary liquidation in 1895 to effect a capital reorganization, given a failure to service debentures.[7]

From these rather unpromising beginnings — the scramble for the *Andino* and the Villa Maria's temporary financial embarrassment — was to emerge another of the large, regional railway conglomerations of Argentina. The Andean sale provided the incentive for a lateral grouping, while the Pacific's experience with the VM&R showed how that grouping was to be achieved. The process of fusion, however, did not progress smoothly. In spite of the fundamental advantages to be obtained from unified working, the prevailing economic situation inevitably engendered a mood of caution. Like many lines constructed during the hectic 1880s the VM&R was built in anticipation of demand. When these prospects failed to materialize, the company made substantial losses. Consequently, the Pacific found its agreement with the Villa Maria onerous, and allowed it to lapse after two years.[8] During the ensuing period of independent operation the VM&R sustained deficits of approximately £11,000 per annum which were gradually reduced until a gross profit of £3,000 was secured in 1899. Profitable operations provided the opportunity for a renewed approach to the BA&P. The company understood the benefits to be derived from economies of scale, and appreciated that its line could be worked more efficiently by a larger undertaking. Despite the ill-feeling generated by the Pacific's abrogation of the earlier agreement, the Villa Maria was pre-

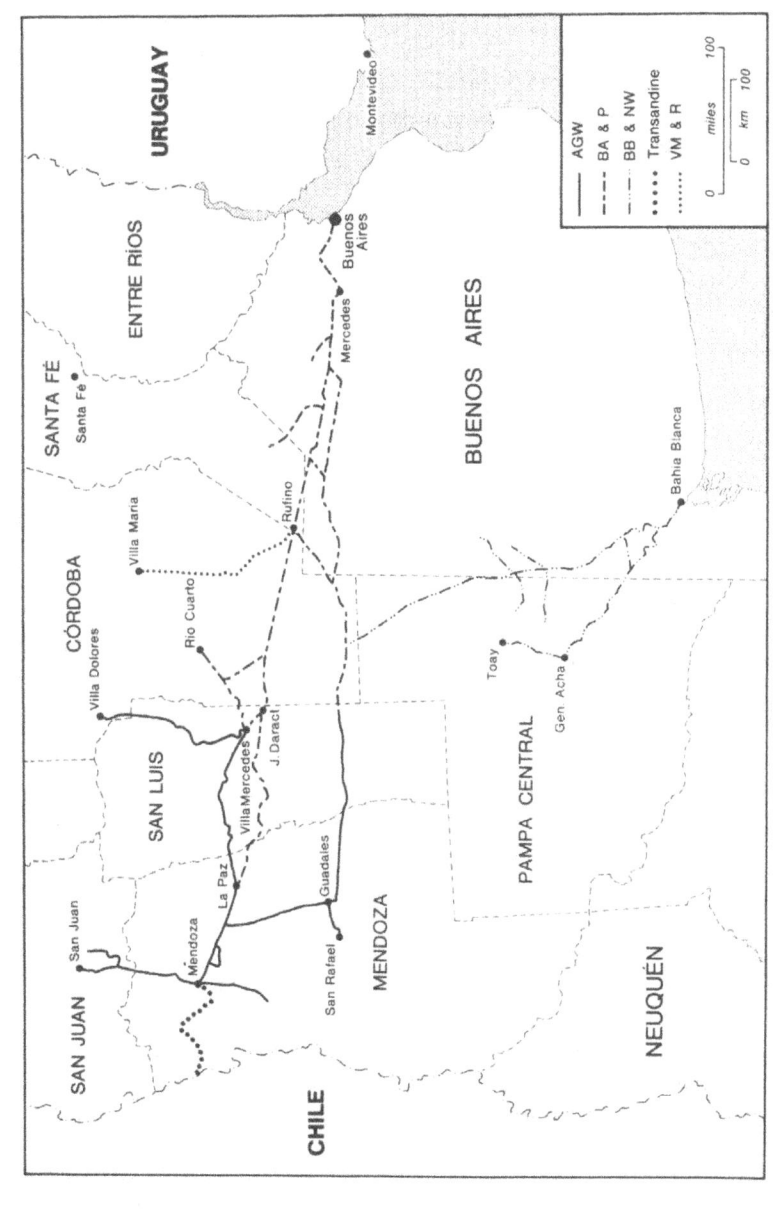

Map 4: The consolidation of the Pacific group, 1895–1910

pared to consider a new arrangement while the company's apparent viability was sufficient to rekindle BA&P interest.[9]

At this juncture John Wynford Phillips joined the Pacific as chairman, a position he retained until 1938.[10] It was under his direction that the BA&P developed into a regional agglomeration of companies and dependent lines reaching from Buenos Aires to the *cordillera*, and stretching from San Juan to Bahía Blanca. Like his brother, Owen Phillips, who played a similar role in the development of the Royal Mail Steamship Company, J.W. possessed a determination and quality of leadership that enabled him to dominate his own group of companies and secure an important position in Anglo-Argentine railway affairs. Indeed, he became the 'strong man' who was held by some to be the individual responsible for the recovery and rise to profitability of the Pacific Group after the turn of the century.[11] Unlike Parish of the Great Southern, he did not own property in Argentina, nor did he come from a family with long-standing River Plate connections. Phillips represented the new generation of railway men who were interested in British-owned Argentine railways for their own sake, as a source of investment and profit. A financier, he manipulated and channelled the growing supply of savings available in the London money market towards enterprises offering the moderate, but regular, return attractive to small and institutional lenders.

Yet, in many respects, the absorption of the Villa Maria was a peripheral affair. The main objective of Pacific policy remained the consolidation of its hold upon the trunk route to Chile. The VM&R episode was interesting because it demonstrated to the Pacific the means of realizing that objective. Working agreements and undertakings to service capital were the devices subsequently employed by the BA&P to secure control over neighbouring companies. Conditions were favourable to such a policy. Since its formation in 1887 the Argentine Great Western had been criticized for the high tariffs it levied. During the difficult years of the early 1890s, the economic stagnation of *Cuyo* was blamed upon maladministration and the onerous freight rates charged by the company.[12] Although the complaints made against the railway were often exaggerated, its tariffs were on the whole higher than those levied by most other lines. Only the Transandine (a special case), the state-owned *Andino*, and the notorious East Argentine subjected their consumers to such exorbitant charges as may be observed in Table 31.

The Great Western countered these complaints with the argument that its shareholders did not receive an adequate income upon investment due to the underdeveloped nature of the region. High tariffs would ensure a reasonable return and were the only means of attracting to the area the investment necessary for economic expansion. The company was little disposed to consider the alternative view that lower tariffs would encourage a general increase in traffic sufficient to generate substantial total earnings.[13] On the other hand, with the return of more prosperous times, the company sought to vindicate its past policy by embarking upon a programme of extension building. This would emphasize its commitment to the region and demonstrate the value of infrastructural investment predicated upon solid earnings potential. The scale of the Great Western's subsequent expansion may be judged from the additional capital raised during the early years of the twentieth century.

Much of the new finance was obtained by issues of ordinary stock, and to some extent the acquisition of this 'cheap' capital justified the company's tariff policy. Stockholders would only subscribe to such issues when they considered there was a reasonable chance that their investment would secure a good return. In 1900, as Table 32 demonstrates, more than 88 per cent of the Great Western's capital consisted of prior-charged securities; by 1906 that proportion had fallen to approximately 55 per cent.

Thus the Pacific was presented with an expansionist rival. During the period between 1900 and 1904 the Great Western obtained 562 miles of new concessions.[14] In addition, the company secured its rear by reaching an agreement with the Transandine. The two companies effected a junction in 1901 which provided for an easy interchange of traffic (inasmuch as the break of gauge would allow): two years later the AGW arranged to work the Transandine.[15] The latter's board was reorganized to contain two Great Western directors, one of whom assumed the chair, the other seats being taken by two original Transandine directors and a representative of the Argentine government (the minister in London).[16] There being little incentive to expand westward, the AGW turned its attention towards the east. Relations with the Pacific became strained, and deteriorated further

Table 31: *Argentine Railways: tariff schedules, 1897*

	Passenger class $ paper per km.				Freight category $ paper per metric ton/km.						
	1st	2nd	1st	2nd	3rd	4th	5th	6th	7th	8th
Government lines										
Andean	6.0	3.5	0.15	0.12	0.11	0.1	0.085	0.07	0.06	0.05
Central Northern	2.5	1.5	0.06	0.05	0.045	0.04	0.035	0.03	0.025	0.02
Private Companies										
AGW	3.5	2.0	0.06	0.05	0.04	0.03	0.025	0.02	0.015	—
ANE	3.0	2.0	0.06	0.05	0.045	0.04	0.035	0.03	0.025	0.02
BA&P	2.5	1.65	0.06	0.05	0.045	0.037	0.03	0.02	0.014	—
BA&R	2.5	1.5	0.04	0.04	0.04	0.03	0.03	0.02	0.015	—
BAGS	*2.48	1.65	—	0.046	—	0.037	—	0.02	0.013	—
	†1.27	0.9	—	0.020	—	0.019	—	0.01	0.006	—
BAW	*2.48	1.65	—	0.046	—	0.037	—	0.02	0.013	—
	†1.27	0.9	—	0.020	—	0.019	—	0.01	0.006	—
CA	2.5	1.5	0.06	0.05	0.045	0.04	0.035	0.03	0.025	0.02
EA	4.0	3.0	0.06	0.05	0.045	0.04	0.035	0.03	0.025	0.02
Transandine	15.0	10.0	0.15	0.14	0.13	0.12	0.11	0.1	0.09	—

*for journeys of less than 350 kms. †for journeys of more than 350 kms.

Source: República Argentina, Ministerio de Obras Públicas, Dirección General de Ferrocarriles *Estadística de los ferrocarriles en explotación durante el año 1897* (Buenos Aires 1898) pp. 184–85.

Table 32: *Argentine Great Western: capitalization*

	1900 £	1903 £	1904 £	1906 £
First debentures	1,655,506	1,665,517	1,675,517	1,675,517
Second debentures	1,550,000	1,700,000	1,700,000	1,700,000
5% Cumulative preference stock	500,000	750,000	750,000	875,000
Ordinary stock	500,000	750,000	750,000	1,750,000
New shares	—	—	250,000	1,625,000
	4,205,506	4,865,517	5,125,517	7,625,517

Source: *Statist* 30 June 1900, XLV, 975, 7 November 1903, LII, 846, 13 May 1905, LV, 894, 17 November 1906, LVIII, 922.

when the AGW began to redirect its Buenos Aires traffic over *Andino* and Central Argentine rails. This route to the federal capital was more circuitous than the direct, Pacific roadway and shippers could only have been persuaded to utilize it if the railways concerned had offered substantial rebates — an exercise which the BA&P considered distinctly unfriendly. Charging lower tariffs than the AGW, the Pacific was anxious to maintain rates, and was usually exercised by rate cutting amongst its competitors.[17] Indignities were heaped upon the protesting BA&P when Central Argentine carriages were permitted to run through to Mendoza, while passengers travelling via the Pacific were obliged to detrain at Villa Mercedes and continue their journey in Great Western stock. It was also rumoured that the Great Western general manager was attempting to force shippers to load exclusively into Central wagons.[18]

Further hostile acts followed as the Great Western embarked upon its extension building programme. Branch lines were constructed in northern San Luis and pushed southward through Mendoza. In addition numerous short feeders were built. Gradually the railway was transformed from a trunk route linking the cities of San Juan, Mendoza and Villa Mercedes into an extensive regional system geared to the requirements of the wine producing area of the Argentine. Its main branches ran longitudinally through the ranges of the *cordillera*, with feeders penetrating the short, lateral valleys. The results of this programme were soon observable in traffic returns which showed a dramatic increase in the output of the wine industry, and a growth in ancillary activities, as well as a general rise in the volume of merchandise handled by the company: between 1895 and 1905 total goods tonnage grew from a little below 140,000 metric tons to over half a million, the volume of wine shipped quadrupling from some 50,000 to nearly 200,000 tons.[19]

While the Pacific remained the sole link between an expanding Great Western and the city of Buenos Aires, it was favourably disposed to its vigorous neighbour. Unfortunately some of the more lengthy Great Western branches performed a variety of functions: not only did they open up new areas, but they also afforded the Great Western contacts with third parties. Indeed, they were hardly branch lines at all, but embryonic trunk routes. If the AGW's branches to Villa Dolores and Guadales could be portrayed as developmental lines, designed to extend the frontiers of cultivation, they could equally be viewed as a means of establishing an area of exclusive influence, and an attempt to pre-empt the construction of similar lines by prospective competitors. So the BA&P observed the AGW busily constructing extensive branch lines to the north and south on the western extremities of its zone, and, furthermore, negotiating traffic agreements with state-owned and private enterprises. Such action was construed as an attempt to secure alternative access to Buenos Aires and could only be viewed as hostile to the Pacific. Great Western expansion generated a valuable new item of revenue, and demonstrated the future potential of the wine producing industry. But the bulk of the BA&P's wine traffic originated on the AGW and would be jeopardized if the latter continued to pursue an independent policy.[20] After a marked increase during the preceding period, the volume of wine (and allied commodities) handled by the Pacific stagnated around the turn of the century, and declined after 1901. This reduction was largely due to the Great Western's re-routing policy.

But the latter was ill-equipped to maintain this position in the face of the Pacific's determination to retain a share of the lucrative wine trade. The BA&P line east from Villa Mercedes represented the most direct route to Buenos Aires. Arrangements with the *Andino* and Central were poor substitutes, as were any other alternatives that the Great Western might offer in co-operation with third parties. Moreover, the AGW's past reputation counted against it. Although the company was able to raise new capital easily, and obtained new concessions, there was little support for its schemes amongst the main shippers. Despite the increased traffic that the Great Western offered the Andean, the national government was hardly disposed to favour it before other lines. The Argentine authorities wished to stimulate competition between the foreign-owned railways, but it would not grant special privileges to a line with a reputation for levying high rates. The Great Western's tariff policy had occasioned a great deal of ill-will inside the *Direccion General de Ferrocarriles*, with whom the company enjoyed far from cordial relations.[21] Consequently, every facility was offered to the Pacific in order that it might reply to the challenge mounted by the AGW, and encouragement was given to the former to extend its own main line to Mendoza.[22]

The Pacific attempted to turn the Great Western's flank and carry the struggle directly to the heart of the latter's zone. Old concessions which had been held for some years were hastened to completion so as to contain AGW expansion and prevent an effecting of convenient junctions with other companies. Finally, the BA&P assumed extensive powers to penetrate the Great Western's profitable wine-growing region. At an extra-ordinary general meeting held in August 1902 the Pacific obtained the sanction of its shareholders virtually to duplicate the Great Western trunk line. A comprehensive series of resolutions allowed the directors to acquire or purchase any concessions; to construct and work any railway; or to subscribe funds or take over the stock of any company which might have concessions or own lines in the following regions:

a) between Mendoza and La Paz
b) between La Paz and a point on the Pacific near Villa Mercedes
c) between San Juan and a point upon the Pacific
d) in the vicinity of the towns of Mendoza and San Rafael.

As the Great Western main line from Villa Mercedes to San Juan ran via La Paz and Mendoza, and San Rafael was one of the wine-producing districts being opened up by the AGW, there was little doubt as to the intention of these measures, which were approved by a large majority. On 2 October 1902 the BA&P obtained from the Argentine government a concession for a line from Justo Daract (east of Villa Mercedes) to La Paz, on the Great Western trunk line. This concession ran some way south of the existing Great Western route between Villa Mercedes and La Paz, and approached to within 90 miles of Mendoza itself.[23]

The Great Western had little room in which to manoeuvre. Criticized over its tariff policy in Argentina, the company only hoped that such schemes would not find support among English capitalists.[24] The logical outcome was for both companies to effect an equitable arrangement that shared the costs of developing the railway network of *Cuyo*, and also provided for a reasonable distribution of the returns obtainable. The first steps in this direction were taken in 1904 when the chairman of the Pacific was co-opted on to the Great Western board.[25]

In retrospect, 1904 was an eventful year. It saw the implementation of a series of agreements and arrangements that determined the shape of the Pacific group. The company's abiding interest in the unity of the international route was exhibited when, after reaching its understanding with the AGW, both the Pacific and the Great Western offered a joint-guarantee to the Transandine company in order to facilitate the completion of the latter's main line through to Chile. The Great Western, it will be recalled, had been working the Transandine since 17 October 1903; this new guarantee was as much an offer of support to the Great Western as it was to the Transandine. Both broad-gauge lines undertood to service the Transandine A Debentures, and so allow Argentine government guarantee recession bonds, the income from which had hitherto been earmarked for these securities, to be sold and the proceeds devoted to the completion of the trans-andean railway.[26] Thus the Pacific had tentatively secured its interests along the whole of the route between Chile and the River Plate. Perhaps it is significant that at this stage the Buenos Ayres and Valparaiso Transandine Railway Company Limited elected to change its name to the more prosaic, if realistic, Argentine Transandine Railway Company Limited.

The Pacific Group and the Western Pampas
This objective achieved, the BA&P unveiled further plans. For some time *estancieros* in the west of the province of Buenos Aires, along the border with the territory of *Pampa Central*, had been pressing for the construction of lines in their area. They had witnessed the beneficial results of railway development in other regions, and wished to secure similar opportunities themselves. This zone had been largely neglected by the major broad-gauge companies which radiated from the federal capital. With the exception of the area immediately to the north of the port of Bahía Blanca, the principal lines had barely begun to penetrate the region before the turn of the century. The Pacific and the Western had pushed their trunk routes westward through the northern districts of Buenos Aires and the southern regions of Córdoba, while the Great Southern had constructed in a south-westerly direction across the bulging coastline of Buenos Aires province. Consequently, as these companies built from the centre, there remained large tracts of camp devoid of effective rail communications. This omission was most keenly felt at the ends of the major trunk routes, where the radial nature of pampean railway development exhibited its worst limitations.

Structural imperfections of this nature in the national rail network had long been recognized; there had been several attempts to solve the problem. Established companies were encouraged to construct more lines and build lateral connections between their main trunk routes so as to transform the radial system into one that more resembled a grid. Before the turn of the century this policy obtained a moderate success in certain regions, particularly in the area close to Buenos Aires where main lines were relatively close together, and it was not too difficult or costly to effect new junctions. In other regions a more radical solution was required — namely the construction of circumferential lines, cutting across and uniting the terminal points of radial routes. The Bahia Blanca and North Western Railway Company Limited was one such expedient. Registered in May 1889, it assumed concessions for lines from the port of Bahía Blanca to Río Cuarto, located on the *Andino*, and Villa Mercedes on the BA&P, via General Acha, La Verde, Toay and Victoria. It was anticipated that this spinal route would form the basis for a regional network complete with connecting branch lines eastwards to the radial trunk routes emanating from the federal capital, and feeder lines westward into *Pampa Central*.[27]

These expectations proved premature. As was the case with projects commenced during the late 1880s, the company was overtaken by the Baring Crisis. Although the original concessions provided that 738 miles of track should be completed by 11 April 1895, when the railway company took over the line from the bankrupt contractor on 1 January 1894, its rails had not reached General Acha, some 128 miles out of Bahía Blanca. Undoubtedly a viable concern, the enterprise was unfortunate in the timing of incorporation. As the main line was pushed northward the company exhibited an increasing anxiety to secure accommodation with a more prosperous entity. There had been moves in 1892 to amalgamate with the Great Southern. Subsequently, the Western was seen as a likely benefactor. Thus, although the Bahia Blanca continued to construct its main line, the company expressed little desire to engage in any works which would involve further capital expenditure.

This timorous policy was maintained until the turn of the century when *estancieros*, despairing of the BB, turned instead to the Great Southern which had already developed extensive interests about the port of Bahía Blanca. The BAGS readily agreed to continue its existing lines in western Buenos Aires province still farther. It was with much unease that the Bahia Blanca learnt from Frank Parish that the Southern intended to take up concessions within its zone. Small comfort was derived from the Great Southern's protestations that such lines would not be constructed in a spirit of hostility, 'but merely as a matter of business and in a friendly way'.[28] The likely repercussions of the Great Southern's action were obvious, and encouraged the BB&NW once again to seek out a powerful sponsor. A suitable partner appeared in the guise of the Western. Negotiations between the two lines were already at an advanced stage. An *ad referendum* agreement had been reached by the respective boards, providing for an exchange of stocks, subject to the approval of the shareholders of both companies. At the eleventh hour, however, the BAW board reneged on its agreement and announced that it would be unable to recommend acceptance of the scheme to its shareholders. The BAW directors explained that a thorough examination of the Bahia Blanca revealed what was only to be expected: the permanent way was in poor condition. It was estimated that £700,000 would be required to raise Bahia Blanca track and rolling stock to the standards prevailing upon the Western. This was a double blow to the BB&NW whose shareholders were already disturbed by rumours that the scheme had been rejected by the BAW as it conflicted with the Great Southern's plans for the region.[29]

The harsh words with which the Bahia Blanca chairman castigated the Western's behaviour brought little comfort to his shareholders. They were aware of their company's vulnerability. Its past record was not good; they had offended local interests with their repeated refusal to construct branch lines; their zone required a substantial infusion of capital which they were unwilling, or unable, to provide. In short, they were ill-prepared to face an intrusion into the region by a large and powerful neighbour. At this juncture the Pacific offered to replace the Western as the BB&NW's saviour. Unlike the latter, the BA&P did not recommend an exchange of stock, but proposed to work the Bahia Blanca, guaranteeing investors' income. Debenture service would be met in full, while the preference stockholders were offered a rate of return that would increase from 3 to $4\frac{1}{2}$ per cent over a 14-year period. BB&NW stockholders (there were no ordinary shares) agreed with alacrity, and the line was worked by the Pacific from 1 July 1904.[30] Despite the Western's assessment, this arrangement had several advantages for the BA&P. The Bahia Blanca's concession, as we have seen, provided for a trunk railway between the port of Bahía Blanca itself, and Villa Mercedes on the BA&P main line. Although the project had not been realized, pressure was once again mounting during the early twentieth century for the establishment of railway lines in precisely this region. The national government indicated that it desired the fulfilment of the original intention, if not the letter, of the BB&NW concession — namely, that the western pampas should be provided with a north-to-south link railway whose branches would connect existing radial routes. By assuming responsibility for the BB&NW, the Pacific ensured that these extensions were constructed by a client, under its auspices, without the intervention of the state.

However, if these were the Pacific's long-term objectives, there were more pressing strategic reasons. The BA&P had only recently secured its arrangement with the Great Western which, although chastened, appears by no means to have abandoned its expansionist desires. One of the AGW's many concessions provided for construction between its San Rafael branch and the Bahia Blanca, either at Toay or General Acha. Toay was already an important Western railhead and it was intended the town become a major junction for all three enterprises. A connection to Toay would have provided the Great Western with further access to Buenos Aires. Consequently, by effecting a working agreement with the BB&NW, the Pacific was able to forestall any future hostile acts by the Great Western. Constructing branches between its own trunk lines and the Bahia Blanca railhead, the Pacific effectively prevented the AGW from thrusting eastwards to establish a junction with one of the trunk routes pushing out from the federal capital. The prize of the *Cuyo* wine traffic was enough for the Pacific to risk offending both the BAW and Southern.[31] Possession of the BB&NW also consolidated the company's position as a grain carrier.

Thus, during the course of 1904, the outline of the Pacific network was established. Subsequent policy was confined to strengthening the hold which it had acquired over its subsidiary lines. A new, retrospective lease agreement was offered to, and accepted by, the VM&R. The BA&P undertook to provide the owners of Villa Maria scrip with a return of 3 per cent upon the nominal value of their investment, rising to $4\frac{1}{2}$ per cent over twelve years.[32] Meanwhile the AGW granted the Transandine a new lease, previously reversing the practice favoured by the Pacific: the Transandine, upon the abrogation of the guarantee which it enjoyed from the Great Western and Pacific, was offered a profit sharing scheme. For 1 January 1905 the AGW undertook to work the metre-gauge line for a portion of the gross receipts yielded by that company. A sliding scale was established whereby the Great Western would take 90 per cent of gross receipts should the working of the company yield £25,999 per annum or less; as earnings rose the AGW's share would decline until, when gross receipts stood at £199,999 per annum or over, the broad-gauge line would receive only 65 per cent.[33]

Finally, the Great Western itself was brought firmly within the Pacific fold by the offer of a comprehensive guarantee. More sophisticated than the other agreements which the Pacific had concluded, the terms secured by the AGW were an indication of the degree of independence still retained by the company, and the consequent desire of the former to replace the existing 'understanding' with a firm, legally enforceable contractual scheme. Inasmuch as the Great Western arrangement epitomizes the device perfected by the Pacific in the pursuit of its expansionist policy, it is worth examining at some length. The BA&P undertook to provide the following guaranteed income:

1. A sum equal to the annual service of the First and Second 5% debentures.
2. Supply a dividend upon the Argentine Great Western preference stock at the following rate:
    a) a dividend at the same rate as that paid to BA&P 1st 5% preference stockholders.
    b) a dividend at the same rate as any bonus paid over 5% to the BA&P 1st 5% preference stockholders, but not more than 6%.
    c) a dividend of ½% if the ordinary stockholders of the BA&P were paid a dividend of 10% or over.
3. Supply a dividend upon ordinary Argentine Great Western stock at the following rate:
    a) a dividend equal to that declared upon BA&P 2nd 5% preference stock.
    b) a dividend equal to any bonus paid on BA&P 2nd 5% preference stock, but not exceeding 6%.
    c) a dividend of ½% when a dividend in excess of 7% was declared upon Pacific ordinary stock.
    d) a dividend of ½% when a dividend in excess of 10% was declared upon Pacific ordinary stock.[34]

This new agreement took effect from 1 July 1907, and was approved by the Argentine government some years later.

The Pacific Group: Strengths and Weaknesses

The consolidation of this group provided Argentina with another regional railway system. Based in the wine-producing area of *Cuyo* and in the grain belt of the western *pampas*, the Pacific's earning schedule was more diversified than that of the other major groupings. Nevertheless, it also devoted particular attention to the requirements of its extended zone, especially to the demands of the wine industry. Subsequent railway development in the provinces of San Juan, Mendoza and San Luis owed much to the harmony imposed by the Pacific. Unification was particularly beneficial for the Transandine. It is doubtful if that company could ever have completed its line to Chile without the support of the larger railways, especially the BA&P. The guarantee accorded to the metre-gauge line enabled it to raise the necessary capital that would not have been forthcoming had the company stood alone.

But the Pacific group was less of an integrated concern than the other zonal networks. Indeed, this was one of its weaknesses. Not only did the system incorporate in a variety of regions and therefore had to provide a diversity of services, but the manner in which unification had been achieved provided an added element of instability. The group was subject to the conflicting demands of different types of users and beset by the claims of a multitudinous range of stockholders. The Pacific had obtained control over its subsidiary companies by means of a series of working agreements secured upon its guarantee to service the capital accounts of client lines. This method avoided the complicated negotiations that would have preceded an amalgamation involving an exchange of stock, and also circumvented the difficulties that might have been experienced with the Argentine authorities if capital had been written up. Moreover, such schemes meant fixed service charges or financial costs that were unlikely to vary greatly from year to year, as would have been the case with profit-sharing arrangements. These limited advantages, however, were outweighed by the adverse features of the obligations assumed by the BA&P. Precisely because the rental required to service allied enterprises' capital was fixed and immutable, the burden of charges bore little relationship to earning potential. In good years Pacific shareholders could not expect to gain spectacular returns given the extent of the liabilities assumed: in bad seasons they alone would have to forego a return so that commitments to associate companies might be fulfilled. The agreements offered by the BA&P to the Bahia Blanca, Villa Maria and AGW gave their securities a prior claim upon part of its own revenue, second only to that of Pacific prior-charged stocks. The group's capital structure was unbalanced; the entity was dependent upon high earnings to implement a plethora of complex obligations.

These devices bore the hallmark of a financier rather than a

Map 5: Railway rivalry and amalgamation in mesopotamia, 1898–1914

railway expert or an individual familiar with economic conditions in Argentina. As such they reveal the hand of Phillips, the investment banker, whose prime concern was the marketing of securities and not the detailed practicalities of infrastructural development.

Amalgamation in Mesopotamia; the Standard-gauge Lines
With the appearance of the Pacific system the pattern of broad-gauge zoning was firmly established. The last phases of amalgamation were played out in the north and east of the country and were determined as much by gauge as by any other factor. Three British-owned companies comprised the rail network of eastern Argentina. The Entre Rios, which possessed an extensive 390-mile system in the south of the province after which it was named. A separate network operated in the north of the region and consisted of two companies: the East Argentine whose single line of track linked the provinces of Entre Ríos and Corrientes, running northward from Concordia to Monte Caseros where it joined with the Argentine North Eastern which ran a service to the northern extremities of Corrientes.[35] Some 71 miles separated the ER and EA railheads in the late 1890s.

Operating in the same region, the fortunes of all companies were closely linked. Yet there was little co-operation between them, either to develop the region or fully integrate their systems. Although far from prosperous, the Entre Rios served a homogeneous district that was the most developed part of mesopotamia, and enjoyed reasonable communications with the remainder of the country. Consequently, it pursued an independent policy and saw little to recommend fusion with the other railways. Neither were the East Argentine and Argentine North Eastern any more favourably disposed towards each other. The North Eastern, as we have seen, emerged as the result of the EA's non-fulfilment of its original concessionary obligations. The East Argentine concession provided for the construction of lines in northern Corrientes, but the company never ventured beyond Monte Caseros. The national government, despairing of the railway's willingness or ability to honour its commitments, had drawn up a new schedule of concessions for the area, including the lapsed EA branches, which was awarded to the North Eastern.

Relations between the two lines remained cool as a result of this unfortunate beginning.

Adversity, however, tempered antagonism. As a result of the Baring Crisis both the EA and the ANE lost their guarantees, while the ensuing dislocation served to emphasize the similarities of the situation in which all three lines found themselves. The differences between the companies were further reduced towards the end of the century when the region once again enjoyed a measure of prosperity. On this occasion the centre and the north began to develop more rapidly, and share in the process of growth that had previously been largely confined to southern Entre Ríos. This last factor was particularly instrumental in altering the ER's view of its sister companies. The northern lines were now regarded as possible partners in a mutually beneficial enterprise. The advantages of the economies of scale encouraged all companies to view a system of joint administration and operation with favour. The difficulty lay in the implementation of such a scheme — an issue soon to be resolved in a trial of strength between the Entre Rios and the Argentine North Eastern. The East Argentine became a pawn in the battle for regional supremacy waged with some ferocity by the contestants. The struggle was all the more hard-fought because the parties were evenly matched. The topography of the region ensured that neither line had a special strategic advantage; the Entre Rios and Argentine North Eastern zones were largely self-sufficient, and both were able to obtain independent communication with the federal capital by means of river steamers.

Effectively, mesopotamian standard-gauge amalgamation dates from the turn of the century when the Argentine North Eastern sought to impose a working agreement upon the East Argentine. Hitherto both companies had operated a unified tariff schedule and facilitated the easy exchange of traffic between their systems. In 1898 the ANE opened a river port at Empedrado on the Paraná and threatened to re-route its traffic unless the East Argentine agreed to negotiate a joint-administration agreement. Should the East Argentine prove intransigent, the North Eastern proposed to dispatch all its traffic via the river Paraná and thus wholly over its own system, thereby replacing the river Uruguay route to Buenos Aires which served the combined EA and ANE network. Shippers were encouraged to utilize the new route by the introduction of a preferential tariff for goods moved via Empedrado. The East Argentine had therefore been forced to reduce its own rates and suffered a marked decline in earnings.[36] This situation prevailed for a couple of years, the ANE representing to the EA the advantages of joint-administration, while the latter — although desirous of reaching some accommodation with the former — was not prepared to countenance amalgamation. The point at issue for the EA was that around the turn of the century it began to declare a return upon equity capital: at that juncture the North Eastern could do no better than operate at the border of prosperity. The East Argentine feared that an arrangement with the North Eastern might compromise its new-found, modest prosperity. In 1900 the EA obtained a measure of relief when the national government was prevailed upon to compel the ANE to withdraw the preferential rates.[37]

Despite this rebuttal the North Eastern continued to advocate joint working, which served only to drive the East Argentine into the arms of the Entre Rios. The southern concern was more than pleased to accommodate the EA. On 18 March 1901, the Entre Rios secured a provincial concession for a branch from its Villaguay railhead to the East Argentine terminus at Concordia, construction being inaugurated by the provincial governor.[38] Agreeing to accord special facilities to the ER at Concordia, the East Argentine also promised to place its own line in first-class working order. A joint service to Buenos Aires was projected from Puerto Ruiz, a small landing point on the Gualeguay tributary of the Paraná; amalgamation was to be considered.[39] When the ER Concordia extension was opened on 30 June 1902 there was every indication that the two companies would not halt at the mere junction of their rails. Continuing to view the ANE with hostility, the East Argentine directors favoured even closer contact with the Entre Rios.[40] Towards the end of 1903 the EA board secured an *ad referendum* agreement with its new southern ally, for the latter to work their line, and placed a bill before the British parliament to alter the company's articles of association to permit the leasing of their railway.[41]

These developments forced the Argentine North Eastern to take drastic action. Some 25 per cent of the East Argentine's equity was acquired in an attempt to forestall the acceptance of the scheme at the EA meeting.[42] From a position of strength, the North Eastern made renewed overtures to the East Argentine. On this occasion it was more successful, despite a spirited rearguard action fought by Entre Rios interests. Because of its substantial equity holding the ANE was allowed to appoint directors to the East Argentine board.[43] In 1905 the chairman of the North Eastern took his place on the EA board.[44] From this vantage point, he informed his respective shareholders that both lines would benefit from joint working — implying that the East Argentine would readily accept the rationality of this point of view.[45] East Argentine shareholders were indeed convinced, but the board of that company continued to procrastinate. The *impasse* was not resolved until two further ANE directors were elected on to the EA board, despite the vehement protests of the East Argentine chairman who accordingly resigned the chair (but not his directorship) and was replaced by the North Eastern chairman.[46]

Subsequently matters proceeded apace. Joint working was speedily implemented and rapid progress made along the path of amalgamation. In this the North Eastern was supported by the Argentine government which was favourably disposed to the project.[47] An agreement was finally concluded in January 1907 when East Argentine shareholders agreed to accept North Eastern scrip. After making due provision for its own debenture holders, the North Eastern proposed that East Argentine ordinary shareholders should exchange their paper for an equal amount of ANE 5 per cent A debentures. In addition, a special scrip was distributed amongst ex-East Argentine shareholders on a *pro rata* basis allowing them one-seventh of profits available as a dividend for Argentine North Eastern shareholders after all prior charges had been met. Existing North Eastern debentures would be split, one half becoming 5 per cent A debentures (ranking *pari passu* with the paper issued to EA ordinary shareholders) and the remainder 5 per cent debentures. Furthermore, after both categories of debentures received their full interest for five consecutive years they might be redeemed at £110.[48] Due to certain peculiarities surrounding some of the East Argentine's issues it was not proposed to effect a full amalgamation until later in the year.

Nevertheless, the North Eastern at last secured its long-cherished objective. The amalgamated company commanded the northern zone of mesopotamia. One branch paralleled the river Uruguay north of Concordia and, when completed to Posadas, would provide a connection with the Paraguay Central. This international route was actively supported by the government at Buenos Aires, a factor which may further explain the cordial relations the company enjoyed with the national authorities.[49] From Monte Caseros another branch of the railway struck north-westwards through the province of Corrientes till it gained the Paraná. The line was thus well situated to dominate the upper reaches of both rivers. In part, the fusion of the two companies, the relatively active construction programme currently being employed by the ANE, and in particular the extent to which the North Eastern appeared poised to transform itself into a substantial regional network constituted the final vindication of the assumption upon which the issue of the original East Argentine concession had been predicated. The amalgamated entity was considered well-placed to exploit the potential of the region and was thought to constitute a dynamic impetus making for the continued prosperity of the area.

There remained the Entre Rios. Prevented from effecting a working arrangement or an amalgamation with the East Argentine, the company turned to the development of its own zone. Of all the regions of mesopotamia, it was probably the province of Entre Ríos that most benefited from rivalry between the British-owned standard-gauge railways at this juncture. The battle between the ER and ANE for possession of the East Argentine was to result in a substantial increase in southern mesopotamia railway mileage during the first decade or so of the twentieth century. As related above, initial contacts between the ER and EA had produced the construction of a branch linking the former's network with the latter's trunk line, and proposals for the provision of a combined ferry service to Buenos Aires. Given the collapse of these schemes, when possibilities of a fusion with the East Argentine no longer proved feasible, the Entre Rios determined to secure independent access to the national capital, and consolidate its position in the southern province of mesopotamia, thereby attempting to pre-empt further acts of hostility anticipated from the North Eastern. A general programme of construction was envisaged including the siting of a new ferry port at

Ibicuy a short distance up-stream from the Buenos Aires Central Railway's terminus on the opposite bank of the Paraná at Zarate.[50]

The ANE's rejoinder came in 1909 when this expansionist company sought a concession to extend its main line southward beyond Concordia along the Uruguay on to Concepción, an Entre Rios railhead.[51] The new route duplicated a more circuitous ER line serving off-river districts. With this invasion of Entre Rios territory came further rumours of amalgamation. The ER redoubled efforts to safeguard its position with a flurry of additional construction designed to open up new regions and bind existing producers more closely to the company by offering an improved service. Soon Entre Rios construction gangs were engaged upon several projects located within the centre and south of the province. In this the ER probably enjoyed an advantage over the North Eastern — the zone was more settled as was soon reflected in the company's traffic returns. For the ANE rapid expansion appears to have had a less immediately beneficial impact; in the short term the cost of additional construction was onerous. It was probably for this reason that the line was the first British-owned Argentine railway to fall victim to the Farquhar Syndicate.

The ramifications of the Syndicate's activities are to be observed in virtually every South American country during the years immediately prior to the First World War as its grandiose schemes for railway expansion were floated.[52] In Argentina the activities of this European-financed, north American-administered consortium were confined to the weaker, less profitable concerns. Exhausted by its struggle to gain control of the East Argentine, the North Eastern succumbed to Farquhar's overtures in 1912 to be followed shortly thereafter by the Entre Rios. Subsequently, although Farquhar's projects crashed due to lack of finance and the outbreak of hostilities in Europe, the ER and ANE were operated as a single concern (yet retaining their separate legal identities) — a monument to the rationality of some of the Syndicate's schemes. In 1915 a joint general manager was appointed and both lines concentrated their local administrations at Concordia, the old headquarters of the East Argentine. Ultimately the Entre Rios, which had acquired a substantial equity interest in the North Eastern during the Farquhar era, obtained the chairmanship of, and several directorates on, the latter's board — a suitable revenge for its earlier defeat.

Thus was the railway map of southern Entre Ríos transformed. In the short space of a few years the ER had evolved from a light local line into an extensive intra-province concern enjoying major inter-province connections, critically with the federal capital — the principal location for export outlets and an expanding market in its own right for a wide range of mesopotamian products.[53] Between 1906 and 1913, a period of remarkable railway construction in Argentina, the ER increased its network at a rate slightly above the national average.[54] This was a major feat for a company operating in a region that had hitherto not been regarded as one of the most favourably factor-endowed.

The significance of railway fusion in mesopotamia was largely determined by the method employed to effect regional unity. The steamer services plying on the rivers Uruguay and Paraná could not serve all the transport needs of the region. They were restricted by climate and river conditions to a limited number of towns. Integration of the standard-gauge railway network meant more than a mere physical union of the previously separate systems; it served to unite the various districts of the region, especially those of the interior, with the main centres. Moreover, an integrated railway network placed the services of the region's few good ports at the disposal of all districts. Hitherto the proliferation of small, inadequate docks and landing stages added a degree of confusion to the area's developing communications industry. Differing facilities, the application of a variety of standards, and a multiplicity of loading points made for small-scale operations and high costs. Railway amalgamation fostered the growth of mesopotamia's major ports. An application of the economies of scale stimulated the development of more effective communications within the region and provided an efficient link with the rest of the country. The subsequent growth of Entre Ríos, Corrientes and even Misiones was largely due to the formation of a zonal railway system. Most of the agricultural pursuits that expanded during the twentieth century, many of which were directly encouraged by the railways, depended upon efficient means of communication with the federal capital, a service that the individual railway companies had rarely been able to provide.

Metre-gauge Amalgamation: the Cordoba Central System
If the Farquhar Syndicate had imposed unity upon the standard-gauge lines of Entre Ríos and Corrientes, the consortium obtained a more favourable reception amongst the British-owned metre-gauge companies. The final grouping to emerge at this juncture was based upon the Cordoba Central which had been registered in 1887, and had later acquired the formerly state-owned Central Northern.[55] The original company was over-capitalized like so many other railways dependent upon the guarantee, and had languished after the abrogation of the system. Its position was not improved by the proliferation of lines that had occurred during the years immediately before the Baring Crisis. In addition to the broad-gauge trunk routes which traversed its region there were a number of local, narrow-gauge lines all of which competed for the limited trade of the area. The company only recovered slowly from the effects of the 1890s depression, yet by the end of the nineteenth century it exhibited signs of improvement as its traffic returns began to increase. With the prospect of better times the railway sought to consolidate its position. Gradually pursuing a policy of absorption, the Cordoba Central unified the British-owned metre-gauge lines in the provinces of Córdoba and Sante Fé.

By the turn of the century the CC had taken over the Rafaela Steam Tramway Limited, and the Cordoba and North West Argentine Railway Company Limited. With the purchase of the latter, the Central acquired an arrangement with the Cordoba and Rosario Railway Company Limited that in 1903 evolved into a joint working agreement between the Central and the Rosario.[56] Finally, in 1905, the Cordoba Central floated a separate entity to construct a line from Rosario to Buenos Aires.[57] Yet it was left to the Farquhar Syndicate to bring a degree of order to the affairs of this expanding company. The system operated by the Cordoba Central was hardly integrated. The subsidiary companies retained a large measure of autonomy. Separate accounts were kept and the Cordoba Central network bore the stamp of a collection of semi-independent, leased concerns, rather than that of a unified railway network. A multiplicity of stocks prevailed which entailed a complicated system of income-sharing. Indeed, the creation of an additional unit to effect a connection between this loose consortium and the federal capital was symptomatic of the prevailing structure. This system was terminated under the influence of Farquhar. Accounting anomalies were removed and the scrip of the various branches amalgamated, thereby simplifying the capital account. Whereas previously there existed some 16 different types of stocks and shares, the amalgamated Cordoba Central of 1912 acknowledged but five; in addition to ordinary capital there were two sets of preference stock and two sets of debentures.[58]

The Farquhar Syndicate acted as a catalyst, fostering the completion of merger schemes earlier than might otherwise have been the case. As a result, the zoning of the Argentine railway system was finalized, and the regional structure established at this juncture remained virtually unchanged until the inter-war period when modifications were effected in the administration of some of the groupings. The scope and form of the national network evolved during these years would survive beyond nationalization after the Second World War. With but a few minor exceptions, subsequent developments confirmed zonal arrangements; future changes were largely intra-regional, designed to provide even greater cohesion.

What might have been the most spectacular example of the principle of zonal amalgamation was, however, not to be effected during this period. Between 1898 and 1900 the BAGS began to rationalize railway operations in the region of Ensenada. The Buenos Ayres & Ensenada Port Railway Company Limited was purchased, bringing with it a lease on Buenos Ayres, Ensenada & South Coast Railway Company Limited track.[59] Shortly thereafter the Great Southern and the BAW entered into an arrangement for the joint administration of their respective lines in and around Ensenada. Both firms would pool their own, and associated companies' rails which would be worked by the BAGS, profits being distributed on a *pro rata* basis.[60] This tidying-up operation was but the prelude to more ambitious projects — the fusion of the Western and Southern. They were already closely allied; operating in similar regions of the *pampas*, the systems were contiguous and possessed common directors and shareholders. Equally significant, both companies enjoyed a reputation for sustained profitability and their respective capital accounts were compatible. Permission to merge was sought from the national government in 1912: bills were placed before Congress and made rapid progress through both houses.[61] A new title, the Argentine Southern & Western Railway Company Limited, had even been selected for the enlarged entity. But the scheme aroused antagonism in La Plata: local interests feared that an obnoxious monopoly would result. Confronted by a rising tide of provincial opposition, the resolve of the federal government weakened; enabling legislation became bogged down. The La Plata authorities threatened to construct some 3,000 miles of new track, penetrating the regions served by both British-owned companies should the scheme be sanctioned by the national Congress. The Great Southern and the Western bowed to the inevitable. In the face of *bonarense* opposition the project was abandoned, and the companies decided to confine their activities to friendly co-operation rather than risk further alienating powerful local interests.[62]

Despite this setback, the concept of regional railway integration was already well-entrenched. Company prosperity would come to be determined by the specialized services provided by the several zonal groupings, and the nature of Argentine agricultural expansion was an added incentive to the process of regionalization and rationalization. By the First World War each of the British-owned systems, although handling a variety of traffic, tended to depend upon a narrow range of principal items. In 1913 some two-thirds of the BAW's revenue was derived from animal traffic, while the Great Southern obtained almost one half of its revenue from a similar source. Grain traffic in 1915 provided over 20 per cent of the Central's total revenue, with maize alone contributing 12 per cent: 22 per cent of the Pacific system's gross receipts came from wine. In the same year sugar and sugar cane accounted for 43 per cent of the freight carried by the Cordoba Central. As the result of bumper harvests in 1913 grain accounted for 44 per cent of the Entre Rios's traffic and 18 per cent of that of the Argentine North Eastern.[63] The detailed consideration which the railway groupings devoted to fostering these commodities accounts for the success of the zonal concept, and explains both its development and survival. Established in their respective regions of the country, and concentrating upon the requirements of their zones, the British-owned railways enjoyed a remarkable degree of prosperity that enabled them to supply the service most suited to the individual needs of their specialist traffic.

VIII

INTEGRATION AND PROSPERITY

A new view of foreign investment pervaded Argentine national thinking in the early twentieth century. Conditioned by changes which had taken place during the preceding period, it was essentially a re-formulation of traditional policy. Foreign investment had first been welcomed, conforming as it did with the liberal, *laissez-faire* theories prevailing in the mid-nineteenth century. The concept then became discredited. Events culminating in the Baring Crisis — the weight of debt service payments, railway speculation and the burden of the guarantees — stimulated a reconsideration of the benefits obtained from an application of the theory of economic specialization and its corollary, the international division of labour. Foreign sponsorship was perceived as engendering a transport monopoly inimical to the interests of the nation. The crash appeared to justify the worse of these fears, indicating the 'true' cost of foreign borrowing. Paradoxically, however, the Crisis had a cathartic effect. Within the governing classes it induced a spirit of caution and encouraged a more realistic appraisal of the nature of the external nexus. Equally, it warned the railway companies that Argentina's view of large-scale foreign investment in key sectors of the economy was not unquestioning. At the same time it fostered a more rational assessment of the potential of the *pampas*. Ultimately, these changes produced a mood of realism conducive to the continuation of foreign investment and ushered in a 'golden era' for Argentina and railway investors.

As related above, the immediate consequences of reappraisal were the abrogation of railway guarantees, the partial withdrawal of the state from active railway development, and the subsequent formation of zonal railway systems. The national government's reaction to the emergence of regional 'railway monopolies' characterized the new attitude. From obstructionism, as exhibited at some stages of Central/Rosario amalgamation, its position changed to one of essential support, provided the companies involved accepted specific safeguards designed to prevent monopolistic excesses as witnessed by the Western/Southern merger scheme. This attitude was institutionalized with the Mitre Law. It was a symbolic enactment which marked the renewed expansion of the railway network. Due to the viable position achieved by the various groupings as the result of amalgamation and regionalization, the period immediately before the First World War saw the last phase of major growth undertaken by foreign-owned Argentine railway companies prior to nationalization.

The Mitre Law
Essentially, Ley No. 5315 — to give the law its correct title — was a re-capitulation and re-codification of previous legislation. It did not supersede earlier enactment but was an attempt to rationalize and simplify the multitude of concession laws and general regulations under whose terms the railways of Argentina had been constructed and which governed their day-to-day operations. With one major exception, the Mitre Law did not establish any new principles. Its significance lay not in what it did, but in the ideals which occasioned its inscription upon the statute books. The law was an official vindication of the original concepts and undertakings which had first attracted foreign funds to the country. It was a remarkable gesture, one calculated to benefit Argentina, given the prevailing international financial situation. It would be an over-simplification to argue that the Mitre Law was responsible for the rapid increase in railway investment during the years immediately preceeding the First World War. Nevertheless, Ley No. 5315 expressed sentiments that were fully appreciated by investors at a time when their purses were replete with capital seeking a remunerative outlet. The law represented a covenant between the elite and railway investors, the psychological importance of which was enhanced by the unprecedented wave of social unrest that occurred in Argentina during the second and third decades of the twentieth century. The years following 1907 witnessed a series of bitter disputes between the railway companies and their employees concerning union recognition, conditions of employment and fringe benefits.[1] The new

legislation, which received congressional sanction in 1907, following the establishment of the national labour department in the same year, appeared to reassure investors of the benevolent attitude of the state. And, not least, this new codification was interpreted as implicitly sanctioning the process of amalgamation.

The new Law ran to some 20 sections, and covered most of the features already contained in existing concessions. But it accorded companies a single, unified franchise which would govern their operations for 40 years: it offered one set of rules and regulations where before there had been many. The new enactment established safety regulations; reiterated the procedure to be followed when applying for new concessions; restated existing laws regarding the expropriation of land necessary for railway operations; confirmed the companies' freedom from customs duties when importing commodities for extension building and the operation of railway services; provided for government regulation of tariffs and profits; ensured that railway services should be supplied to the state at reduced rates or *gratis*; re-stated the government's right to remove track where lines obstructed movement upon navigable waterways, and re-established the government's power to expropriate the railways upon payment of due compensation; emphasized that this new legislation did not supersede the existing *Ley General de Ferrocarriles*; allowed some discretion to the companies in the construction of minor branch lines; finally it made provision for the private railways to accede to the act, encouraging them to do so by ensuring that upon the termination of current privileges, non-acceding lines would be liable to the full burden of taxation imposed by Argentine commercial legislation. The only novel item was a 3 per cent tax upon net profits in lieu of all national, provincial and municipal charges. This revenue was to be collected by the companies themselves and applied to the construction and improvement of station access roads. Although the railways had been accorded exemption from taxation under the terms of their original concessions, the approaching expiration of many of those concessions encouraged a ready acceptance of the Law which thus freed the companies from a wide range of imposts until 1947.

Despite these generous provisions, it was the spirit of the act, rather than the terms of the legislation, which represented a renewal and reaffirmation of earlier views. This was the construction placed upon the Law by Deputy Emilio Mitre. Introducing the debate in Congress he stated that the act would impose uniformity upon prevailing concessions, and remove the confusion which governed railway operations, especially in matters concerning exemption from taxation and customs duties. Mitre's moderate and reasoned approach ensured the easy passage of the act through the Chamber. Although some had misgivings most parliamentarians accepted these principles, despite disagreements over detail. The intention, as Mitre said, was to balance the interests and desires of both parties.

> I believe that it is a fair regulation. On the one hand, it allows the companies sufficient profit upon investment; they may have the remuneration to which they legitimately aspire. On the other, the act completely prevents the possibility of exorbitant profits which would constitute an extra-ordinary burden in the freights borne by producers.

His words echoed sentiments expressed half a century earlier.[2] For the railways the law was a restatement of the principles of fair and equitable treatment, sentiments which they considered had not been conspicuous in their recent relations with the Argentine state. Therefore it was hardly surprising that most of the British-owned lines rapidly acceded to the new regime. The only railways to delay were the standard-gauge mesopotamian lines whose original concession still had several years to run. The provision extending the exemption from all national, provincial and municipal taxation (subject to the 3 per cent profits levy) was undoubtedly a major factor in producing this rapid acceptance. Such was the opinion of the Pacific.[3] A trifle less direct, the BAGS considered that the new legislation would be 'of great help' to the future development of the line.[4] Equally far reaching, however, was the government's generous interpretation of the clause applying to mergers and crypto-fusions, as the post-1907 process of amalgamation indicates. The law signalled the re-establishment of harmony between foreign capitalists and the Argentine government; it finally repaired the damage occasioned to company–state relations by the Baring Crisis.

The 'Golden Era' — Development and Prosperity

The benefits were plainly visible; investors continued to regard Argentina, particularly the railways, as a remunerative outlet for capital. The passage of the Mitre Law and the creation of zonal networks provided an added incentive for further construction, both to effect amalgamation and stimulate the growth of regions recently incorporated within the railway system. Between 1900 and the outbreak of the First World War total Argentine railway route mileage increased from 10,285 to 20,857 miles, while capital account grew from £105.3 to £262.7 millions.[5] But the greater part of this expansion occurred in the seven years before the commencement of hostilities in Europe. The annual rate of new British investment abroad more than doubled between 1907 and 1913, rising from £89.4 to £196.7 millions. During this period some £118.3 millions, 10.5 per cent of the total, was invested in Argentina.[6] Much of this capital was subscribed to British-owned Argentine railway development. The Rosario's capital account increased threefold between 1899 and 1914. The BAW almost doubled its capital between 1906 and 1914 as did the Great Southern during the years from 1903 to 1914. In 1900 some £6.3 millions were invested in the BA&P; by 1914 the combined Pacific group was capitalized at over £50 millions.

Virtually all the British-owned lines embarked upon major building programmes at this juncture, as Table 33 illustrates, and the amount of new construction completed was almost twice as great as that undertaken during the late 1880s. In 1908 the BAGS considered expansion an 'essential' prerequisite of continued prosperity and raised some £5½ millions for the construction of new track, mainly branch lines running to over 750 miles.[7] The Western was similarly occupied. Indeed, the sentiments expressed in the Mitre Law did much to encourage these two companies to expand despite the equivocal attitude of the Buenos Aires provincial government.[8] Even the small lines were infected with the same fervour. The Cordoba Central, having barely completed its independent access to the federal capital, considered the moment opportune to embark upon substantial new construction.[9] But these extensions were not based solely upon the availability of new funds nor the favour with which the national government viewed the process of foreign investment: they were determined by the potential of the country.

Table 33: *Argentine Railways: expansion of British-owned lines (route mileage)*

	National total	British total*	British as % of national total	BAGS	BAW	CA and BA&R	BA&P	CC	ANE and ER
1900	10,286	8,006	78	2,229	570	2,011	1,415	990	792
1901	10,499	8,356	80	2,298	591	2,105	1,461	990	910
1902	10,791	8,622	80	2,303	628	2,170	1,549	990	982
1903	11,429	9,030	80	2,304	732	2,316	1,707	990	982
1904	12,065	9,380	78	2,478	816	2,347	1,767	990	982
1905	12,292	9,647	79	2,481	966	2,347	1,882	990	982
1906	12,768	9,866	77	2,506	966	2,361	2,014	990	1,029
1907	13,740	10,486	76	2,529	1,111	2,390	2,403	990	1,063
1908	14,743	10,982	75	2,613	1,219	2,392	2,652	990	1,116
1909	15,389	11,412	74	2,716	1,305	2,392	2,859	990	1,150
1910	17,384	12,010	69	2,770	1,305	2,482	3,073	1,176	1,205
1911	18,667	12,888	69	3,044	1,586	2,644	3,176	1,176	1,262
1912	19,537	13,729	70	3,380	1,659	2,870	3,298	1,176	1,346
1913	20,179	14,233	71	3,544	1,781	2,994	3,393	1,176	1,346
1914	20,857	14,630	70	3,655	1,792	3,151	3,419	1,184	1,482

Financial years ending 30 June, excepting CC and ANE (until 1905) and CA (until 1907) whose financial years terminated on 31 December.
* Total of mileage operated by major groupings listed, but excluding peripheral private lines.

Source: Compiled from respective companies' *Annual Reports*; República Argentina, Ministerio de Obras Públicas, Dirección General de Ferrocarriles *Estadística de los ferrocarriles en explotación durante el año 1913* (Buenos Aires 1916) p. 398; *SAJ* various dates.

Buoyant markets and the extension of the frontier provided the incentive for, and the means of supporting, an inflow of capital. The realization of this potential may be seen in the expansion of the area under cultivation, the rise in agricultural output, and the mounting volume of freight moved by the railway system. The availability of land for profitable exploitation was determined by the scope of the railway network, as a comparison of Table 33 and the data contained in Table 34 will indicate. The annual increase in the combined area devoted to the production of wheat and maize — the main cash crops of the period — bears a marked resemblance to the rate of growth of the national system, given a brief time lag. But the dynamic effects of the moving frontier were not confined to a few, select arable crops. The growth of the network facilitated a general increase in rural output, stimulated as much by the demand of Argentina's own burgeoning urban centres as by export markets.[10] Railway extension increased the margin of profitable cultivation and permitted an expansion in rural output which in turn generated the additional traffic necessary to sustain the momentum of the whole

Table 34:   Argentina: area under cultivation, select arable products (thousands of hectares)

	Wheat	Maize	Linseed	Oats	Barley
1900	3,250	1,009	355	23	49
1901	3,380	1,225	607	33	52
1902	3,296	1,406	783	33	52
1903	3,695	1,802	1,307	56	13
1904	4,320	2,107	1,488	48	31
1905	4,903	2,287	1,083	51	48
1906	5,675	2,717	1,023	72	50
1907	5,692	2,851	1,191	146	50
1908	5,760	2,719	1,391	386	94
1909	6,063	2,974	1,534	633	61
1910	5,837	3,005	1,456	575	60
1911	6,253	3,215	1,504	801	60
1912	6,897	3,422	1,630	1,031	68
1913	6,918	3,830	1,900	1,192	108
1914	6,574	4,152	1,834	1,249	169

Source: C.F. Díaz Alejandro *Essays on the economic history of the Argentine Republic* (London 1970) p. 441.

process. As the indices of agricultural output rose so the traffic accounts of the railway companies registered a rise in the volume of goods moved along their lines.

Increased freight and other types of traffic produced a steady growth in railway revenues which was readily translated into profits for shareholders. Improving net earnings were the basis of the 'golden era' when individual companies established their reputations as sound fields for investment, capable of yielding a reasonable, regular return, as Table 35 demonstrates. Due to the establishment of zonal systems these years were ones of increasing prosperity for British-owned enterprises. Provided with a

Table 35: *Argentine Railways: global yield and ordinary dividends declared by major British-owned companies*

	% Return on total Railway Investment	BAGS	BAW	CA/ BA&R	* BA&P	CC	ANE	ER
1900	3.3	†7	6	3	2	2	nil	nil
1901	3.6	†7	6	3	nil	5	nil	nil
1902	3.6	†7	6	2½	nil	nil	nil	nil
1903	4.5	†7	7	5	5	5	nil	nil
1904	4.9	†7	7	6	4	8	1½	nil
1905	5.1	†7	7	6	7	8	2½	nil
1906	4.9	†7	7	6	7	9	3	nil
1907	4.3	†7	7	6	7	9	nil	nil
1908	4.6	†7	7	6	7	9	‡1½	nil
1909	4.7	†7	7	6	5	—	nil	nil
1910	4.3	†7	7	6	3	§5	nil	nil
1911	3.9	†7	7½	6	3½	5	nil	nil
1912	4.1	†7	7	6	2	2½	nil	nil
1913	4.1	†7	7	6	3	nil	nil	nil
1914	2.7	†5	5	5	nil	nil	nil	nil

Financial years ending 30 June excepting CC and ANE (until 1905) and CA (until 1907) whose fiscal years terminated on 31 December.
† After tax.
* Dividend declared on BA&P ordinary stock.
§ 5% dividend for 18 months ending 30 June 1910.
‡ For half year January – June 1908.

Source: Compiled from respective companies' *Annual Reports* and República Argentina, Ministero de Obras Públicas, Dirección General de Ferrocarriles, *Estadística de los ferrocarriles en explotación durante el año 1913* (Buenos Aires 1916) p. 398.

secure base the railways were able to reorganize their finances, where necessary, and justified the confidence requested of shareholders during subsequent, repeated calls for capital. Expansion of the national railway network during this period was occasioned by the realization of regional potential and benign official policy.

There was, however, an exception to this rule of prosperity: while even the standard- and narrow-gauge companies exhibited a degree of dynamism, the BA&P's earning capacity languished. Running counter to the general pattern of rising returns, the Pacific's performance appears incongruous when it is recalled that the network's most rapid expansion occurred during a period that was particularly conducive to sustained growth (see Table 36). Concomitant increases in the size and scope of the company's network, and substantially improved gross revenues were confounded by a declining rate of increase in net receipts and an absolute fall in dividend payments. An explanation of this phenomenon must be sought in the structure of the railway's capital account. The device employed by the Pacific when pursuing its expansionist policies was not to absorb other lines but, as indicated, to offer shareholders of allied companies a dividend guarantee. Effectively this created a 'top heavy' capital account loaded with prior-charged stocks. Arrangements with subsidiaries converted their ordinary scrip into a special type of preference stock. Given this rigid structure, the Pacific was less able to respond to changes in the economic situation, as a large proportion of its total revenue was eaten up by fixed charges. Failure to honour these commitments would inevitably mean the disintegration of its network. Not only did this situation imply reduced flexibility in operational strategy, but it led to a degree of conservatism in management and administration. The objectives of policy were to obtain a return sufficient to meet the network's financial obligations, while at the same time inhibiting innovations which might, in the short term, jeopardize the realization of that paramount consideration.

By 1914, for example, while the capital account of the BA&P itself was composed of some £18 millions of prior-charged stocks, and £10 millions of ordinary capital — a weighting in favour of the former which was already excessive by comparison with the other broad-gauge lines — the ratio of prior-charged to ordinary

Table 36: BA&P: expansion of system

	1905	1908	1913
Route mileage	1,767	2,427	3,416
Gross receipts	£1,263,636	£3,655,772	£5,590,613
Net receipts	£544,325	£1,354,990	£2,130,692
Passenger traffic			
Numbers	862,532	5,631,521	16,601,148
Revenue	£119,257	£652,713	£1,174,578
Goods traffic			
Tonnage	1,018,992	3,875,694	6,162,209
Revenue	£575,036	£2,567,929	£3,888,402

Source: Compiled from *PP* 1914, LXXXIX 510; Buenos Ayres and Pacific Railway Company Limited, *Annual Reports 1905, 1908, 1913* (London 1905, 1908 & 1913).

stocks for the whole group was effectively 4:1.[11] Due to the underdeveloped nature of sections of its zone, this capital account structure placed a strain upon earnings not experienced by other broad-gauge concerns. The inflexibility of its service schedule became even more burdensome after 1909 when all the guarantee schemes were fully operational and the company beset by a series of natural disasters (inclement weather, locust plagues and other adversities) and labour disputes which frustrated the anticipated growth in revenue, placing the additional weight of extra service payments firmly upon the shoulders of Pacific ordinary stockholders.

Excepting the BA&P, long-term prospects were sound and likely to encourage continued expansion as evidenced by the quotation of British-owned Argentine railway securities upon the London Stock Exchange. An expression of shareholders' confidence and the market's assessment of the earning potential of various lines, these valuations explain why investors were prepared to place so much capital into Argentine railway development at this time.

The quotations in Table 37 illustrate the overall position of Argentine railways and the particular characteristics of individual companies. Profitability made for increased firmness in share prices. In 1900, for example, the valuation of Great Southern ordinary stock fluctuated by 18 points, or approximately 13

Table 37: Argentine Railways: London Stock Exchange quotations of selec

		1900		*1901*		*1902*		*1903*		*1904*		*190*	
		H	*L*	*H*	*L*	*H*	*L*	*H*	*L*	*H*	*L*	*H*	
AGW	Ords.			104	97	96	88	107	98	106½	99	128	1
	1st Debs.	93	85	105	101	106	99	105	100	107	99	109	1
ANE	Ords.												
	Debs.	28		25½	31	30							
BAGS	Ords.	155	137	155	133	139	126	140	132	136½	129	147	1
	Debs.	119	111	113½	109	113	109	109½	105	112	105	111	1
BA&P	Ords.	81	52	69	61	59	52	114	61	119	110	140	1
	1st Debs.	106	99	105	103	103	98	104	100	105	100	108	1
BA&R	Ords.	82	62	71½	62	72½	59	90½	74½	101¼	88½	114¾	1
	4% Debs.	110	99	105	100	104	101	108	102	107	101	109	1
BAW	Ords.†	11¾	9¾	11	9¾	119	105	131	118	130	123	139	1
	Debs.	111	107	113	103	108	103	108	103	110	103	110	1
CA	Ords.	116	98	114½	105	116½	106						
	Debs.												
CC	Ords.												
	Income debs.	43	34	41	32	33	29	42½	33½	60¼	37	72½	
ER	Ords.			11	8	12½	9	12	10	16	13	43	
	1st Prefs.			44	41	57	46	64	47	74	58	105	

H = High L = Low † Ordinary share, £10 converted into ordinary stock, £10

Source: *The Times*, various dates.

British-owned stocks

1906		1907		1908		1909		1910		1911		1912		1913	
H	*L*	*H*	*L*	*H*	*L*	*H*	*L*	*H*	*L*	*H*	*L*	*H*	*L*	*H*	*L*
8½	111½	113½	104	114	106	110½	100	108	101	110	101	107	100¼	102½	87½
6	101	104	98	106	99	106	100	105	101	115	110	115½	108	112	103¼
3	124	128	119	128½	120	126	121½	125½	116½	125	119½	129¾	120¾	129¾	109¾
9	103	106	101	108	100	107	103	108	101	105	100	103½	99	101¾	93
5½	122	123½	107	121	109	114½	88	95½	85½	101	91	100¾	84½	92½	64½
7	101	106	99	108	100	107	101	107	101	106½	102	106½	100	102½	93
6½	112¼	111¼	99	111½	105½	see CA									
7½	102	106	100	107	101										
9	124	129	117	130	120½	132	125	131	126	134	124	135	119½	128½	109¼
8	102	106	99	108	101	107	103	107	101	105	100	103	99	101½	93¼
						109	99½	109	96½	108½	104½	111½	103	113¼	100
						106	102	106	100	103	100	102	98½	100	94
								97	80						
3½	66½	71½	53	63	56										
2½	30	44	36	48	41	48	39	45	40	78½	44½	90½	72½	78½	54
5	85	94	83	95	89	98	91	101	91	98	93				
2.															

per cent; in 1911 the difference between the year's 'high' and 'low' quotations was only 5½ points — roughly 5 per cent. A similar trend may be observed generally. Entre Rios ordinary and preference quotations, for instance, indicate the gradual improvement in that company's prospects. With reference to the Pacific's difficulties, it is instructive to compare the valuation accorded to AGW ordinaries with that placed upon BA&P debentures.

Railway Modernization
The expansion of the railway network during this period was due, as has been seen, to the renewed mood of optimism prevailing in British-Argentine railway circles, and this was occasioned in part by the liberal attitude of the national government. But the foreign-owned railways did not abuse their improved position. The companies were not activated exclusively by dictates of the profit motive: while responsive to their shareholders, they were not unmindful of obligations towards users. If the companies considered the establishment of zones of influence and the construction of new branch lines as a means of improving financial viability, the returns generated were devoted to improving the quality of railway services as much as to extending the quantity of the network. The prosperity enjoyed in the period immediately prior to 1914 underpinned a programme of experimentation, the application of technical innovation, and the implementation of policies designed to answer past criticisms.

Complaints had often been made concerning the railways' inability to handle the volume of freight generated by the development of the Argentine economy. Comment was especially critical in the late 1880s after the rapid expansion of the network, and matters reached a head in 1889 with the publication of a Presidential Decree suspending the guarantee of railways without sufficient rolling stock to meet traffic requirements. The railways maintained that the charge was unfounded; many lines priding themselves, with some justice, upon the quality of their equipment.[12] In this, however, they missed the point, for the criticism was not directed at the style or quality of their rolling stock, but rather concerned their ability to ship bulk cargoes. Rolling stock ratios had undoubtedly been allowed to slip in the 1880s as individual companies channelled funds into expanding their systems (in order to penetrate new zones or pre-empt competition) without paying due regard to the size of rolling stock parks. After the crash there had been little incentive, or ability, to make good this deficiency. Although Table 38 does not indicate the power of locomotives or the capacity of wagons, it nevertheless illustrates the deplorable conditions prevailing on certain lines, especially in contrast with the provincially-owned *Oeste*, though not necessarily with the nationally-owned *Andino*, as was acknowledged in a contemporary official report.[13]

Table 38: Argentine Railways: rolling stock ratios of select lines, 1889

	Mileage In service	Mileage Under construction	Locomotives	Carriages	Wagons
British-owned lines					
AGW	318	—	58(5.5:1)	40(8.0:1)	654(0.49:1)
BA&P	425	—	41(10.4:1)	43(9.9:1)	989(0.43:1)
BA&R	344	588	81(4.2:1)	83(4.2:1)	3,177(0.11:1)
BAGS	839	—	114(7.4:1)	255(3.3:1)	4,498(0.19:1)
BAN	19	—	23(0.8:1)	61(0.31:1)	370(0.05:1)
BA&EP	66	—	22(3.0:1)	44(1.5:1)	724(0.09:1)
CA	273	141	86(3.2:1)	58(4.7:1)	2,038(0.13:1)
EA	99	6	10(9.9:1)	24(4.1:1)	217(0.46:1)
State-owned lines					
Oeste	751	617	124(6.1:1)	227(3.3:1)	3,758(0.20:1)
Andino	158	—	13(12.2:1)	16(9.9:1)	121(1.31:1)

* Ratio : miles of track per unit of rolling stock.

Source: Compiled and calculated from PP 1890/91 LXXXIV 8.

In reply to these complaints the British enterprises began to import more equipment and fabricate wagons and locomotives at their workshops in Buenos Aires and Rosario. It was a slow process given the financial stringency imposed by prevailing hardships. The fundamental problem of the availability of rolling stock at harvest time lay in the seasonal nature of traffic, the enormous fluctuations from year to year in the quantity of commodities produced and the implications of the moving frontier. For example, the 1906 maize harvest yielded 4.9 million metric tons while the following year only 1.8 millions were garnered: the linseed crop almost doubled between 1912 and 1913: wheat output fell from 5.1 million metric tons in 1913 to 2.8 millions in 1914.[14] It required a nice calculation as to the exact amount of investment to be diverted into the purchase or manufacture of rolling stock when, for the greater part of the year, much of that equipment would lie idle.[15] In addition, operating efficiency was influenced by more mundane factors such as the length of time required to turn trains around at the ports, pressure upon marshalling yards, and the provision of storage facilities at the dockside and up-country stations — all of which had a bearing upon the availability of wagons at railheads in the camp during harvest time.

Nevertheless, criticism was stilled by an improvement in the rolling stock ratio, though this was but a partial solution which brought only temporary relief. Sustained increases in rural output at the turn of the century once again occasioned similar complaints, which became more vociferous and vehement when the scale of the problem was exacerbated by bountiful harvests and further expansion of the network. Certainly, by the early 1900s the volume of abuse heaped upon the companies required careful consideration. It was generally recognized that a more permanent solution would have to be found to the problem of moving rural output.[16] The situation in Buenos Aires was particularly bad, due as much to want of wagons as to congestion in the ports.[17] Steamers at Bahía Blanca had to wait from five to eight weeks while cargoes came down from the interior, and at the end of the 1904/5 season some 400,000 tons of grain awaited shipment in that province alone.[18] Immediate relief was once again sought by purchasing additional equipment. This improvement was based upon the prosperous position acquired by the companies; in the late 1900s large-scale increases in the rolling stock park were financed from current earnings whereas previously they had been written off against capital account.[19] The obvious answer was to use rolling stock more effectively, reduce average journey times, and minimize delays and bottlenecks along the line and at the ports. In short, the companies devoted equal attention to the quality of traction and the structure of their networks. Given the special characteristics of its zone the Pacific was well situated to experiment with more powerful locomotives. The latitudinal nature of the network, and the fact that most of its traffic originated at one end of the system but was destined for the other, meant that average hauls on the BA&P were amongst the longest in Argentina. In 1905 the company commissioned 'giant' decapod engines which were especially suited to long, heavy hauls.[20] Most railways introduced more powerful locomotives during this period to cope with the increasing volume of traffic.[21] Of even greater significance were the modifications undertaken with regard to the structure and scope of the networks, both in terms of the quality of the permanent way, and the construction of extensions. Improvements in the quality and quantity of the track permitted greater efficiency in the use of new locomotives and wagons.

One of the main features of railway expansion during the period 1890–1914 was the creation of direct links between the federal capital and various regions of the country. Most of the zonal systems sought to secure independent access to Buenos Aires; not only were broad-gauge lines like the Pacific and Central anxious to push their rails through to the city, but lesser companies similarly wished to control their own approaches. The last of these connections was established in May 1912, when the Cordoba Central's Buenos Ayres Extension Railway was permanently opened to traffic. Thus routes to the capital became less congested, and in the case of the standard- and metre-gauge lines, independent access also meant that through journeys could be accomplished without the expense and inconvenience imposed by breaks of gauge. New construction thus facilitated communications between zonal networks, the port and metropolitan district of Buenos Aires where most produce was consigned for internal consumption or export.

To some extent it might be argued that these developments merely eradicated one bottleneck at the expense of creating another; the point of congestion was shifted from the approaches to Buenos Aires into the port area. But while the companies were building their lines into the federal capital they had not neglected other areas. Precisely because of the pressure at Buenos Aires, the railways attempted to establish alternative outlets. Bahía Blanca was one of the more successful examples of diversification. The port there was used by the Great Southern to relieve facilities at Buenos Aires. With the completion of the BB&NW, Bahía Blanca became a viable alternative to the national capital for an even

Table 39: *Argentine Railways: rolling stock ratios of select British-owned companies*

Buenos Ayres Great Southern

	A	B	R	C	R	D'	R	D"	R
1898	1,702	186	9.2	310	5.5	7,565	.22		
1899	2,132	233	9.2	422	5.1	8,590	.25		
1900	2,132								
1901	2,298	260	8.8	457	5.0	9,132	.25		
1902	2,303	272	8.5	485	4.7	9,663	.24	115,596	.02
1903	2,304	291	7.9	463	5.0	9,673	.24	116,389	.02
1904	2,478	291	8.5	467	5.3	9,883	.25	122,590	.02
1905	2,481	291	8.5	476	5.2	9,981	.25	128,127	.02
1906	2,506	414	6.1	509	4.9	11,025	.23	177,085	.01
1907	2,529	526	4.8	708	3.6	11,793	.21	205,328	.01
1908	2,613	561	4.7	813	3.2	12,109	.22	266,841	.01
1909	2,716	549	4.9	827	3.3	12,320	.22	224,324	.01
1910	2,770	546	5.1	834	3.3	12,615	.22	260,881	.01
1911	3,044	546	5.6	867	3.5	12,490	.24	261,458	.01
1912	3,380	548	6.2	955	3.5	12,884	.26	287,214	.01
1913	3,544	573	6.2	1,007	3.5	13,495	.26	305,702	.01
1914	3,665	650	5.6	1,084	3.4	15,175	.24	396,565	.01

Buenos Ayres Western

	A	B	R	C	R	D'	R	D"	R
1898	602	105	5.7	181	3.3	3,887	.15	37,000	.02
1899	602	116	5.2	201	3.0	3,877	.16		
1900	570	110	5.2	196	2.9	3,887	.15	47,000	0.1
1901	591								
1902	628	117	5.4	199	3.2	3,943	.16		
1903	732	123	6.0	196	3.7	3,741	.20		
1904	816	141	5.8	186	4.4	4,048	.20	64,000	.01
1905	966	153	6.3	186	5.2	4,538	.21	77,000	.01
1906	966	194	5.0	199	4.9	5,024	.19	100,000	.01
1907	1,111	270	4.1	233	4.8	5,873	.19		
1908	1,219	292	4.2	281	4.3	6,031	.20		
1909	1,305	293	4.5	305	4.3	6,611	.20		
1910	1,305	310	4.2	344	3.8	7,367	.18		
1911	1,586	312	5.1	364	4.4	8,065	.20		
1912	1,659	311	5.3	366	4.5	8,145	.20		
1913	1,781	327	5.4	425	4.2	9,242	.19		
1914	1,792	347	5.2	432	4.1	9,509	.19		

Table 39: contd.

	Buenos Ayres & Pacific								
	A	B	R	C	R	D'	R	D"	R
1898									
1899						1,804		16,920	
1900						1,913		18,428	
1901						2,262		23,771	
1902						2,378		27,225	
1903		98		107		2,498		31,081	
1904		114		132		2,923		49,882	
1905	1,030	168	6.1	132	7.8	3,756	.27	70,623	.01
1906	1,098	225	4.9	165	6.7	4,248	.26	86,369	.01
1907	1,886	514	3.7	253	7.5	8,377	.23	188,467	.01
1908	2,250	563	4.0	285	7.9	9,290	.24	225,143	.01
1909	2,505	654	3.8	343	7.3	10,169	.25	241,829	.01
1910	3,004	674	4.5	345	8.7	11,106	.27	263,787	.01
1911	3,186	679	4.7	368	8.7	11,571	.28	273,301	.01
1912	3,240	679	4.8	370	8.8	11,542	.28	272,901	.01
1913	3,404	702	4.8	381	8.9	11,473	.30	271,142	.01
1914	3,473	706	4.9	379	9.2	11,403	.30	270,119	.01

R = Ratio, miles of track per unit of rolling stock/capacity of wagons
A = Mileage
B = Locomotives, numbers
C = Carriages, numbers
D' = Wagons, numbers
D" = Wagons, capacity (metric tons)
*BA&P, original line and allied companies from date of working/leasing agreements
Source: Compiled from respective companies' *Annual Reports*.

larger region and was well-placed to tap the new grain areas of the Western *pampas*.[22] The process was repeated at several of the Plate riverine ports.

These developments confound repeated charges that the British-owned railway companies discriminated in favour of the port of Buenos Aires, either through the manipulation of tariff schedules, or in the siting of their extensions.[23] Argentine railway tariff scales conformed to usual practice and declined relatively over distance, although in contrast to those applied in North America they were especially cheap for hauls of 100 miles or less.

Nevertheless, as average hauls in Argentina were shorter than in the USA, there was little inducement for shippers to favour a longer route to Buenos Aires over the shorter journey to a local port.[24] Improvement of port facilities outside the federal capital provided example incentive to avoid the continuing pressure at Buenos Aires. Indeed, these criticisms are even more effectively refuted by an examination of the export returns of various ports. In 1884 approximately 60 per cent of total maize exports was shipped through Buenos Aires; by 1910 more than 84 per cent was being moved through other ports. Virtually the whole of oats exports were shipped via Buenos Aires in 1900, but only 40 per cent in 1911. Although in the case of wheat and linseed the relative proportion of exports dispatched via Buenos Aires was roughly the same in 1884 and 1910, in absolute terms increasing quantities were exported from alternative ports.[25] Given the integration of the national network, this was precisely the period when Buenos Aires could have eclipsed other ports had the railways applied discriminatory freight rates.

Despite such diversification, companies did not ignore the danger of congestion in the province of Buenos Aires and at major junctions elsewhere. These difficulties were eased by the construction of new branches, which provided alternative routes or by-passed the worst bottlenecks, and double or quadruple tracking over the sections where traffic was heaviest.[26] By 1914 the Central had double-tracked the whole of its busy line between Buenos Aires and Rosario; the Great Southern enjoyed a four-line approach to Buenos Aires — a luxury hitherto unimagined in Latin America. The Western had similar plans for a quadruple entry into the capital, and an underground access to the port. The Pacific, as has been related, was also engaged in improving its last section from Palermo to provide direct access to Retiro and the port, and also envisaged a quadruple-track entry into its terminus.[27] Attention was also paid to the quality of the line itself. During this period the permanent way was much improved; heavier rails laid, longer sections ballasted, station facilities increased and extensive repairs and renewals undertaken. While the Pacific was engaged in replacing its 50-pound rails with 70- and 100-pound track, the Western enjoyed a particularly good reputation for improving existing station facilities, and opening new depots. In 1903, when capital account stood at approximately £26.5 millions, the Great Southern estimated that it had spent some £15 millions upon repairs and renewals during the previous 40 years.[28] There can be little doubt that, as their *Annual Reports* indicated, the majority of British-owned railway companies were at this time devoting substantial sums to depreciation, and the improvement of existing services. The result of this policy may be seen in increased train-mileage. Heavier rails, better ballasting and the laying of *quebracho* sleepers allowed faster running speeds; the creation of more direct routes, the eradication of bottlenecks, and the beginning of grain elevator construction facilitated the introduction of a more efficient service and faster turn-arounds at termini.

Although designed to cater for grain traffic many of these improvements benefited all classes of traffic. Yet the railways stood or fell upon their ability to move cereals; the sheer volume of the crops, the seasonal nature of production peaks, and the layout of the networks, with their complex pattern of junctions, meant that sustained grain blockages could disrupt the whole traffic schedule and dislocate rail services almost indefinitely. Prosperity, however, did not only mean a solution to the perennial rolling stock problem. Experimentation and the application of innovations became the order of the day as railway management attempted to meet the country's transport needs. The profitable years before 1914 enabled the companies to expand and diversify their activities. Increased earnings allowed the railways to anticipate future problems. Attention was paid to passenger requirements; the Central and Western (possibly because their suburban passenger traffic was most susceptible to competition from the tramways) investigated the potential of electrification while the Southern introduced oil-powered rail cars in order to develop faster commuter services.[29]

Yet, perhaps the most important development of these years was the extension of ancillary operations. If adverse conditions in the past had encouraged horizontal integration, sustained prosperity before the First World War was responsible for vertical expansion. The major companies applied themselves to the provisions of a more complete service for shippers, particularly those concerned with the export sector. The Southern and Pacific offered a wide range of port facilities at Buenos Aires, La Plata and Bahía Blanca, including storage, loading, power and shipping services. In addition, the railways acquired interests in various utilities — urban transport, electricity generation, and water works — associated functions of railway operation. The BAGS and BA&P also ran their own steamer service, loading grain in Argentina, and returning with British coal.[30] Government approval for this diversification was accorded when the state commissioned several of the British-owned railways to construct irrigation works within their respective zones.[31]

The Railways and the National Economy
Railway prosperity during the early twentieth century was instrumental in effecting the final stage of Argentina's incorporation within the world economy. While the period between the late 1890s and the First World War saw expanding markets for her principal commodities, it was the intensification of the railway network which determined the realization of the productive potential of the *pampas*. Profitability generated the flow of funds responsible for new construction and improvements that provided the country with an integrated, sophisticated infrastructure capable of handling vast quantities of produce cheaply and efficiently. Refinements effected at this stage meant a real reduction in the costs of railway operation and allowed the companies to maintain low-cost services in less favourable times when the availability of cheap transport facilities cushioned the declining profit margins of primary producers.

These policies showed that the profits enjoyed by the British-owned railways did not merely result from general economic expansion: their prosperity did not depend upon a fortuitous juxtaposition of factors. The companies stimulated the development of the national economy; they responded to its needs and requirements; they shared in the returns that accrued. The private lines were conscious of their duties and obligations, great and small. They did not always lead, and sometimes had to be coerced, but broadly, in their attention to detail and overall consideration, the railways demonstrated a fine appreciation of the requirements of the situation. Not only did the companies extend their networks, but they attended to the minutiae upon which prosperity was based. The individual needs of specialized traffic were not neglected in the general pattern of expansion.[32] The companies struggled to achieve solutions to the perennial problems of

Table 40: Argentine Railways: operating data of British-owned companies

	BAGS		BAW		BA&P		CA/BA&R		ER		ANE		CC	
	Working expenses £	W. ratio %	Working expenses £	W. ratio %	Working expenses £	W. ratio %	Working expenses £	W. ratio %	Working expenses £	W. ratio %	Working expenses £	W. ratio %	Working expenses £	W. ratio %
1900	1,105,000	48.6	423,000	49.6	297,000	53.4			77,600	77.4	79,700	90.6		
1901	1,159,000	49.0	383,000	46.8	332,000	55.3			69,200	77.7	84,300	89.2		
1902	1,097,000	46.3	454,000	48.5	304,000	52.2	1,215,000	52.9	70,400	78.7	85,500	89.0		
1903	1,184,000	46.7	562,000	47.6	347,000	48.4	1,632,000	50.2	91,600	72.6	87,800	83.4		
1904	1,314,000	46.1	667,000	48.2	532,000	55.6	1,963,000	52.2	104,900	65.0	98,000	72.5		
1905	1,670,000	49.9	731,000	48.3	719,000	56.9	2,060,000	51.6	116,000	56.5	95,000	65.3		
1906	2,239,000	57.5	940,000	52.8	882,000	54.5	2,553,000	56.3	119,000	59.9	110,000	65.3		
1907	2,449,000	57.6	1,122,000	56.3	1,892,000	61.8	2,727,000	59.2	140,000	52.8	120,000	65.1		
1908	2,474,000	55.7	1,214,000	55.1	2,300,000	62.9	2,934,000	59.7	166,000	55.4	111,000	63.6		62.5
1909	2,531,000	54.4	1,269,000	55.3	2,575,000	62.3	2,884,000	58.5	220,000	60.1	120,000	57.2		65.9
1910	2,516,000	56.7	1,300,000	56.5	2,465,000	57.4	2,763,000	58.2	226,000	55.8	140,000	57.1		70.5
1911	2,694,000	54.0	1,392,000	52.9	2,806,000	58.2	3,009,000	55.5	254,000	53.1	164,000	56.2		67.8
1912	3,016,000	55.9	1,339,000	55.1	3,152,000	63.4	2,930,000	56.1	292,000	61.8	195,000	61.4		76.1
1913	3,698,000	56.3	1,659,000	57.1	3,459,000	61.9	3,719,000	57.3	346,000	56.6	222,000	60.6		73.7
1914	3,200,000	58.9	1,487,000	58.8	3,057,000	62.6	3,547,000	58.5	332,000	54.5	237,000	68.1		68.5

Financial years ending 30 June, excepting CC and ANE (until 1905) and CA (until 1907) whose fiscal years terminated on 31 December.
Source: Compiled and calculated from respective companies' *Annual Reports*.

Argentine railway development, diversified their activities and integrated their operations precisely because they recognized their responsibility to do so. Shareholders' dividends were dependent upon the service provided to consumers. If the British-owned companies were to maximize their profits, of necessity they had to provide Argentine shippers with efficient and reasonable transportation facilities. The success of their action may be seen in companies' working ratios. Despite pressures to the contrary, railway prosperity was achieved and maintained due to operational efficiencies occasioned by substantial new investment, and by an attention to the requirements of zonal development which also necessitated access to additional capital. Despite rising costs — dearer labour (due to wage increases and the provision of extra fringe benefits), the need to 'carry' new branches, increased depreciation costs, and the extension of services — the railway companies nevertheless largely maintained their working ratios, absorbing increased expenses through more efficient working.

With the exception of the Pacific, broad-gauge working ratios demonstrated a remarkable degree of stability in the face of rising costs which increased in both relative and absolute terms. Between 1900 and 1913 the Western's gross receipts grew by approximately 245 per cent, but operating costs rose by some 300 per cent. Similarly, although the Great Southern enjoyed a 190 per cent increase in gross revenue during these years, costs climbed by 240 per cent. The returns for the other lines pursued a parallel course. Operating efficiency alone maintained profit levels, but for most of the period was dependent upon new investment. It was a circular process. Prosperity generated confidence and encouraged investors to subscribe to the new issues required by an expansionist policy. Expansion and integration facilitated the emergence of zonal groupings conducive to efficient and profitable operations.

CONCLUSION

Whether Argentina could, or should, have financed railway construction from domestic sources is a sterile debate. Claims that provincial and central government railway building, the early beginnings of the *Oeste*, direct national investment in the Central, and the weight of guarantee payments made to some companies (particularly the East Argentine) indicate that Argentina did indeed fund initial development are equally specious. Such considerations overlook companies like the Great Southern and Rosario. Also, they do not relate total guarantee payments to aggregate British investment in all railways. Above all these arguments conveniently ignore the fact that much of the capital employed in the construction of national lines was obtained from foreign borrowing. Moreover, these discussions miss the fundamental point that even in the 1860s Argentina, or the economic interests which comprised the governing classes, was more concerned with the derived effects of railway development rather than the profits which accrued to railway operations *per se*.

The basic questions to be answered relate to the impact of infrastructural development upon the domestic economy, and the extent to which foreign-owned companies provided the services appropriate to local requirements. Similarly, an examination of the profits earned by foreign investors will indicate the extent to which *their* objectives were realized, and also illustrate the true 'cost' to Argentina consequent upon foreign domination of the transport industry.

Argentine Railway Profits
Local capitalists (native and foreign-born) were interested in early railway schemes as a means of fostering the expansion of their primary interests in commerce and agriculture. A wide general involvement in railway projects characterized the

investment portfolio of entrepreneurs like Fair and Gowland, signifying an apparent lack of preference for any one particular scheme. They were concerned that railway companies should be speedily established as profitable entities, capable of attracting capital from other quarters, thereby allowing them to devote their attention to more lucrative fields. Hence an insistence upon the importance of guarantees and dependence upon state financing during the formative phase of railway construction. As the early history of the *Oeste* illustrates, local entrepreneurs were hardly commited to railways when there were more profitable areas of investment. Railways rarely yielded the return provided by alternative, traditional outlets, or allowed such scope for capital gains. Only after the initial period of development, during the 1870s and 1880s, was investment attracted by the prospect of the income yielded as a result of railway operations, and it is in this sense that the question of the return upon railway capital must be considered.

In view of the disparity between individual companies it is difficult to generalize with regard to the rate of return upon British railway investment throughout the whole period. But the concentration which arose as the result of amalgamation, and the uniformity imposed by the formation of zonal networks, particularly the emergence of the 'big four', make for an easier analysis of trends after the Baring Crisis. Despite marked differences during the 1880s, dividend rates, for example, assumed a degree of similarity in the 1890s. By 1916 funds invested in the 'big four' accounted for some 74 per cent of the total nominal capitalization of all British-owned Argentine railways, while the Great Southern and Central were individually responsible for approximately 28 per cent.[1]

Gauge may be taken as a rough guide to profitability. The broad-gauge lines of the *pampas* enjoyed the best records for sustained prosperity, while the medium- and metre-gauge companies were less fortunate. Indeed, notwithstanding the haphazard determination of the *FCO* gauge, other standards were introduced as a means of reducing construction costs, and were chosen because the traffic potential of these regions was considered to be less than that of the more fertile *pampas*. Mesopotamia and the north-west were thought unlikely to require the additional capacity which came with wider track, and were consequently viewed as incapable of generating sufficient revenue to cover the extra cost of broad-gauge construction. These original estimates were usually correct. However, allowing due consideration for the differences between individual companies, a general view of Anglo-Argentine railway profitability may be obtained from an examination of select case-studies. At opposite ends of the earning spectrum were the BAGS and the Argentine North Eastern; the former was the most profitable British company, and the latter one of the least prosperous mesopotamian lines.

Official Argentine government statistics indicate that prior to the First World War the average return upon total recognized investment in the national railway network (state-owned lines, foreign and domestically-financed companies) rarely exceeded 6 per cent, though the yield was usually substantially lower.[2] Despite its well-deserved reputation as the premier British-owned concern, further official data demonstrates that the net return on Great Southern capital was normally little more than a couple of percentage points above the global figure: conversely, the ANE yielded substantially less than the national average, often operating at a loss, or barely managing to service debenture scrip.[3] The higher ordinary dividends declared by the BAGS were due to the structure of its capital account, rather than to an ability to earn 'monopoly profits', a large proportion of its stocks bearing fixed low rates of interest. Over the long term even the ordinary dividends declared by the company were not a great deal higher (save for the years immediately prior to the Great War when road competition undermined the position of home-based lines) than those paid by the more profitable companies operating in Britain, as Table 41 indicates.

Investments in railway securities did not yield excessive profits. The remuneration obtained by British capitalists from the broad-gauge lines was usually little more than the premium expected for venturing to place funds abroad; often they were denied even that. Argentine railway profits were just sufficient to maintain the process of foreign investment, but equally, for most of the period the major companies were able to pay dividends with a regularity which converted their securities into prime scrip. By the 1870s companies such as the Southern rose above the ordinary because they could provide a reasonable rate of

Table 41: *Comparative dividends declared upon ordinary stock by British and Argentine railway companies*

	BAGS	BA&R	CA	London & North Western	Great Western	Great Southern & Western of Ireland
	%	%	%	%	%	%
1868–72	7.8			7.0	3.4	5.1
1873–77	7.7		4.6	6.8	4.8	5.4
1878–82	8.0		4.6	7.0	5.3	4.5
1883–87	10.0	9.0	10.0	6.7	5.8	4.4
1888–92	8.6	5.0	5.0	6.7	6.4	4.7
1893–97	5.1	2.2	2.0	6.5	5.4	5.3
1898–1902	6.8	3.0	4.8	6.8	4.6	5.0

Source: Compiled and calculated from *Bradshaw's*, various issues.

return despite adverse local or international conditions. The enviable reputation for prosperity enjoyed by the major British-owned Argentine railway companies was based upon a solid yield sustained for long periods. It was not occasioned by spectacular profits, or excessively high dividend payments. Moreover, it was the average yield which appeared so promising. The metre-gauge Córdoba lines and the standard-gauge companies of mesopotamia did not share this reputation. Although relatively peripheral in terms of capitalization and mileage, certainly prior to the process of amalgamation and expansion in which they participated at the turn of the century, the experience of these lines sets that of the broad-gauge companies into perspective. Dividends of between 10 and 12 per cent obtained by Central and Southern shareholders during the 1880s were countered by the years when smaller lines declared no return whatsoever upon ordinary capital. Similarly, investment in Anglo-Argentine railway securities did not provide spectacular capital gains. Given an element of security, capital values were influenced by yields, in conjunction with prevailing interest rates. The Great Southern again serves as a useful example. Fluctuations in the value of its securities were determined by income which made for stability rather than capital appreciation, and are representative of the relative values accorded to the issue of other companies. They emphasize that British investment in Argentine railways was a profitable exercise, but not one that obtained abnormal rewards.

The moderate nature of foreign shareholders' expectations had important implications for Argentina. In 1900 the British-owned companies accounted for 88 per cent of aggregate railway investment, and some 14.7 per cent of Argentina's total capital stock. The paramount position achieved by these companies within the context of domestic transport facilities (which represented 16.3 per cent of total national capital stock) allowed the industry to provide an efficient, low-cost service to other sectors of the economy.[4] In this sense British funding of Argentine railway development had a dual effect. Firstly, it released domestic capital for investment in the more profitable fields to which local interests had almost exclusive access. Secondly, the comparatively low profit margins of the railway companies (as evidenced by average profit rates and dividend payments) made for a cheap, efficient (as implied by working ratios) service which encouraged expansion in other areas. Not only did efficient transport facilities stimulate general economic development, but the high profits accruing to other activities were retained within those sectors because they were not required to channel funds into low-yielding infrastructure projects, nor indeed pay a high price to foreign capitalists for transport services.

Railways and the Domestic Economy

Although counter-factual model building is an interesting academic occupation, economic actuality in the Argentina of the mid-nineteenth century provides little scope for such pursuits. Geophysical conditions and the current level of technological achievement ensured that railway construction was the only viable method of solving the transportation requirements of the *pampas*.[5] But railway development was only one of the factors responsible for economic growth. The relatively minor impact of initial railway projects upon the course of economic expansion indicates that the dynamic impulses occasioned by the railways were not sufficient in themselves to effect fundamental changes in the economic structure of the country. The impact of railway development is rather to be discovered in its causal relationship with the mix of factors which brought about that change.

The economic transformation of Argentina is usually dated

from the last quarter of the nineteenth century which witnessed the country's incorporation within the world economy. That incorporation was effected by several interdependent instruments; railway development was a function of the country's participation in the international, multilateral system. It was technological innovation which permitted market forces to operate more effectively. However, although consequent upon that transformation, within the context of the domestic economy railway construction had a dynamic of its own. It is a truism to state that large-scale agricultural expansion necessitated the provision of infrastructural services; the question of causality can only be answered by a consideration of the interconnection of factors which facilitated economic change. 'T'-tested correlation coefficients reveal a substantial positive relationship between rates of expansion of the railway network, the movement of the frontier and net immigration.[6] As is to be anticipated, the closest relationship is that between the growth of the railways and the expansion of the arable sector during the period between the 1890s and 1914. The linkage between the pastoral economy and railway development is disguised by the existence of the shifting 'interior' cattle frontier, particularly for the years before the turn of the century, although there is a close correlation thereafter. Inevitably, the degree of association between the growth of the railway system and population increase (48 per cent of which was occasioned by net immigration during the years from 1870 to 1913) is less apparent though no less real. However, while the impact of railway development was most directly experienced by areas of the economy related to export activities, other sectors and the 'internal' economy also responded to the dynamism of infrastructure modernization. As related above, expansion and amalgamation facilitated economic integration within Argentina. The network provided intra-regional linkages, besides establishing more direct means of communications between the provinces and the centre. This process was responsible for the expansion of the *Cuyo* wine industry and it should not be ignored that many export activities were in addition major local suppliers.

The spin-off from British-financed railway expansion was thus substantial. And this contribution was founded upon sustained, reasonable profits. The British-owned companies sought to provide an effective service for local consumers and in order to do so were required to expand their networks, catering for the interests of the dominant groups in Argentina. This does not mean that there were no instances when some, or most, lines failed to provide a consistently efficient service, or that there were no occasions when individual companies did not engage in questionable or even reprehensible activities. As has been indicated, chicanery and malpractice were not unknown in Anglo-Argentine railway circles, particularly during the formative era. Yet, over time, the connection between British capitalists and Argentina was based upon mutual advantage. Railway investors obtained a moderate return with some regularity; *estancieros* were spared the necessity of placing funds in low-yield projects. The companies' participation in the process of Argentine economic growth was occasioned by methods controlled — if not selected — in Argentina. Established upon the concept of reciprocal benefit, as stated in the early guaranteed concessions, the duration of the relationship was dependent upon a common acceptance of the roles and functions ascribed to both parties, as evidenced by the late nineteenth and early twentieth centuries. But the determination and definition of those roles had not been easy, as events during the formative phase of Argentine railway development demonstrate.

ABBREVIATIONS

British-owned railway companies		gauge
Argentine Great Western Railway Company Limited	AGW	b
Argentine North Eastern Railway Company Limited	ANE	s
Argentine Transandine Railway Company Limited	Transandine	m
Bahia Blanca and North Western Railway Company Limited	BB&NW	b
Buenos Ayres and Campana Railway Company Limited	BA&C	b
Buenos Ayres and Ensenada Port Railway Company Limited	BA&EP	b
Buenos Ayres and Pacific Railway Company Limited	BA&P	b
Buenos Ayres and Rosario Railway Company Limited	BA&R	b
Buenos Ayres and San Fernanda Railway Company Limited	BA&SF	b
Buenos Ayres and Valparaiso Transandine Railway Company Limited	Transandine	m
Buenos Ayres, Ensenada and South Coast Railway Company Limited	BAE&SC	b
Buenos Ayres Great Southern Railway Company Limited	BAGS	b
Buenos Ayres Northern Railway Company Limited	BAN	b
Buenos Ayres Western Railway Company Limited	BAW	b
Central Argentine Railway Company Limited	CA	b
Cordoba and North Western Railway Company Limited	C&NW	m
Cordoba and Rosario Railway Company Limited	C&R	m
Cordoba Central Railway Company Limited	CC	m
Cordoba Central Buenos Ayres Extension Railway Company Limited	CCBAE	m
East Argentine Railway Company Limited	EA	s
Entre Rios Railway Company Limited	ER	s
North West Argentine Railway Company Limited	NWA	m

ABBREVIATIONS

Sante Fe and Cordoba Great Southern Railway Company Limited	SF&CGS	m
Villa Maria and Rufino Railway Company Limited	VM&R	b
Western of Santa Fe Railway Company Limited	WSF	b

State lines

Ferrocarril Andino	FCA	b
Ferrocarril Central Norte	FCCN	m
Ferrocarril Oeste	FCO	b

Gauge
b broad gauge, 5 feet 6 inches
s standard (medium) gauge, 4 feet 8½ inches
m metre gauge, 3 feet 3½ inches

NOTES

CHAPTER I

1 Alejandro E. Bunge *Ferrocarriles argentinos: contribución al estudio del patrimonio nacional* (Buenos Aires 1918) pp. 145–47.
2 Reginald Lloyd (ed.) *Impresiones de la República Argentina en el Siglo Veinte* (London 1911) p. 304. Several versions of this episode survive. See also Diego A. Santillan (ed.) *Gran Enciclopedia Argentina* (Buenos Aires 1957) II p. 313 cited in Winthrop R. Wright *British-owned railways in Argentina: their effects on the growth of economic nationalism, 1854–1948* (Austin 1974) pp. 23–24; *The Times* 28 January 1948, 5f.
3 Juan Bautista Alberdi *Obras completas. Vol. III. Bases y puntos de partida para la organizacion de la República Argentina* (Buenos Aires 1886) pp. 433–35.
4 República Argentina, Ministerio de Relaciones Exteriores y Culto *Constitution of the Argentine Republic* (Buenos Aires 1926) p. 20. Translated by Dr Mario A. Carranza.
5 William Hadfield *Brazil, the River Plate and the Falkland Islands; with the Cape Horn Route to Australia. Including Notices of Lisbon, Madeira, the Canaries and Cape Verde* (London 1854) p. 281.
6 *Brazil and River Plate Mail* (hereafter *B&RPM*) 22 March 1864, I, 180.
7 *The Times* 28 January 1948, 5f.
8 For a detailed account of the political events of the period, and their economic consequences, see A.J. Walford, 'Economic aspects of the Argentine War of Secession 1857–61' *Inter-American Economic Affairs* (hereafter *IAEA*) I 2 (1947) 70–96; James R. Scobie *La Lucha por la consolidacion de la nacionalidad argentina, 1852–1862* (Buenos Aires 1964) and by the same author 'The aftermath of Pavon' *Hispanic American Historical Review* (hereafter *HAHR*) XXXV 2 (1955) 153–74; 'The uneasy triumvirate; Derqui, Mitre and Urquiza' *HAHR* XXXVIII 3 (1958) 327–52; 'The significance of the September Revolution' *HAHR* XLI 2 (1961) 236–58.
9 El Consejo de Obras Públicas de la Provincia de Buenos Aires to Bartolome Mitre, 30 November 1852. Archivo General de la Nación, 1852/10/28/2/4/1723b.
10 Provincia de Buenos Aires *Registro Oficial de la Provincia, 1854* (hereafter *Registro* . . .) (Buenos Aires 1854) p. 5.
11 Confederacion Argentina *Registro Oficial, 1855* (Buenos Aires 1855) No. 3441 p. 207; República Argentina, Ministerio de Obras Públicas, Dirección General de Ferrocarriles *Estadística de los ferrocarriles en explotación durante el año 1893* (Buenos Aires 1895) p. 69.
12 Provincia de Buenos Aires *Registro* . . . *1857* pp. 55 & 77.
13 Provincia de Buenos Aires *Registro* . . . *1854* p. 104; Raul Scalabrini Ortíz *Historia de los Ferrocarriles Argentinos* (Buenos Aires 1958) pp. 27–28.
14 Provincia de Buenos Aires *Mensaje(s) del gobierno del estado a la asamblea general lejislativa, 1° de mayo de 1856* (Buenos Aires 1856) p. 47, *1857* (Buenos Aires 1857) p. 24, *Registro* . . . *1857* p. 75; Scalabrini Ortíz *Historia* p. 29.

[15] Provincia de Buenos Aires *Registro . . . 1858* p. 94.
[16] Provincia de Buenos Aires *Registro . . . 1862* p. 188; M.G. & E.T. Mulhall *Handbook of the River Plate* (Buenos Aires 1869) I 107.
[17] For an account of the protracted difficulties experienced in promoting this concession, see Wright *British-owned Railways* pp. 18–20.
[18] William Wheelwright (ed.) *Introductory remarks on the provinces of La Plata and the cultivation of cotton: Parana and the Cordoba Railway, report of Allen Campbell: proposals for an Interoceanic Railway between the Rio de la Plata and the Pacific. Being a Paper read at a Meeting of the Royal Geographic Society, 23 January 1860* (London 1881).
[19] República Argentina, Congreso Nacional *Comisión encargada del estudio de la cuenta capital de los ferrocarriles de régimen de sus gastos* (Buenos Aires 1933) *passim*: Bunge *Ferrocarriles* Ch. III; Scalabrini Ortíz *Historia passim*.
[20] *The Times* 6 December 1869, 6e; *Railway Times* (hereafter *RT*) 23 January 1897 LXXI, 119. Calculations by the Argentine Railway Board undertaken during the early 1890s indicate the following average costs of railway construction, per mile, for select countries, United Kingdom — £43,600, France — £27,000, Germany — £20,400, Italy — £17,800, Spain — £15,800, USA — £12,500, Canada — £11,900, India — £9,500, Australia — £9,300, South Africa — £8,900, European average — £23,400, World average — £16,100, Argentina — £11,000. Obviously these are crude figures, based upon nominal capitalization returns and take no account of differences in gauge, terrain, etc.
[21] República Argentina *Registro Nacional, 1862* (Buenos Aires 1862) IV, 5668.
[22] J.S. Duncan *Public and private operation of railways in Brazil* (New York 1932) p. 24.
[23] *Burdett's Official Intelligence* (hereafter *BOI*) III (1882) 357.
[24] Norberto de la Riestra to David Robertson, 25 May 1863. Baring Archive, House Correspondence (hereafter BAHC) 4.1.29 Pt.III.
[25] Provincia de Buenos Aires *Registro . . . 1862* p. 140.
[26] *B&RPM* 22 April 1864, I, 221–24.
[27] *Railway and Travel Monthly* 18 February 1914, VIII, 90.
[28] John Fair to Robertson, 27 June 1863. BAHC 4.1.29 Pt.III.
[29] Robertson to Baring Young, 26 October 1863. BAHC 4.1.29 Pt.III.
[30] Riestra to Robertson, 27 July 1863. BAHC 4.1.29 Pt.III.
[31] Robertson to Baring Young, 29 October 1863. BAHC 4.1.29 Pt.III.
[32] Robertson to Riestra, 21 December 1863. BAHC 4.1.29 Pt.III.
[33] Provincia de Buenos Aires *Registro . . . 1863* p. 256.
[34] John Fair *Some notes on my Early Connection with the Buenos Ayres Great Southern Railway* (Bournemouth 1899).
[35] *B&RPM* 7 August 1867, IV, 14; Hadfield *Brazil and the River Plate in 1868* (London 1869) p. 146.
[36] *The Times* 20 November 1869, 6f.
[37] Fair to Robertson, 27 June 1863. BAHC 4.1.29 Pt.III; *The Times* 27 May 1870, 10e; *B&RPM* 7 June 1870, VII, 10; Fair *op.cit.*; Hadfield *Brazil . . . 1868* p. 146.
[38] Robertson to Baring Young, 29 October 1863. BAHC 4.1.29 Pt.III.
[39] *The Times* 6 February 1869, 7f, 17 February 1869, 10a.
[40] Provincia de Buenos Aires *Registro . . . 1869* p. 540.
[41] Buenos Ayres Great Southern Railway Company Limited (hereafter BAGS) *Report of the Directors to the Shareholders for the half-year ended June 30, 1869* (hereafter *Half-year report . . .*) (London 1869); BAGS *Report of the Directors to the Shareholders and Statement of the Revenue and Capital Accounts for the year ended December 31, 1869* (hereafter *Annual Report . . .*) (London 1870); *BOI* III (1882) 355.

[42] *RT* 27 November 1869, XXXII, 1162.
[43] Riestra to Robertson, 27 July 1863. BAHC 4.1.29 Pt.III.
[44] Buenos Aires *Standard* 18 May 1870.
[45] R. Wood and others to the General Purposes Committee of the London Stock Exchange, 22 March 1860. London Stock Exchange Archive, Quotation Department Records (hereafter Stock Exchange, QDR), 21A. 775.
[46] *RT* 16 June 1860, XXIII, 680, 30 June, 747–49, 7 July, 775–76.
[47] Provincia de Buenos Aires,*Registro* . . . *1862* pp. 60 & 65; *RT* 12 April 1862 XXIV, 525, 2 August 1862 XXIV, 1114; *Bradshaw's Railway Manual, Shareholders Guide and Directory* (hereafter *Bradshaw's*) XV (1863) 380.
[48] *The Times* 21 January 1863, 9d.
[49] *The Times* 3 August 1863, 7d.
[50] *The Times* 24 August 1865, 5a, 8 September 1865, 6f; *B&RPM* 7 September 1865, II, 495–97, 22 September, 522–23.
[51] *RT* 12 May 1866, XXIX, 562; *B&RPM* 22 August 1865, II, 469.
[52] *The Times* 18 September 1866, 5e; *B&RPM* 22 September 1866, III, 425.
[53] *B&RPM* 22 August 1865, II, 469.
[54] *The Times* 7 December 1866, 4c & d, 8 April 1867, 7b, 11 April 1867, 7a, 11 September 1867, 5d, 18 September 1867, 5d, 22 July 1868, 10f, 29 October 1868, 6f.
[55] M.G. & E.T. Mulhall *Handbook of the River Plate Republics* p. 65.
[56] Provincia de Buenos Aires *Registro* . . . *1868* p. 430; Northern Railway of Buenos Ayres Company Limited (hereafter BAN) *Report of the Directors to the Shareholders for the Year ended December 31, 1868* (London 1869); *B&RPM* 22 January 1869, VI, 19.
[57] Lloyd (ed.) *op cit*. p. 303; Scalabrini Ortíz *Historia* p. 25.
[58] *The Times* 28 January 1948, 5f; Scalabrini Ortíz, *Historia* p. 28.
[59] *RT* 12 November 1864, XXVII, 1461.
[60] *The Times* 10 February 1864, 7b; *B&RPM* 23 March 1865, II, 22–25.
[61] *The Times* 22 March 1867, 22e.
[62] *B&RPM* 22 October 1867, IV, 15, 7 December, 15; *Parliamentary Papers, Accounts and Papers* (hereafter *PP*) 1872 LIV 373; Ferns *Britain and Argentina* p. 33.
[63] *The Times* 25 March 1868, 11d, 24 September 1868, 4e.
[64] *The Times* 18 March 1869, 10d.
[65] George Woolcott, secretary, Central Argentine, to Baring Brothers, 27 August 1875. BAHC 4.1.52.
[66] *B&RPM* 6 April 1867, IV, 13.
[67] Thomas Armstrong to Robertson, 26 August 1863. BAHC 4.1.29 Pt.III.
[68] Robertson to Thomas Baring, 13 July 1863. BAHC 4.1.29 Pt.III.
[69] Fair *op. cit. passim*.
[70] Robertson to Baring Young, 21 July 1863. BAHC 4.1.29 Pt.III.
[71] M.G. & E.T. Mulhall, *Handbook of the River Plate* I 106; Fair *op.cit.*
[72] *Bradshaw's* XIX (1867) 417, XX (1868) 403.
[73] *The Times* 1 August 1867, 7d.
[74] Ferns *Britain and Argentina* pp. 333–38.
[75] Robertson to Thomas Baring, 13 July 1863. BAHC 4.1.29 Pt.III.
[76] República Argentina, Congreso Nacional, Camara de Diputados, *Diario de Sesiones de la Camara de Diputados, 1864* (hereafter *Sesiones*) (Buenos Aires 1865) Tomo Unico pp. 91–96; *PP* 1867 LXIX 288; Alberdi, *op.cit.* pp. 433–35.
[77] *B&RPM* 8 October 1870, VII, 1 & 13; *The Times* 25 May 1877, 7c.
[78] C.O. Barker, secretary, BAGS, to Baring Brothers, 18 January 1877. BAHC 4.1.67; *PP* 1875 LXXVI 316.
[79] J.R. Scobie *Revolution on the pampa. A social history of Argentine Wheat,*

1860–1910 (Austin Texas 1964) p. 11; Hadfield *Brazil and the River Plate, 1870–76* (London 1877) p. 104.

[80] Thomas J. Hutchinson *Buenos Ayres and Argentine Gleanings* (London 1865) p. 36.

[81] *B&RPM* 22 February 1865, II, 173.

[82] *B&RPM* 22 February 1865, II, 174.

[83] Hadfield *Brazil and the River Plate, 1870–76* p. 114.

[84] Buenos Ayres & San Fernando Railway Company Limited (hereafter BA&SF) *Prospectus*. Stock Exchange, QDR 21A. 775.

[85] Scalabrini Ortíz *Historia* p. 39. While Scalabrini Ortíz argues that the *Oeste* consistently charged lower rates than the Great Southern, the data he provides, for 1866, indicate that on short hauls, the former company applied to second-class passenger traffic a mileage charge some 13.6 per cent higher than the latter. Only over long hauls was the *Oeste* markedly cheaper than the BAGS, charging between approximately 56 and 72 per cent of the other company's tariff.

[86] Scobie *Revolution on the Pampas* p. 11.

[87] Hutchinson *op. cit.* pp. 37–60. For a more detailed discussion of the nature of the differential between early rail freights and bullock cart charges see P.B. Goodwin 'The Central Argentine Railway and the economic development of Argentina, 1854–1881' *HAHR* LVII 4 (1977) 613–32, the critique of Goodwin's article presented by S. Damus and the former's rejoinder *HAHR* LVIII 3 (1978) 468–76. Goodwin maintains that there were only limited savings resulting from early railway construction.

[88] *The Times* 7 November 1870, 7e.

[89] *The Times* 22 November 1867, 7f; BAGS *Half-yearly report . . . January–June 1867* (London 1867).

[90] *The Times* 28 October 1873, 7f; and *B&RPM* 22 November 1873, X, 9–11.

[91] *B&RPM* 22 May 1874, XI, 6–7.

[92] *The Times* 25 May 1877, 7c.

[93] Nicolas Bouwer to Baring Brothers, 8 September 1877. BAHC 4.1.65 Pt.I.

[94] Bouwer to Barings, 7 November 1877. BAHC 4.1.65 Pt.II; BAGS *Annual Report . . . 1877* (London 1878).

[95] *B&RPM* 5 April 1871, VIII, 16.

[96] Bouwer to Barings, 8 September 1877. BAHC 4.1.65. Pt.I.

[97] *PP* 1866 LXIX 201.

[98] *PP* 1867/68 LXVIII 257.

[99] *PP* 1875 LXXVI 317.

[100] *B&RPM* 22 March 1871, VIII, 6. These statistics are taken from the Bateman Report presented to the Buenos Aires provincial government, soliciting a concession for the construction of a new port.

[101] BAGS *Annual Report . . . 1867* (London 1868); *The Times* 6 June 1868, 10e.

[102] *PP* 1875 LXXVI 321.

[103] For an account of the development of the wool economy see Herbert Gibson *The History and Present State of the Sheep-breeding industry in the Argentine Republic* (Buenos Aires 1893) *passim*; and Jose Chiaramonte *Nacionalismo y liberalismo economicos en la Argentina 1860–1880* (Buenos Aires 1971) Ch. 1.

[104] *B&RPM* 21 November 1868, V, 15–16; BAGS *Annual Report . . . 1868* (London 1869).

[105] M.G. & E. T. Mulhall *Handbook of the River Plate* I 107; Scalabrini Ortíz *Historia* pp. 25–85. Such statements ignore the sums of capital raised abroad, initially by the province of Buenos Aires, and subsequently by the company itself.

[106] *PP* 1878 LXXII 24; Francisco Barres 'Reseña de los ferrocarriles argentinos; Ferrocarril Entre Ríos' *Boletin de la asociación internacional permanente del*

congreso panamericano de ferrocarriles, XXVI, 71 (1942) 96–104.
[107] Bouwer to Barings, 31 July 1877. BAHC 4.1.65 Pt.I.
[108] *The Times* 14 January 1871, 7a; *B&RPM* 23 January 1871, VIII, 7.
[109] *PP* 1878 LXXVII 24–25; J.T. Carter *South American Railways: Argentina and Uruguay* (London 1891) n.p.
[110] *The Times* 28 July 1873, 6c.
[111] *PP* 1873 LXVII 6; Ferns *Britain and Argentina* p. 331.
[112] *PP* 1878 LXXII 25.
[113] *PP* 1877 LXXXIII 4.
[114] Bouwer to Barings, 26 December 1876. BAHC 4.1.65 Pt.I.
[115] For insight into the episode and an indication of the conflicting interests involved, see W. Gordon, representative for London Agent of Cordoba and Tucuman Railway contractor, to R. Bourke 30 July 1877. Public Records Office (hereafter PRO), London, Foreign Office Correspondence (hereafter FO) 6/344:90, J. Barker, London Agent for contractor, to Earl of Derby, 1 August 1877, and related correspondence. FO 6/344: 92–99, 117–29, L.S. Sackville West, British Minister at Buenos Aires, to Derby, 7 September 1877 and related correspondence. FO 6/340: 88–91, 220–21; Bouwer to Barings, 14 January 1878, 19 January 1879. BAHC 4.1.65 Pt.II.
[116] Bouwer to Barings 23 July 1879. BAHC 4.1.65 Pt.IV; *Echo de Córdoba* 5 May 1878, reprinted in *B&RPM* 6 July 1878 XV, 13.
[117] Due to fortuitous geographical, technical and legal factors the San Paulo (Brazilian) Railway Company Limited, which joined the coffee port of Santos to its hinterland, long enjoyed a monopoly of rail communications between the coffee producing regions of the province of São Paulo and the coast. Although its main line was comparatively short, other railways constructed lines from its railhead into the coffee districts so that virtually the whole of the coffee export of the region passed over its tracks at some stage of shipment. Its profit record was legion in the annals of Latin American railways. For an account of the company see Richard Graham, *Britain and the onset of modernization in Brazil, 1850–1914* (Cambridge 1968) pp. 60–66.
[118] República Argentina, Ministerior de Obras Públicas, Direccion General de Ferrocarriles, *Estadística de los ferrocarriles en explotación durante el año 1893* (Buenos Aires 1895) p. 63; Francisco Barres 'Reseña de los ferrocarriles argentinos; Ferrocarril Nordeste Argentino' *Boletin de la asociación internacional permanente del congreso panamericano de ferrocarriles* XXVI 72 (1942) 27–33; *The Times* 21 August 1873, 7c; *B&RPM* 6 January 1872, VIII, 4–5 states that the Argentine Government viewed with distaste the transfer of the concession to a British Company, possibly as the result of its difficulties with the Central Argentine. This factor and some irregularities in the deed of transfer may account for delayed official sanction.
[119] Edward Thornton, British Minister at Buenos Aires, to the Earl Russell, 20 October 1864 (copy of concession enclosed). FO 6/251: 187–95; *The Times* 11 May 1871, 7a; *RT* 13 May 1871, XXXIV, 471; *Bradshaw's* XXIV (1872) 377.
[120] *The Times* 14 October 1875, 6e.
[121] *PP* 1878 LXXII 32; *RT* 13 June 1874, XXXVII, 616.
[122] *The Times* 28 December 1876, 5d; Francisco Barres 'Reseña de los ferrocarriles argentinos; Ferrocarril Central Argentino' *Boletin de la associación internacional permanente del congreso panamericano de ferrocarriles*, XXVIII, 82 (1944) 33–59.
[123] Bouwer to Barings, 30 September 1877. BAHC 4.1.65 Pt.I.
[124] *BOI* III (1882) 353.
[125] West to Derby, 3 June 1874, FO 6/320; *PP* 1878 LXXII 13.

NOTES

[126] Provincia de Buenos Aires *Registro . . . 1877* p. 77, *Registro . . . 1863* p. 75; *Sesiones* 1863 I 441–42 & 447.

[127] *RT* 29 June 1871, XXXV, 672; *The Times* 29 June 1871, 10a.

[128] *PP* 1878 LXXII 11–13.

[129] BAGS *Memorandum of association and articles of association* (London, no date) p. 39, Stock Exchange, QDA 21A 793; BAGS *Half-yearly report . . . January to June, 1870* (London 1870); República Argentina, Ministerio de Obras Públicas, Dirección General de Ferrocarriles, *Estadística de los ferrocarriles en explotación durante el año 1893* (Buenos Aires, 1895) p. 66.

[130] Armstrong to Robertson 26 August 1863. BAHC 4.1.29 Pt.III.

[131] BAGS *Half-yearly report . . . January to June, 1870* (London 1870); *Buenos Aires Standard* 30 August 1870.

[132] BAGS *Half-yearly report . . . January to June, 1870* (London 1870); *B&RPM* 8 October 1870, VII, 1 & 13; *The Times* 1 November 1870, 7f.

[133] BAGS *Half-yearly report . . . January to June, 1871* (London 1871); BAGS *Report of Mr Drabble on his mission to Buenos Ayres, 1872* (London 1872) pp. 17–18. In the final event the province only paid a subvention on the main line prolongation.

[134] BAGS *Annual Report . . . 1872* (London 1873); *B&RPM* 8 May 1973, X, 17.

[135] BAGS *Annual Report . . . 1874* (London 1875); *The Times* 15 May 1875, 9c.

[136] BAGS *Annual Report . . . 1876* (London 1877); Hadfield *Brazil and the River Plate, 1870–76* p. 226.

[137] For an account of the changing structure of the Argentine economy during the first half of the nineteenth century see Miron Burgin *Economic aspects of Argentine federalism, 1820–1852* (Cambridge, Mass., 1946).

[138] J.R. Scobie *Argentina: A city and a nation* (New York 1971) pp. 113–14.

[139] *The Times* 6 February 1869, 7f, 22 February 1869, 6e.

[140] *The Times* 27 June, 1870, 9a, 2 July 1870, 10f, 27 October 1870, 7a.

[141] BAGS *Annual Report . . . 1872* (London 1873).

[142] BAGS *Annual Report . . . 1872* (London 1873); *Half-yearly report . . . January to June, 1874* (London 1874); *Annual Report, 1874* (London 1875); *Half-yearly report . . . January to June, 1875* (London 1875); *The Times* 31 May 1873, 7e, 15 May 1875, 9c. A succession of somewhat contradictory statements were issued by the company and it appears that it was necessary to raise additional capital to complete the line to the standard required by the provincial government. Difficulties in the London money market prevented the company from raising capital as cheaply as originally envisaged, while some unfortunate accidents also increased costs. The true cost of construction was probably between £8,743 and £8,750 per mile.

[143] *PP* 1878 LXXII 23. This estimate differs from that of the company which indicates a total capital expenditure of almost £2,500,000 or £9,260 per mile, BAGS *Annual Report . . . 1877* (London 1878). The difference is probably due to the company's inclusion of capital raised for 'work in hand' but not formally recognized by the local authorities.

[144] Ferns *Britain and Argentina* p. 352.

[145] *The Times* 25 May 1874, 8c.

[146] Hadfield *Brazil . . . 1868* p. 115.

[147] *RT* 24 December 1870, XXXIII, 1262, 14 October 1871, XXXIV, 1004; *The Times* 14 January 1871, 7f, 1 December 1871, 7f.

[148] *B&RPM* 7 October 1871, VIII, 13.

[149] *RT* 23 May 1874, XXXVII, 533.

[150] *RT* 18 July 1874, XXXVII, 726.

[151] *B&RPM* 8 August 1874, XI, 7–11.

[152] Bouwer to Barings, 31 October 1884. BAHC 4.1.65 Pt.XI; *South American Journal* (hereafter *SAJ*) 21 February 1885, XXII, 94.

NOTES

[153] Bouwer to Barings, 31 January 1877. BAHC 4.1.65 Pt.I; Emerson R. Johnson *The Railways of Argentina* (Washington 1943) p. 124; República Argentina, Ministerio de Obras Públicas, Dirección General de Ferrocarriles, *Estadística de los ferrocarriles en explotación durante el año 1893* (Buenos Aires 1895) p. 63.

[154] *The Times* 4 December 1876, 7a; *BOI* III (1882) 369.

[155] Carter *South American Railways*.

[156] Bouwer to Barings, 21 January 1882. BAHC 4.1.65 Pt.I.

[157] *RT* 13 June 1874, XXXVII, 616.

[158] *PP* 1878 LXXII 8.

[159] The total was made up as follows,

	BAGS	£2,250,000
	BA&EP	700,000
	BA&C	900,000
	BAN	455,000
	CA	2,000,000
	EA	1,000,000
		£7,305,000

[160] *B&RPM* 21 October 1873, X, 8.

[161] The *canard* that the initial equipment and material used in the construction of the line were ex-military supplies, destined for the use of the British army in the Crimea, has been disproved, but there can be little doubt that much of the material was second-hand and already obsolete. This was particularly true of the iron rails. See George Pendle, 'Railways in Argentina' *History Today* VIII 2 (1958) 119–25 and R.M. Robbins, 'The Balaclava Railway' *Journal of Transport History* I 1 (1953) 28–43.

[162] *PP* 1878 LXXII 8.

[163] Juan Carlos Walther *La conquista del desierto* (Buenos Aires 1970) *passim*; Alfred Hasbrouck 'The conquest of the desert' *HAHR* XV 2 (1935) 195–228; Cesar Bustos-Videla, 'The conquest of the Argentine desert and its religious aspect' *The Americas* XXI 1 (1964) 36–57.

[164] Ferns *Britain and Argentina* p. 392.

CHAPTER II

[1] Central Argentine Railway Company Limited (hereafter CA) *Report of the Directors and Statement of Accounts for the year ended 31st December, 1880* (hereafter *Annual Report* . . .) (London 1881).

[2] BAGS *Half-yearly report . . . January to June, 1880* (London 1880) *Annual Report . . . 1880* (London 1881); *The Times* 23 October 1880, 7b, 22 April 1881, 6d.

[3] Bouwer to Barings, 14 July 1880. BAHC 4.1.65 Pt.VI; Sir H. Rumbold, British Minister at Buenos Aires, to Earl Granville, 23 February 1881. FO 6/364: 61–76.

[4] *The Times* 23 October 1880, 7d.

[5] BAGS *Annual Report . . . 1880* (London 1881).

[6] CA Annual Report . . . 1880 (London 1881); *The Times* 27 July 1881, 11f.

[7] *SAJ* 21 February 1885, XXII, 94.

[8] Bouwer to Barings, 23 June 1884. BAHC 4.1.65 Pt. XI.

[9] CA *Annual Report(s)* (respective years).

[10] *The Times* 19 October 1883, 9e.

[11] República Argentina, Ministerio de Obras Públicas, Dirección General de Ferrocarriles *Estadística de los ferrocarriles en explotación, 1913* (Buenos Aires 1916).

[12] William Ashworth *An economic history of England, 1870–1939* (London 1967), p. 35. See also R. Cortés Conde and E. Gallo *La formación de la Argentina moderna*, (Buenos Aires 1967) *passim*.; V. Vázquez-Presedo *El caso argentino: migración de factores comercio exterior y desarrollo, 1875–1914* (Buenos Aires 1971) *passim*.

[13] Simon G. Hanson *Argentine meat and the British market. Chapter in the history of the Argentine meat industry* (Palo Alto 1938) pp. 18ff.

[14] For the increase in real incomes which occurred in Great Britain during the 1880s, see S.B. Saul *The myth of the Great Depression, 1873–1896* (London 1969) pp. 30–34.

[15] Scobie *Revolution on the pampas* p. 169; Vázquez-Presedo *El caso* Ch. III.

[16] *PP* 1893/4 XCII 158.

[17] BAGS *Annual report . . . 1880* (London 1881); Carter *South American Railways*.

[18] *The Times* 26 April 1884, 13d.

[19] Bouwer to Barings, 4 May 1881. BAHC 4.1.65 Pt.VII; BAGS *Half-yearly report . . . January to June, 1881* (London 1881).

[20] Bouwer to Barings, 10 September 1881. BAHC 4.1.65 Pt.VIII; BAGS *Half-yearly report . . . January to June, 1881* (London, 1881).

[21] Bouwer to Barings, 4 May 1881, 7 September 1881. BAHC 4.1.65 Pts.VII & VIII.

[22] Bouwer to Barings, 10 September 1881. BAHC 4.1.65 Pt.VIII; BAGS *Annual Report . . . 1881* (London 1882). The tariffs levied during 1881 were, on average, approximately 12 per cent below those applied in 1880.

[23] Bouwer to Barings, 17 October 1881. BAHC 4.1.65 Pt.VIII; *The Times* 22 October 1881, 7e.

[24] *The Times* 13 February 1882, 6f.

[25] *PP* 1883 LXXI 591.

[26] Bouwer to Barings, 24 December 1880. BAHC 4.1.65. Pt.VI.

[27] Bouwer to Barings, 3 May 1884. BAHC 4.1.65. Pt.XI; BAGS *Annual Report . . . 1884* (London 1884).

[28] BAGS *Half-yearly report . . . July to December, 1883* (London 1884); *The Times* 26 April 1884, 13d; Carter *South American Railways*.

[29] Provincia de Buenos Aires *Registro oficial . . . 1871* 527 & 710; República de Argentina, Ministerio de Obras Públicas, Direccion General de Ferrocarriles, *Estadística de los ferrocarriles en explotación durante el ano 1893* (Buenos Aires 1895) pp. 68–69; *The Times* 28 July 1873, 6c, 7 November 1873, 6a; *B&RPM* 8 December 1873, X, 8.

[30] St John to Granville, 6 May 1873. FO 6/315: 49–51; *The Times* 12 June 1874, 10a.

[31] Bouwer to Barings, 4 August 1883. BAHC 4.1.65. Pt.X; *The Times* 12 June 1874, 10a.

[32] Bouwer to Barings, 30 September 1877, 26 August 1878. BAHC 4.1.65. Pts.I & III.

[33] Bouwer to Barings, 4 August 1882, 11 August 1883. BAHC 4.1.65. Pt.X; *RT* 23 February 1884, XXXXVII, 244.

[34] *RT* 1 March 1884, XXXVII, 288.

[35] *RT* 17 May 1884, XXXXVII, 627; Bouwer to Barings, 4 August 1883. BAHC 4.1.65 Pt.X.

[36] *The Times* 18 October 1884, 11c.

[37] F. Barres 'Reseña de los ferrocarriles argentinos; Ferrocarril Central Argentino' *Boletin de la asociación internacional permanente del congreso paramericano de ferrocarriles* XXVIII 82 (1944) 33–58.

[38] *The Times* 1 May 1886, 13d, 30 April 1887, 13d.

[39] Bouwer to Barings, 28 January 1886. BAHC 4.1.65 Pt.XIII.

[40] Buenos Aires and Pacific Railway Company Limited (hereafter BA&P) *Memorandum and Articles of Association, Construction, Contract and Translation of Concession* Biblioteca del FCNGSM Vol. 12.50; London Stock Exchange, QDR, 6B 154; F. Barres 'Reseña de los ferrocarriles argentinos; Ferrocarril de Buenos Aires al Pacifico' *Boletin de la asociación internacional permanente del congreso panamericano de ferrocarriles* XXVII 78(1943) 41–55.

[41] *BOI* II (1883) 387.
[42] London Stock Exchange, QDR, 6B 154; *RT* 14 October 1882, XXXXV, 967.
[43] *RT* 14 October 1882, XXXXV, 967.
[44] *BOI* II (1883) 387.
[45] Bouwer to Barings, 14 April 1883. BAHC 4.1.65 Pt.X.
[46] *The Times* 20 April 1887, 16d.
[47] *RT* 1 May 1886, XXXXIX, 562.
[48] *The Times* 21 April 1886, 11d.
[49] *SAJ* 26 June 1886, XXIII, 299 & 302.
[50] *SAJ* 7 August 1886, XXIII, 372.
[51] E. Monson, British Minister at Buenos Aires, to Granville, 11 November 1884. FO 6/380: 71–74; Bouwer to Barings, 22 December 1884. BAHC 4.1.65 Pt.XI; Ferns *Britain and Argentina* pp.401–2.
[52] Bouwer to Barings, 13 January 1885. BAHC 4.1.65 Pt.XII; Monson to Granville, 16 January 1885. FO 6/385: 13–22.
[53] Bouwer to Barings, 27 June 1885. BAHC 4.1.65 Pt.XII; *RT* 2 October 1886, L, 442 & 446.
[54] *The Times* 25 September 1886, 11d, 2 October 1886, 11b.
[55] *SAJ* 12 May 1888, XXV, 264.
[56] Bouwer to Barings, 22 October 1881. BAHC 4.1.65 Pt. VIII.
[57] *PP* 1881 LXXXIX 171.
[58] *PP* 1881 LXXXIX 433.
[59] *PP* 1884 LXXX 6.
[60] For slightly different intepretations of the Line's situation, based upon the same data, see *PP* 1883 LXXI 592, 1884/5 LXXVIII 160; Scalabrini Ortíz *Historia* pp. 277–79.
[61] *PP* 1883 LXXIII 385.
[62] *The Times* 9 July 1886, 11c; *SAJ* 10 July 1886, XXIII, 320–21.
[63] *Sesiones* 1884 Tomo II p. 1006.
[64] Lawrence Baker, chairman, East Argentine Railway Company Limited (hereafter EA), to Baring Brothers, 21 March 1882. BAHC 4.1.65 Pt. XI.
[65] *PP* 1883 LXXI 588.
[66] *SAJ* 10 August 1889, XXII, 186; see also Vázquez-Presedo, *Estadísticas* pp. 65, 67, 74, 75,; J.H. Williams *Argentine International Trade under Inconvertible Paper Money, 1880–1900* (Cambridge, Mass. 1920).
[67] *RT* 24 January 1885, XXXXVIII, 122. Reprinted from the Buenos Aires *Standard*.
[68] Bouwer to Barings, 16 March 1885. BAHC 4.1.65 Pt.XII.
[69] Bouwer to Barings, 13 March 1885. BAHC 4.1.65 Pt. XII.
[70] Bouwer to Barings, 11 January 1885. BAHC 4.1.65 Pt. XII.
[71] Ferns *Britain and Argentina* pp. 402–4.
[72] *The Times* 4 May 1885, 11c.
[73] *RT* 15 May 1886, XXXXIX, 625.
[74] *The Times* 28 October 1887, 11c.
[75] *The Times* 22 April 1892, 10c.
[76] Carter *South American Railways*.
[77] *RT* 10 September 1887, LII, 355.

[78] *The Times* 28 January 1889, 11d.
[79] *RT* 20 February 1892, LXI, 260.
[80] *The Times* 7 March 1885, 11b.
[81] Carter *South American Railways*. The figure does not include the capitalization of the line leased (and later purchased) from the BAN or the BAW; CA *Annual Report . . . 1889* (London 1890).
[82] *RT* 8 October 1892, LXII, 474.
[83] *SAJ* 11 July 1885, XXII, 345.
[84] *RT* 28 November 1891, LX, 553; *PP* 1890/91 LXXXIV 4.
[85] Carter *South American Railways*. This figure does not include the line leased from the BAN. See also F. Barres 'Reseña de los ferrocarriles argentinos; Ferrocarril Central Argentino' *Boletin de la asociación internacional permanente del congreso panamericano de ferrocarriles* XXVIII 82 (1944) 33–58.
[86] *Bradshaw's* XLIII (1891); *Economist* 28 May 1892, L, 698; *Statist* 11 June 1892, XXIX, 667.
[87] Buenos Aires and Rosario Railway Company Limited (hereafter BA&R) *Report of the Directors to the Shareholders for the half-year ending June 30, 1889* (hereafter *Half-yearly report . . .*) (London 1889), *Report of the Directors to the Shareholders and Statement of Accounts for the year ending December 31, 1889* (hereafter *Annual Report . . .*) (London 1890); *PP* 1890/91 LXXXIV 4.
[88] BAGS *Annual Report . . . 1886/87* (London 1887); *The Times* 4 April 1887, 11b.
[89] BAGS *Annual report . . . 1889* (London 1889).
[90] *PP* 1892 LXXXI 150.
[91] Carter *South American Railways*.
[92] *The Times* 29 April 1886, 11c.
[93] *RT* 11 April 1885, XXXXVIII, 473.
[94] *RT* 18 April 1885, XXXXVIII, 508.
[95] *RT* 28 August 1886, L, 281, 9 October, 457, 23 October, 538, 6 November, 603, 20 November, 667.
[96] *RT* 19 November 1887, LII, 887, 28 January 1888, LIII, 122.
[97] Bouwer to Barings, 28 November 1887. BAHC 4.1.65 Pt.XIV.
[98] *RT* 19 November 1887, LII, 665. Reprinted from *La Prensa*.
[99] *RT* 26 November 1887, LII, 700.
[100] *RT* 21 July 1888, LIV, 80.
[101] *RT* 12 May 1888, LIII, 643.
[102] *SAJ* 1 September 1888, XXV, 571. Reprinted from the Buenos Aires *Standard* 23 June 1888.
[103] *Sesiones* 1892, I, p. 282.
[104] *PP* 1890/91 LXXXIV 3.
[105] *PP* 1892 LXXXI 11–12.
[106] *RT* 29 November 1891, LVIII, 631.
[107] *RT* 3 December 1892, LXII, 731.
[108] República Argentina, Ministerio de Obras Públicas, Dirección General de Ferrocarriles, *Estadística de los ferrocarriles en explotación, 1913* (Buenos Aires 1916) pp. 396–98.

CHAPTER III

[1] *SAJ* 29 September 1888, XXV 667–69.
[2] *The Times* 23 January 1889, 11d.

[3] *SAJ* 19 April 1890, XXVIII, 500–501.
[4] CA *Annual Report(s) . . . 1885 & 1889* (London 1886 & 1890).
[5] *The Times* 13 May 1890, 11c.
[6] *RT* 18 February 1888, LIII, 211; *The Times* 12 December 1889, 11c.
[7] A.G. Ford 'Argentina and the Baring Crisis of 1890' *Oxford Economic Papers* VIII 2 (1956) 127–50; J.E. Hodge 'Carlos Pellegrini and the Financial Crisis of 1890' *HAHR* L 3 (1970) 499–523.
[8] *The Times* 31 March 1871, 10f, 22 July 1871, 6a; *B&RPM* 7 October 1871, VII, 13. The initial debenture issue consisted of £100,000 at 6 per cent. Yet even at the end of the decade the ratio of equity to debenture capital was in the order of 6.4:1. See CA *Annual Report . . . 1889* (London 1890); *RT* 12 July 1890, LVIII, 41.
[9] BAGS *Annual Report(s) . . . 1884 & 1885* (London 1884 & 1885).
[10] The Extension shares, 1890, bore interest at 6 per cent; the Extension shares, 1892, at 5 per cent. When this capital was created the dividend being declared upon ordinary stock stood at 11 and 10 per cent respectively.
[11] Stock Exchange, QDR, 14B 97.
[12] Cordoba Central Railway Company Limited (hereafter CC) *Report of the Directors and statement of accounts to 31st December, 1890* (hereafter *Annual Report...*) (London 1891); Carter *South American Railways*.
[13] Argentine North-Eastern Railway Company Limited (hereafter AEN) *Report of the directors to be presented to the shareholders at the second ordinary annual meeting . . . 1890* (hereafter *Annual Report . . .*) (London 1890).
[14] Carter *South American Railways*.
[15] *Economist* 28 November 1891, XLIX, 1527; Ford 'Argentina and the Baring Crisis of 1890'.
[16] Although the rate of dividend upon ordinary stock is a rather crude guide to railway profitability, it nevertheless fairly accurately reflects the state of a company's finances at this juncture. For example, there is a reasonably close correlation between fluctuations in the ordinary dividends paid by the BAGS and the rates, respectively, of net earnings (i.e. less working expenses) and residual income (i.e. net earnings less fixed service payments, but including balances carried forward from previous years' operations and income generated from other sources, from which transfers to the reserves and ordinary dividend payments effected) to *paid-up* capital. Viz.

BAGS

	Net earnings(%)	Residual income(%)
1883/4	6.3	3.7
1884/5	5.6	2.3
1885/6	6.1	2.8
1886/7	7.2	3.5
1887/8	8.0	4.0
1888/9	8.0	3.8
1889/90	5.3	2.0
1890/1	4.1	1.6
1891/2	3.8	1.2
1892/3	3.9	0.9
1893/4	4.1	0.9
1894/5	4.7	1.8
1895/6	5.1	2.9

Source Compiled and calculated from BAGS *Annual Report(s)*

[17] For an account of Argentina's recovery, see Ferns *Britain and Argentina* pp. 470–84.

[18] Díaz Alejandro *Essays* pp.5, 148–51, 474; Vázquez-Presedo *El caso* Ch. IV; A.G. Ford 'Export Price Indices for the Argentine Republic, 1881–1914' *IAEA* IX 2 (1955) 42–54.

[19] Díaz Alejandro *Essays* p. 18; Vázquez-Presedo *Estadísticas* pp. 69–71, *El caso* pp. 150–51, 157–75.

[20] República Argentina, Ministerio de Agricultura, Dirección General de Inmigración *Memoria de la Dirección General de Inmigración correspondiente al año 1913* (Buenos Aires 1915) pp. 50–54; Díaz Alejandro *Essays* p. 421.

[21] For an account of the impact of immigration upon Argentine economic development see, Scobie, *Revolution on the pampas* and C. Solberg *Immigration and nationalism Argentina and Chile, 1890–1914* (Austin 1970). And for a description of the grain industry see William Goodwin *Wheat Growing in the Argentine Republic* (Liverpool 1895).

[22] E. Gallo 'Ocupación de tierras y colonización agrícola en Santa Fe (1870–1895)' in Alvaro Jara (ed.) *Tierras Nuevas: expansion territorial y ocupación del suelo en America (Siglos XVI–XIX)* (Mexico 1969).

[23] BAGS *Half-Yearly report . . . July–December, 1893* (London 1894), *Annual Report . . . 1894* (London 1894).

[24] *The Times* 27 April 1895, 15f; 25 April 1896, 15c, 1 May 1897, 7e.

[25] BA&P *Thirteenth Annual Report: Report and Accounts for the Year Ending 30th June, 1895* (hereafter *Annual Report . . .*) (London 1895), *Annual Report . . . 1896* (London 1896); *The Times* 10 December 1895, 4d, 17 December 1895, 13b, 3 November 1896, 12b, 11 November 1896, 10a.

[26] BAGS *Annual Report(s) 1884 & 1885* (London 1884 & 1885).

[27] For a discussion of this process, especially the expansion of BA, see J.R. Scobie *Buenos Aires: plaza to suburb, 1870–1910* (New York 1974); N. Besio Moreno *Buenos Aires: estudio critico de su población, 1536–1936* (Buenos Aires 1939).

[28] BAGS *Annual Report(s) 1883, 1884, 1889, Half-yearly report, July–December, 1885* (London 1883, 1884, 1889, 1886).

[29] Calculated from various *Annual Report(s)*.

[30] Buenos Aires Western Railway Company Limited (hereafter BAW) *Report of the Directors to the Proprietors, and Statement of the Revenue and Capital Accounts fot the Year ended 30th June, 1900* (hereafter *Annual Report . . .*) (London 1900); CA *Annual Report . . . 1891* (London 1892).

[31] República Argentina, Ministerio de Obras Públicas, Dirección General de Ferrocarriles *Estadística de los ferrocarriles en explotación 1913* (Buenos Aires 1916) pp. 396–98; Bunge *Ferrocarriles* pp. 119–21.

[32] BAGS *Annual Report . . . 1895* (London 1895); *RT* 28 September 1895, LXVIII, 412; *The Times* 25 October 1895, 3f.

CHAPTER IV

[1] *Sesiones* 1891 I 665.

[2] *RT* 14 November 1891, LX, 507.

[3] See above, pp. 7–10.

[4] BAGS *Memorandum of Association and Articles of Association*. pp. 36–38. London Stock Exchange, QDA 21A 796.

[5] Calculated and compiled from BAGS *Annual Report(s)*; CA *Annual Report . . . 1895* (London 1896).

[6] Compiled and calculated from BAN *Annual Report . . . 1882* (London 1883).

[7] Compiled and calculated from Buenos Ayres and Ensenada Port Railway Company Limited (hereafter BA&EP) *Report of the Directors and Statement of Accounts to be presented to the Shareholders for the year ending 31st December, 1895* (hereafter *Annual Report . . .*) (London 1896).

[8] That is under normal conditions. During the 1890s BAGS was able to operate a working ratio well below 40 per cent by failing to make adequate allowances for depreciation.

[9] Bouwer to Barings, 17 April 1878. BAHC 4.1.65 Pt.II.

[10] *The Times* 22 July 1867, 7c, 22 November 1876, 7f, 27 November 1868, 7b.

[11] *The Times* 25 July 1872, 7c.

[12] Bouwer to Barings, 17 April 1878. BAHC 4.1.65 Pt.II.

[13] BAN *Annual Report . . . 1865* (London 1866); *The Times* 7 December 1866, 4c & d, 8 April 1867, 7b.

[14] BAN *Annual Report . . . 1866* (London 1867); *The Times* 14 July 1868, 10f.

[15] *The Times* 11 September 1867, 5d.

[16] BAN *Annual Report . . . 1867* (London 1868); *The Times* 22 October, 4f.

[17] Provincia de Buenos Aires, *Registro Oficial . . . 1868* p. 430; BAN *Annual Report . . . 1868 & 1871* (London 1869 & 1872); *The Times* 4 May 1871, 10c.

[18] Bouwer to Barings, 31 January 1877. BAHC 4.1.65 Pt.1.

[19] Bouwer to Barings, 7 May 1877. BAHC 4.1.65 Pt.1.

[20] For an account of the escalation of the guarantee claims and desultory payments by the national government, see EA *Report(s) of the Directors to be presented to the Shareholders at the fifth Ordinary Ceseral Meeting for the year(s) ending 31st December 1875 (–1882)* (hereafter *Annual Report . . .*) (London 1876–83); *The Times* 8 December 1876, 7c, 30 May 1877, 7e, 12 June 1878, 7d, 7 June 1879, 9c, 12 June 1879, 9c, 8 July 1880, 9e, 23 July 1881, 13b, 10 August 1881, 11e, 22 June 1882, 11e. For measures adopted by the company at this stage to secure a settlement of its claims, see W.N. Massey, chairman, EA, to Barings, 2 March 1878, 2 May 1878, L.J. Baker, chairman, EA, to Barings, 21 March 1882, 28 March 1882, H.B. Templar Powell, secretary, EA, to Barings, 7 February 1881, 25 April 1882. BAHC 4.1.68; Bouwer to Barings, 19 March 1878, 20 April 1878, 1 April 1881, 24 May 1881. BAHC 4.1.65 Pts II & VII; *The Times* 6 January 1881, 7d.

[21] BA&SF *Prospectus* Stock Exchange, QDR, 21A 775; *RT* 25 February 1860, XXIII, 236.

[22] BA&C *Prospectus* reproduced in *RT* 13 June 1874, XXXVII, 616.

[23] BAGS *Memorandum* Stock Exchange, QDR, 21A 796 reproduced in *RT* 9 August 1862, XXV, 1149.

[24] Bouwer to Barings, 7 May 1877. BAHC 4.1.65 Pt.I. This situation lay at the root of disputes between several companies and the national government during the late 1870s.

[25] Buenos Aires *Standard*. 12 October 1868. Reprinted in *The Times* 27 November 1868, 7b.

[26] For various accounts of the company's difficulties, and a sample of press coverage, see *The Times* 24 August 1865, 5a, 8 September 1865, 6f, 7 December 1866, 4c & d, 27 March 1867, 11c, 8 April 1867, 7b, 11 April 1867, 7a, 29 October 1868, 6f, 25 November 1869, 6e; *RT* 12 May 1866, XXIX, 562, 2 June, 649; *B&RPM* 22 August 1865, II, 469, 7 September, 495–97, 22 September, 522–23, 7 May 1868, V, 19.

[27] Provincia de Buenos Aires *Registro oficial . . . 1868* 430; BAN *Annual Report . . . 1868* (London 1869); *B&RPM* 22 January 1869, VI, 16. At the annual general meeting held in 1866, the chairman had called for a quiet and orderly meeting, given the adverse impression which was being created in Argentina. It was

reported that the Minister of Finance had informed the Assembly that in various organs of the British press it was being stated that the chairman had been called a swindler. See, *The Times* 18 September 1866, 5e; *B&RPM* 22 September 1866, III, 425.

[28] C. Seale Hayne, chairman, BA Northern to Barings, 22 November 1881. BAHC 4.1.78.

[29] Edmund Ayres, secretary, BAN to Barings, 6 December 1881. BAHC 4.1.78.

[30] Barings to BAN, 8 December 1881. BA Letter Book 62 (1881) p. 146.

[31] Bouwer to Barings, 21 January 1882. BAHC 4.1.65 Pt.VIII.

[32] Bouwer to Barings, 10 February 1882. BAHC 4.1.65 Pt.VIII; J. Wilson Theobald, secretary, BAN to Barings, 21 March 1882. BAHC 4.1.78.

[33] Bouwer to Barings, 17 April 1878. BAHC 4.1.65 Pt.II.

[34] L.S. Sackville West, British Minister at Buenos Aires, to the Earl of Derby 6 October 1877 FO 6/340: 134–40, H. Brockett, chairman, CA, to West 25 April 1878, copy enclosed Sackville West to the Marquis of Salisbury, 29 April 1878 FO 6/347: 73.

[35] Bouwer to Barings, 1 April 1886. BAHC 4.1.65 Pt. XIII.

[36] Baker to Barings, 21 March 1882. BAHC 4.1.68.

[37] Baker to Barings, 28 March 1882, Templar Powell to Barings, 25 April 1882. BAHC 4.1.68.

[38] *Sesiones* 1883 I 310–12, 1006; Bouwer to Barings, 4 August 1883, BAHC 4.1.65 Pt.X; *The Times* 19 June 1884, 11d.

[39] Bouwer to Barings, 26 October 1886. BAHC 4.1.65 Pt. XIII; *RT* 12 November 1887, LII, 641.

[40] Templar Powell to Barings, 7 February 1881. BAHC 4.1.68.

[41] For a more detailed discussion of this point see C.M. Lewis 'British Railway companies and the Argentine Government', in D.C.M. Platt (ed.) *Business Imperialism, 1840–1930: an inquiry based on British experience in Latin America* (Oxford 1977).

[42] Fair *Some Notes* p. 9.

[43] At the time some commentators considered that the promoters of the line were foolhardy to forgo the guarantee. St. John to Granville 6 May 1873. FO 6/315: 49–51.

[44] *PP* 1892 LXXXI 67; *Economist* 21 February 1891, XLIX, 237–38; *SAJ* 5 July 1890, XXIX, 19.

[45] *SAJ* 5 July 1890, XXIX, 19.

[46] G. Jenner, Chargé d'Affaires, to Marquis of Salisbury, 25 May 1888. FO 6/398: 39–64, Jenner to Salisbury, 26 & 27 May 1888. FO 6/399: 78–100 & 102–112; H. Mabragaña (ed.) *Los mensajes: historia del desenvolvimento de la nación argentina redactada cronologicamente por sus gobernates, 1810–1910* (Buenos Aires 1910) IV 220; Ferns *Britain and Argentina* pp. 412–13; *Economist* 30 June 1888, XLVI, 824. Members of Congress appear to have taken the hint and during its thirteenth ordinary session the lower house spent more time discussing railway matters — new projects, reforming the administration of the guarantee system, remedying inefficiencies and inconsistencies in the application of existing legislation, etc. — than hitherto. See *Sesiones* 1888 I *passim*. Similar criticisms were voiced, with even greater force, the following year. See Jenner to Salisbury, 10 May 1889. FO 6/405: 261–263; F. Pakenham, British Minister at Buenos Aires, to Salisbury, 17 August 1889. FO 6/405: 424–426; Sir Thomas Villiers Lister, Assistant Under Secretary, FO, to various railway companies, 26 September 1889. FO 6/408: 457–58; *RT* 21 September 1889, LVI, 372.

[47] Jenner to Salisbury, 28 May, 11 June & 13 September 1888. FO 6/399: 114–15, 141–44 & 240–41; *RT* 20 October 1888, LIV, 542; *SAJ* 3 November 1888, XXV, 821. The sources are unclear as to whether this legislation applied only to

the Argentine Great Western Railway Company Limited (hereafter AGW) or a general enactment was invoked against that company.

⁴⁸ Buenos Aires *Standard* 4 October 1888, reprinted in *SAJ* 3 November 1888, XXV, 833; *RT* 3 November 1888, LV, 605.

⁴⁹ Templer Powell to Under Secretary of State, FO, 1 August 1888. FO 6/402: 128–32; Templer Powell to the editor, 30 October 1888, *The Times* 31 October 1888, 11b. Similar protests were addressed by various directors and officials of the company to a number of commercial and financial journals: for a selection see, *RT* 3 November 1888, LV, 605; *SAJ* 3 November 1888, XXV, 821. The EA argued that its rolling stock park was adequate; that its expenditure upon equipment went beyond the capital sums guaranteed by the government. In addition, the company implied that official procrastination in the settlement of guarantee claims, and a refusal to extend guarantee cover, frustrated attempts to obtain new capital to finance the purchase of rolling stock. Other British-owned guaranteed lines echoed these complaints: see W. Heald, secretary, AGW, to Under Secretary of State, 5 July 1888. FO 6/402: 97–103. And for a less partial appraisal, Jenner to Salisbury, 27 May 1888, unsigned enclosed memorandum, 23 May 1888. FO 6/399: 108A–112.

⁵⁰ Telegram, S.B. Hale & Co. to Barings, 28 October 1888. BAHC 4.1.71 Pt.I.

⁵¹ *The Times* 22 November 1888, 12b.

⁵² *The Times* 7 December 1889, 11e; *Economist* 4 January 1890, XLVII, 6–8.

⁵³ *Economist* 4 January 1890, XLVIII, 6–8.

⁵⁴ Buenos Aires *Standard* 30 March 1890, reprinted in *SAJ* 26 April 1890, XXVIII, 539; *RT* 31 May 1890, LVII, 702.

⁵⁵ BA&P *Annual Report . . . 1891* (London 1892); *The Times* 27 September 1892, 9b.

⁵⁶ Ferns *Britain and Argentina* p. 471.

⁵⁷ *RT* 9 July 1892, LXII, 50.

⁵⁸ *RT* 30 July 1892, LXII, 148.

⁵⁹ Telegram, Lord Rothschild to President Sáenz Peña, 2 February 1893. Copy enclosed, F.O. Smithers, secretary, Villa Maria & Rufino Railway Company Limited (hereafter VM&R), to local board in Buenos Aires, 2 February 1893. VM&R Correspondence, Letter Bundle A, letters 1–23, letter A/4 (consignment no. 71). Archivo del Ferrocarril Nacional General San Martin, (hereafter FCNGSM).

⁶⁰ Telegrams; Rothschild to Sáenz Peña, 3 February 1893, J.F. Romero, Argentine Minister of Finance, to Rothschild, 17 February 1893. Copies enclosed, Smithers to local board, 24 February 1893. VM&R Correspondence, letter A/6 (consignment no. 73). Archivo del FCNGSM.

⁶¹ Smithers to local board, 5 April 1893. VM&R Correspondence, letter A/9 (consignment no. 76). Archivo del FCNGSM.

⁶² *RT* 1 April 1893, LXIII, 431.

⁶³ BA&P *Half-yearly report . . . January–June, 1893* (London 1893); *RT* 15 April 1893, LXIII, 495.

⁶⁴ *Economist* 3 June 1893, LI, 663.

⁶⁵ ANE *Annual Report . . . 1893* (London 1894); *RT* 26 August 1893, LXIV, 280–81.

⁶⁶ *RT* 2 December 1893, LXIV, 736.

⁶⁷ Telegrams; London board, VM&R, to local board, 22 December 1893, 24 December 1893. VM&R Correspondence, letter A/21 (no consignment no.). Archivo del FCNGSM.

⁶⁸ *Times of Argentina* 14 July 1893, reprinted in *RT* 15 July 1893, LXIV, 87.

⁶⁹ *Times of Argentina* 6 March 1894, reprinted in *RT* 10 March 1894, LXV, 337.

NOTES

[70] República Argentina *Registro Nacional de la Republica Argentina, año 1894* (Buenos Aires 1894) pp. 278–79.

[71] ANE *Annual Report . . . 1893* (London 1894); CC *Annual Report . . . 1893* (London 1894); Minutes of meeting, 26 July 1894, Minute Book 33. River Plate Loan and Trust Agency archive (hereafter River Plate Agency).

[72] *RT* 28 April 1894, LXV, 563.

[73] *RT* 14 April 1894, LXV, 488.

[74] General manager, Cordoba Central, to F.H.C. Boutell, manager River Plate Trust, 26 May 1894. Cordoba Central Letter Book 226, January 1893 — August 1895. River Plate Agency.

[75] E.E. Reade to Barings, 14 August 1896. BAHC 4.1.124 Pt.XIV.

[76] Reade to John Baring, 1 July 1896. BAHC 4.1.124 Pt.XIV.

CHAPTER V

[1] J. Fuchs *Argentina: su desarrollo capitalista* (Buenos Aires 1965) p. 134. While it would be difficult to sustain this claim, the controversy surrounding the magnitude of official (national and provincial) participation in railway construction is partly explained by recourse to differing data series. Many of the government lines were constructed to the metre gauge; most private entities were at this stage broad-gauge. Obviously construction costs varied. Thus estimates based upon mileage would tend to inflate the state's contribution to railway development; a focus upon capitalization favoured the private sector. The criticism that the private (mainly foreign-owned) concerns were over-capitalized may be set against the complaint that many government lines were inadequately constructed — initial estimates being insufficient for the purpose, disguised capital funding was necessary to place lines in sound order, as has been related. For various assessments of the role of the federal and provincial authorities in railway building and financing see Scalabrini Ortíz *Historia passim*; R.M. Ortíz *El ferrocarril en la economía argentina* (Buenos Aires 1958) pp. 32–34; M.J. Cuccorese *Historia de los ferrocarriles en la Argentina* (Buenos Aires 1969) *passim.* especially pp. 11–12, 24, 37–40, 45–61, 66–67, 69–71, 114–19, 132–34, 137–41.

[2] *SAJ* 5 July 1890, XXIX, 19.

[3] Carter *South American Railways*; Cuccorese *Historia* pp. 47–57. The BA&P provides an interesting case-study of the vacillations in state railway policy. The original concession envisaged the construction of a privately-owned company and was obtained by J.E.&M. Clark & Company. However, the national government subsequently revoked the concession and appointed the Clark brothers to build the line on account, but before construction was completed a further policy change occurred. The finished section of the line was retained by the federal government and incorporated within the *Andino* network, while the balance of the concession was transferred once more to private hands, devolving upon the Pacific.

[4] *RT* 23 January 1897, LXXI, 119.

[5] Bouwer to Barings, 11 January 1885. BAHC 4.1.65 Pt.XII.

[6] Ferns *Britain and Argentina* pp. 450–57, *Argentina* (London 1969) pp. 104–13.

[7] *La Democracia*, Chivilcoy, reprinted *RT* 5 November 1887, LII, 591; *RT* 20 April 1889, LV, 531; Ferns *Britain and Argentina* p. 442. For an account of complaints levied against the company in the Buenos Aires provincial legislature see Cuccorese *Historia* p. 99.

[8] Scalabrini Ortíz *Historia* pp. 39 & 50; *SAJ* 9 February 1889, XXVI, 173. This

was particularly so during periods when the Gold Premium was high, as in the late 1880s. In 1888, for example, when the Great Southern applied to tariff surcharge in order to secure sterling earnings against the depreciation of the paper *peso*, its rates were some 16 to 44 per cent above those of the *FCO*.

⁹ *SAJ* 9 February 1889, XXVI, 173.

¹⁰ Bouwer to Barings, 5 December 1885. BAHC 4.1.65 Pt. XII; *RT* 22 September 1888, LIV, 394, 20 April 1889, LV, 531.

¹¹ Pakenham to Salisbury, 3 February & 30 March 1890. FO 6/410: 35–37 & 228–30; Messrs. Greenwood & Co. to Barings, 28 May 1890. BAHC 4.1.121; *RT* 19 April 1890, LVII, 509; Ferns *Britain and Argentina* p. 452.

¹² Pakenham to Salisbury, 28 April 1890. FO 6/410: 231; D. Joslin *A Century of banking in Latin America: to commemorate the centenary in 1962 of the Bank of London & South America Limited* (London 1963) pp. 40 & 125; Ferns *Britain and Argentina* p. 452.

¹³ Scalabrini Ortíz *Historia* pp. 61, 63–70; *PP* 1890/91 LXXXIV 3; *BOI* XII (1891) 581; *Statist* 25 June 1892, XXIX, 720. There is some dispute concerning the precise data. Spanish language sources indicate that the sterling equivalents of the purchase price and cash payment were £8,134,920 and £3,179,540 respectively; English sources place these figures at £8,284,921 and £3,329,541. All accept that the nominal value of provincial bonds assumed by the company was £4,955,380. The differences may be accounted for by agents' commissions and variations in exchange calculations.

¹⁴ *BOI* XII (1891) 581.

¹⁵ *La Nación* 20 May 1890.

¹⁶ F. Barres 'Reseña de los ferrocarriles argentinos; Ferrocarril Entre Ríos' *Boletin de la asociación internacional permanente del congreso panamericano de ferrocarriles* XXVI 71 (1942) 96–104; *BOI* 1892 X 621.

¹⁷ Barres *op. cit.*

¹⁸ Entre Rios Railway Company Limited (hereafter ER) *Report of the Directors for the period of operating ending 31 June 1892* (hereafter *Half-yearly report* . . .) (London 1892); *The Times* 12 October 1891, 7e, 19 October 1892, 11c; *BOI* XIII (1892) 621.

¹⁹ *RT* 4 January 1896, LXIX, 22.

²⁰ ER *Annual Report* . . . *1899* (London 1899).

²¹ Bouwer to Barings, 20 September 1886. BAHC 4.1.65 Pt.XIII; F. Barres 'Reseña de los ferrocarriles argentinos; Ferrocarril Santa Fé' *Boletin de la asociación internacional permanente del congreso panamericano de ferrocarriles* XXVI 74 (1942) 26–35; Vázquez-Presedo *El caso* p. 65.

²² Bouwer to Barings, 20 September 1886. BAHC 4.1.65 Pt.XIII; *RT* 11 February 1888, LIII, 185.

²³ *PP* 1890/1 LXXXIV 7, 1892 LXXXI 70.

²⁴ *RT* 3 January 1891, LIX, 21 & 24, 24 January, 99.

²⁵ Cuccorese *Historia* pp. 73–75, 77–81; Wright *British-owned Railways* pp. 66–67. Both authors cite the sentiments voiced by the Juárez Celman administration. See also Mabragaña *Los mensajes* IV 179–87.

²⁶ República Argentina, Ministerio de Obras Públicas, Dirección General de Ferrocarriles *Estadística de los ferrocarriles en explotación durante el año 1895* (Buenos Aires 1896); *RT* 23 January 1897, LXXI, 119.

²⁷ Bouwer to Barings, 7 January 1888. BAHC 4.1.65 Pt.XIV; *Buenos Aires Standard* 5 January 1888; *Buenos Aires Herald* 14 January 1888; *RT* 18 February 1888, LIII, 211.

²⁸ *The Times* 19 November 1891, 5b.

²⁹ Reade to Barings, 19 August 1891 & 21 March 1892. BAHC 4.1.124 Pts. I & II; *The Times* 19 November 1891, 5b.

NOTES 241

[30] *RT* 4 January 1896, LXIX, 22, 29 February, 288, 22 July 1899, LXXVI, 190; *The Times* 13 December 1900, 6a.
[31] *The Times, South American Supplement* 29 November 1910 3c.
[32] *RT* 10 September 1892, LXII, 343.
[33] Carter *South American Railways; BOI* X (1889) 319; *PP* 1912/13 XCIV 111–13.
[34] BAGS *Annual Report . . . 1890* (London 1890); *SAJ* 17 May 1890, XXVIII, 632.
[35] *PP* 1890/1 LXXXIV 8.
[36] *SAJ* 5 July 1890, XXIX, 19.
[37] *The Times, South American Supplement* 30 July 1910, 12a.
[38] F. Barres 'Reseña de los ferrocarriles argentinos; Ferocarril Santa Fé' *Boletín de la asociación internacional permanente del congreso panamericano de ferrocarriles* XXVI 74 (1942) 26–35.
[39] *PP* 1901 LXXXI 37.
[40] W.P. Glade *The Latin American economies: a study of their institutional evolution* (New York 1969) pp. 242–47, 297–310, 325–31.
[41] For a selection of literature see N.R. Botana *El orden conservador: la política argentina entre 1880 y 1916* (Buenos Aires 1977); M. Pena *De Mitre a Roca: consolidación de la oligarquía anglo-criolla* (Buenos Aires 1968); J.A. Terry *La crisis* (Buenos Aires 1893). A sample of comments concerning railway denationalization are located as follows: Cuccorese *Historia* Ch. VII; Ferns *The Argentine Republic, 1516–1971* (Newton Abbott 1973) p. 86; Fuchs *Argentina* p. 134; E. Gallo & R. Cortes Conde *Argentina: la república conservadora* (Buenos Aires 1972) p. 49; Ortiz *El ferrocarril* pp. 31–36; M. Pena *La clase dirigente argentina frente al imperialismo: seguido de orígenes y resultados de la nacionalización de los ferrocarriles* (Buenos Aires 1973) *passim.*; Scalabrini Ortíz *Historia* pp. 52–74, 211–34; L.V. Sommi *La revolución del 90* (Buenos Aires 1957) Ch. VI; Wright *British-owned Railways* pp. 66–69. Some authors tend to the view that denationalization signified a resurgence of *laissez-faire* principles, others find evidence of more sinister machinations. In general, less weight is attached to more pragmatic fiscal considerations than above.
[42] Bunge *Ferrocarriles* pp. 41–77 provides, for purposes of comparison, unabridged versions of both the 1872 and 1891 legislation. An indication of the subsequent expansion, scope and complexity of Argentine railway regulations may be obtained from the following works: J.N. Matienzo *La jurisdicción sobre los ferrocarriles en la derecho constitucional argentino* (Buenos Aires 1920); J. Rubianes *Deslinde de las jurisdicciones nacional y provincial en materia de concesiones ferroviarrias* (Buenos Aires 1908); C. Saavedra Lamas *Los ferrocarriles ante la legislación positiva argentina* (Buenos Aires 1918).
[43] Wright *British-owned Railways* Ch. IV; P.B. Goodwin *Los ferrocarriles británicos y la UCR, 1916–1930* (Buenos Aires 1974) *passim.*
[44] Wright *British-owned Railways* p. 97.
[45] *The Times* 17 May 1890, 8c, 20 May 1890, 11e; *RT* 24 May 1890, LVII, 672.

CHAPTER VI

[1] *The Times* 9 July 1886, 11c; *SAJ* 10 July 1886, XXIII, 320–21; Ferns *Britain and Argentina* pp. 411–12.
[2] *SAJ* 21 August 1886, XXIII, 400.
[3] *Bradshaw's* XXXVIII (1886) 445 & 448.
[4] Scalabrini Ortíz *Historia* p. 139 indicates that within five years of opening, the

247-mile Central route from Rosario to Córdoba was fed by approximately 500 miles of other companies' tracks. Several CA *Annual Report(s)* published at this time contain references to the construction being undertaken by neighbouring lines, and the resultant impact upon company profits.

⁵ R.P. Houston to the editor, 3 February 1892. Printed in *The Times* 4 February 1892, 11b; Ferns *Britain and Argentina* p. 412.

⁶ *Economist* 28 May 1892, L, 697–98; *RT* 23 January 1897, LXXI, 119; *PP* 1897 LXXXIX 191. While most sources agree that the BA&R possessed a greater route-mileage, there is some dispute concerning capitalization due to the treatment accorded the Central's leasing arrangement with the BAW. Occasionally the annual rental of Western track is capitalized on the basis of 20-years purchase, sometimes this figure is omitted from the CA capital account as a charge against revenue.

⁷ For a wide selection of views see the following shareholders' letter reproduced in the press, *SAJ* 19 July 1890, XXIX, 73–74, 18 October 1890, XXIX, 468–70; *The Times* 4 February 1892, 11b; *RT* 20 February 1892, LXI, 260, 21 May 1892, LXI, 653.

⁸ *RT* 16 April 1892, LXI, 497.

⁹ *RT* 20 February 1892, LXI, 260.

¹⁰ R.K. Middlemas *The master builders* (London 1963) p. 103; Ferns *Britain and Argentina* pp. 404–06.

¹¹ *SAJ* 24 May 1890, XXVIII, 567.

¹² *RT* 6 May 1893, LXIII, 585.

¹³ For further detail concerning the BA&R's challenge to the Central monopoly see C.M. Lewis 'Problems of railway development in Argentina, 1857–1890' *IAEA* XXII 2 (1968) 55–75.

¹⁴ *The Times* 12 March 1892, 13c; *RT* 12 March 1892, LXI, 352–54.

¹⁵ *The Times* 7 May 1892, 15c; *RT* 21 May 1892, LXI, 653.

¹⁶ *The Times* 4 May 1893, 13f.

¹⁷ *RT* 1 July 1893, LXIV, 25.

¹⁸ *The Times* 15 April 1896, 12c.

¹⁹ *The Times* 14 April 1899, 3c, 29 April 1899, 14c.

²⁰ CA *Half-yearly report . . . January–June, 1899* (London 1899); BA&R *Half-yearly report . . . January–June, 1899* (London 1899). Indirectly the Argentine government was responsible for the joint venture. The Central Station located near the Plaza de Mayo, which the companies shared due to an earlier arrangement between the Camapana and Northern was destroyed by fire. The federal authorities refused to permit rebuilding on this site, so the Central and Rosario were obliged to plan a terminus elsewhere in the city; Retiro (also shared) was considered to be most suitable for redevelopment. Similarly, the construction of a joint approach to the port sprang from the government's order that both companies close their separate routes through Palermo park.

²¹ BA&R *Annual Report . . . 1899* (London 1900); *Statist* 21 September 1903, LII, 470.

²² *The Times* 11 April 1900, 3c.

²³ BA&R *Annual Report . . . 1900* (London 1901).

²⁴ BA&R *Annual Report . . . 1900* (London 1901); *The Times* 13 April 1901, 6e, 20 April 1901, 5d; *PP* 1901 LXXXI 19.

²⁵ CA *Annual Report . . . 1900* (London 1901); *The Times* 20 April 1901, 5d. In the event, the total purchase price was higher, requiring the issue of substantially more stock on account of previously unpaid interest. For details of the final exchange of scrip see *The Times* 16 November 1900, 13c, 26 June 1901, 5d. For an alternative interpretation of the WSF stock transfer see Scalabrini Ortíz *Historia* pp. 163–67.

NOTES

[26] E. Essex Reade to Barings, 19 August 1891. BAHC 4.1.124 Pt.I.
[27] H.T. Thompson, assistant secretary, CA, to C.H. Sanford, 11 February 1897. BAHC 4.1.196; *BOI* XII (1891) 665; *The Times* 26 April 1894, 12c.
[28] Sanford to Barings 21 September 1898. BAHC 4.1.199 Pt. II; *The Times* 16 November 1900, 13c, 20 April 1901, 5d.
[29] *The Times* 16 November 1900, 13c.
[30] *Statist* 30 November 1901, XLVIII, 985; *The Times* 28 January 1902, 12c.
[31] *The Times* 28 January 1902, 12c.
[32] *Ibid.*
[33] *Bradshaw's* LIV (1902) 469 & 473, LV (1903) 462.
[34] *Statist* 30 November 1901, XLVIII, 985.
[35] Scalabrini Ortíz *Historia* pp. 167–71. Bunge *Ferrocarriles* Ch. III contains an interesting discussion on the capitalization of foreign-owned lines. He examines the issue of watering (pp. 101–05) and indicates that the Central was the worst offender, though all of the 'water' amassed in its capital account was not occasioned by the Rosario/Central merger.
[36] *The Times* 13 April 1903, 11d.
[37] F. Fighiera, secretary, BA&R, to J.A. Torrens-Johnson, Stock Exchange, Quotations Department, 1 October 1908. Letter bound in BA&R *Annual Report . . . 1908*, London Stock Exchange Reference Library 'Foreign Railway Reports, 1907/8', vol. A–C; *Statist* 3 October 1908, LXII, 668; *The Times* 30 October 1908, 30c.
[38] BA&R *Half-yearly report . . . January–June, 1903* (London 1903); *Statist* 10 October 1903, LII, 647.
[39] The original Northern lease was terminated in 1898 when the CA purchased the former outright.
[40] Ferrer *Argentine Economy* p. 135.

CHAPTER VII

[1] Clarence Whiting to Barings, 21 May 1864. BAHC 4.1.48.
[2] F. Barres 'Reseña de los ferrocarriles argentinos; Ferrocarril de Buenos Aires al Pacífico' *Boletin de la asociación internacional permanente del congreso panamericano de ferrocarriles* XXVII 78 (1943) 41–58; Scalabrini Ortíz *Historia* pp. 259–79.
[3] Carter *South American Railways* (see sections on BA&P, AGW and Transandine); W.H. Taylor and R.M. Rankin *Ferrocarril de Buenos Aires al Pacifico: reseña historica y características de la empresa* (Buenos Aires 1933) *passim*.
[4] *RT* 3 January 1903, LXXXIII, 18, 14 February, 187.
[5] *Bradshaw's* XLII (1890) 487 & 517.
[6] *The Times* 11 June 1895, 4f.
[7] VM&R *Report of the Directors to the Shareholders and Statement of Accounts for the year ended 31 December 1894* (hereafter *Annual Report . . .*) (London 1895); *The Times* 23 February 1895, 12c, 5 June 1895, 4f.
[8] *The Times* 10 May 1898, 5e.
[9] BA&P *Annual Report . . . 1889/1900* (London 1900); VM&R *Annual Report . . . 1900* (London 1901); *The Times* 29 May 1900, 3d, 17 October 1900, 2d.
[10] *Bradshaw's* LI (1899) 477; *The Universal Directory of Railway Officials and Year Book, 1937/8* (London 1937), p. 132.
[11] *The Tatler* 28 June 1905; L.G. Wickham Legg (ed.) *The Dictionary of National Biography, 1931–1940* (London 1949), pp. 695–96.
[12] *Sesiones* 1891 I 659–60; Scalabrini Ortíz *Historia* p. 291; Cuccorese *Historia* pp. 81–83.

[13] The state had forfeited the right to intervene in fixing the tariffs of the AGW until 1902 under the terms of the original contract negotiated with the company.

[14] F. Barres 'Reseña de los ferrocarriles argentinos; Ferrocarril de Buenos Aires al Pacifico' *Boletin de la asociación internacional permanente del congreso panamericana de ferrocarriles* XXVII 78 (1943) 41–58.

[15] *The Times* 17 October 1901, 13b, 13 August 1903, 11f.

[16] *Bradshaw's* LV (1903) 465.

[17] *The Times* 13 November 1901, 3d.

[18] *RT* 6 September 1902, LXXXII, 252.

[19] *Statist* 30 June 1900, XLV, 975, 29 December 1900, XLVI, 1090, 18 November 1905, LVI, 905. For further detail see also AGW *Annual Report(s)* for the period which contain a wealth of data on concessions acquired.

[20] BA&P *Report of Proceedings at the Ordinary General Meeting held on 11 November 1902* (hereafter *Proceedings* ...) (London 1902); *The Times* 12 November 1902, 13e.

[21] *The Times* 20 October 1898, 9a.

[22] *RT* 6 September 1902, LXXXII, 252.

[23] *The Times* 30 August 1902, 10e; F. Barres 'Reseña de los ferrocarriles argentinos; Ferrocarril de Buenos Aires al Pacifico' *Boletin de la asociación internacional permanente del congreso panamericano de ferrocarriles* XXVII 78 (1943) 41–58.

[24] *The Times* 30 October 1902, 13e, 29 October 1903, 11e.

[25] *The Times* 27 October 1904, 12d; 12d; *Bradshaw's* LVII (1905) 438.

[26] BA&P *Proceedings* ... *1904* (London 1904); AGW *Report of the Proceedings at the Annual General Meeting held on 26 October 1904* (hereafter *Proceedings* ...) (London 1904).

[27] *BOI* XI (1890) 531; Carter *South American Railways*; Bahia Blanca & North-Western Railway Company Limited (hereafter BB&NW) Contract with J.G. Meiggs. PRO Board of Trade Papers (hereafter BT) 31/36784/28900.

[28] *The Times* 11 November 1903, 12a.

[29] BAW *Annual Report* ... *1903* (London 1903); *The Times* 22 October 1903, 12a, 11 November 1903, 12a.

[30] BA&P *Annual Report* ... *1904* (London 1904); *The Times* 11 June 1904, 16c, 18 October 1904, 12d.

[31] *The Times* 11 June 1904, 16b.

[32] *The Times* 4 June 1906, 11b, 13 June 1906, 17b.

[33] *Bradshaw's* LXXV (1923) 424.

[34] *Bradshaw's* LXXV (1923) 419.

[35] *BOI* III (1882) 369, X (1889) 501, XIII (1892) 621; F. Barres 'Reseña de los ferrocarriles argentinos; Ferrocarril Entre Ríos', & 'Ferrocarril Nordeste Argentino' *Boletin de la asociación permanente del congreso panamericano de ferrocarriles* XVI 71 (1942) 96–104, XVI 72 (1942) 27–33.

[36] *The Times* 8 July 1899, 18c, 21 July 1899, 3f; ANE *Report of the Directors to be presented to the Propietors at the Eleventh Annual Ordinary General Meeting* (hereafter *Annual Report* ...) (London 1899). The North Eastern argued that shippers' preference for the Paraná route was due less to 'any slight economy in freight' than the reliability of this circuitous river journey over that afforded by the shifting Uruguay channel.

[37] *The Times* 9 June 1900, 4f.

[38] ER *Annual Report* ... *1901* (London 1901); F. Barres 'Reseña de los ferrocarriles argentinos; Ferrocarril Entre Ríos' *Boletin de la asociación internacional permanente del congreso panamericano de ferrocarriles* XVI 71 (1942) 96–104.

[39] *The Times* 3 July 1902, 12c.

[40] ANE *Annual Report* ... *1904* (London 1904); *The Times* 20 June 1903, 5d.

NOTES

⁴¹ *The Times* 21 November 1903, 4a.
⁴² ANE *Annual Report . . . 1904* (London 1904); *The Times* 31 May 1904, 13e.
⁴³ *The Times* 8 July 1904, 14d.
⁴⁴ ANE *Annual Report . . . 1905* (London 1905); *Bradshaw's* LVII (1905) 440 & 474.
⁴⁵ *The Times* 20 June 1905, 15b.
⁴⁶ *Bradshaw's* LVIII (1906) 444 & 476; *The Times* 3 June 1905, 15a.
⁴⁷ ANE *Annual Report . . . 1907* (London 1907); *The Times* 9 June 1906, 16d.
⁴⁸ *Bradshaw's* LXXV (1923) 421-22.
⁴⁹ ANE *Annual Report . . . 1909* (London 1909). The Argentine government was to assist the company obtain the ferryboats necessary to effect a link with the Paraguay Central in order to permit the through-running of carriages from Buenos Aires to Asunción.
⁵⁰ ER *Annual Report . . . 1905* (London 1905), *Annual Report . . . 1906* (London 1906).
⁵¹ ANE *Annual Report . . . 1910* (London 1910).
⁵² For further details on the operations of the Farquhar Syndicate see C.A. Gauld *The Last Titan* (Stanford 1964) *passim*; S.G. Hanson 'The Farquhar Syndicate in South America' *HAHR* XVIII 3 (1937) 314-26; C.M. Lewis 'Percival Farquhar and the Argentine Railways, 1912-1914' *Transport History* I 3 (1968) 209-231.
⁵³ ER *Annual Report . . . 1908* (London 1908); *Financial News* 3 October 1908.
⁵⁴ República Argentina, Ministerio de Obras Públicas, Dirección General de Ferrocarriles *Estadística de los ferrocarriles en explotación, 1913* (Buenos Aires 1916) pp. 396-98; ER *Annual Report . . . 1921* (London 1921).
⁵⁵ *BOI* X (1889) 319; Carter *South American Railways; PP* 1912/13 XLIV 111-13.
⁵⁶ CC *Annual Report . . . 1903* (London 1904); *The Times* 2 December 1903, 4a.
⁵⁷ F. Barres 'Reseña de los ferrocarriles argentinos; Ferrocarriles del Estado' *Boletin de la asociación internacional permanente del congreso panamericano de ferrocarriles* XXVIII 84 (1944) 57-100.
⁵⁸ *Statist* 17 August 1912, LXXIII, 463, 19 October 1912, LXXIV, 155.
⁵⁹ BAGS *Annual Report . . . 1898* (London 1898); *The Times* 6 May 1898, 3f, 7 May 1898, 5e.
⁶⁰ BAW *Annual Report . . . 1899* (London 1899); BAGS *Annual Report . . . 1899* (London 1899).
⁶¹ Sir R. Towers, British Minister at Buenos Aires, to Sir Edward Grey, 12 July 1912. FO 368/649; Buenos Aires *Standard, Mail Supplement* 19 December 1912, 6a; BAGS *Annual Report . . . 1912* (London 1912).
⁶² BAW *Annual Report . . . 1913* (London 1913); BAGS *Annual Report . . . 1913* (London 1913); *The Times* 8 October 1913, 19f.
⁶³ Calculated from respective companies' *Annual Report(s)*.

CHAPTER VIII

¹ The classic account of railway labour relations remains Bunge *Ferrocarriles* Ch. XII. See also Goodwin *Los ferrocarriles passim*, especially pp. 29-33, 63-148, 231-32, 250-58; D. Rock *Politics in Argentina: the rise and fall of radicalism* (Cambridge 1975) pp. 91-92; R. Thompson 'Organised labour in Argentina; the railway unions to 1922' unpublished DPhil. thesis, Oxford, 1978, *passim*.
² For details of the congressional debate preceding the passage of this legislation, see República Argentina, Congreso Nacional, Senado *Diario de Sesiones del*

Senado 1907, I 1048; *Sesiones* 1907, I 677–83, 1005–24, 1025–58, 1176–85, 1196–212, 1241. The full text of the *Ley Mitre* is reproduced in Bunge *Ferrocarriles* pp. 78–88; a reasoned discussion of the issues raised is located in Ortiz *El ferrocarril passim*. See also Wright *British-owned railways* pp. 85–87.

[3] BA&P *Annual Report . . . 1908* (London 1908).
[4] *The Times* 23 April 1908, 12c.
[5] República Argentina, Ministerio de Obras Públicas, Dirección General de Ferrocarriles *Estadística de los ferrocarriles en explotación, 1913* (Buenos Aires 1916) p. 398.
[6] Sir George Paish 'The export of capital and the cost of living' *Statist Supplement* 14 February 1914, LXXIX.
[7] BAGS *Annual Report . . . 1908* (London 1980); *The Times* 22 October 1908, 15d.
[8] *The Times* 11 October 1906, 12a.
[9] CC *Annual Report . . . 1908* (London 1909).
[10] República Aegentina, Ministerio de Agricultura de la Nación *Informes y estudios de la Dirección de Economía Rural y Estadística* I (1916) 391. Calculations concerning the nature of railway traffic undertaken during the mid-1900s indicate that some 24.75 per cent of total freight carried was destined for local consumption (the figure does not include goods absorbed at the point of production), 34.50 per cent was consigned to foreign markets, imports represented 30.37 per cent and the balance consisted of materials shipped for the railways' own use. See also Vázquez-Presedo *El caso* pp. 48–49; R. Cortés Conde *El progreso argentino, 1880–1914* (Buenos Aires 1979) pp. 90–106.
[11] BA&P *Annual Report . . . 1914* (London 1914); *Statist* 14 November 1914, LXXXII, 313.
[12] *Statist* 28 June 1890, XXV, 774.
[13] Wright *British-owned Railways* pp. 72–73.
[14] República Argentina, Dirección General de Estadística de la Nación *Extracto estadístico de la República Argentina correspondiente al año 1913* (Buenos Aires 1916) p. 352. Quoted in Guideo Di Tella and Manuel Zymelman *Las etapas del desarrollo económico argentino* (Buenos Aires 1967) pp. 237, 260, 281.
[15] For example traffic-flow charts see CA *Half-yearly report . . . July–December, 1908* (London 1909); BAGS *Annual Report . . . 1909* (London 1909); a specimen monthly revenue table is contained in BA&P *Annual Report . . . 1909* (London 1909). All indicate large seasonal fluctuations in traffic as do other reports published at this time.
[16] Walter Townley to Grey, 2 May 1907. FO 371/194; *Statist* 8 April 1905, LV, 632; BA&P *Annual Report . . . 1907* (London 1907).
[17] Miles A. Pasman, resident agent, to chairman, Curamalan Land Co. Ltd., 7 March 1902. BAHC 4.1.170.
[18] *The Times, Financial and Commercial Supplement* 8 May 1905, 370.
[19] *Statist* 15 April 1905, LV, 688, 16 January 1915, LXXXIII, 104.
[20] *RT* 11 November 1905, LXXXVIII, 531, 19 May 1906, LXXXIX, 633.
[21] FFCC Sud, Oeste y BBNO 'Descripciones' p. 3, Memorandum, 24/1/1910. Archivo del FCNGR, Mechanical Department.
[22] BAGS *Report(s) of Proceedings at the Ordinary General Meeting(s) of the proprietors 1885, 1894 & 1895* (London 1885, 1894 & 1895); *RT* 3 September 1892, LXII, 314; BA&P *Annual Report . . . 1904* (London 1904).
[23] Scalabrini Ortíz *Historia* pp. 17–23.
[24] R.R. Kuczynski 'Freight rates on Argentine and North American wheat' *Journal of Political Economics* X 3 (1902) 333–60.
[25] *The Times, South American Supplement* 31 December 1912, ix–x.

[26] *PP* 1912/13 XCIV 108-14.

[27] *The Times* 25 October 1900, 13d, 13 November 1901, 3d, 1 October 1909, 8b; *PP* 1914 LXXXIX 514; BAGS *Annual Report* ... *1912* (London 1912); BA&P *Annual Report* ... *1914* (London 1914); CA *Annual Report* ... *1914* (London 1914).

[28] *The Times* 21 October 1903, 14a.

[29] CA *Annual Report* ... *1911* (London 1911); BAW *Annual Report* ... *1913* (London 1913); *The Times* 6 October 1911, 16d, 16 October 1913, 19c; *RT* 26 August 1905, LXXXVIII, 253.

[30] *PP* 1912/13 XCIV 108-109, 1914 LXXXIX 514 & 555-57; *The Times* 19 April 1901, 3d, 9 October 1902, 12d, 19 April 1905, 13e 10 October 1908, 17e.

[31] BAGS *Annual Report* ... *1910* (London 1910); *PP* 1912/13 XCIV 105, 1914 LXXXIX 498-500; *The Times* 11 February 1910, 17e.

[32] *PP* 1912/13 XCIV 108-109; *The Times* 14 October 1909, 16e.

CONCLUSION

[1] *Statist* 22 January 1916, LXXXVII, 128.

[2] República Argentina, Ministerio de Obras Públicas, Dirección General de Ferrocarriles *Estadística de los ferrocarriles en explotación, 1913* (Buenos Aires 1916) pp. 396-98.

[3] Compiled from, República Argentina, Ministerio de Obras Públicas, Direccion General de Ferrocarriles *Estadística de los ferrocarriles en explotación durante el año 1897* (Buenos Aires 1898) pp. 194-205., *Estadística de los ferrocarriles en explotación durante el año 1935* (Buenos Aires 1938) pp. 362-63; F. Barres 'Reseña de los ferrocarriles argentinos; Ferrocarril Nordeste Argentino', 'Ferrocarril Sud' *Boletin de la asociación internacional permanente del congreso panamericano de ferrocarriles* XXVI 72 (1942) 27-33, XXVIII 83 (1944) 55-80.

[4] Calculated from *PP* 1901 LXXXI 37; United Nations Organization, Economic Commission for Latin America *Analisis y proyecciones del desarrollo económics, V, el desarrollo económico de la Argentina. Parte I, los problemas y perspectives del crecimiento económico argentino* (UN.II.G.1959.3) p. 32.

[5] Despite the conclusions which he advances with regard to the United States of America, Fogel himself states that the validity of his study depends upon 'what the substitutes for railroads could have done'. As Díaz Alejandro indicates, there were no 'substitutes' for Argentina. See R.W. Fogel *Railroads and American economic growth: essays in econometric history* (Baltimore 1964) p. 10; Díaz Alejandro *Essays* p. 45 note 57.

[6] The correlation coefficients were calculated from data contained in the following sources. Bunge *Ferrocarriles* pp. 119-21, 129-31; Di Tella & Zymelman *Las etapas* pp. 89 & 107; Díaz Alejandro *Essays* pp. 421, 440-41; Vázquez-Presedo *Estadísticas* pp. 15-16. Correlation coefficients are as follows:
  railway mileage and population growth (1869-1914) :0.99
  railway mileage and arable acreage (1891-1914) :0.94
For a more detailed, cyclical breakdown of the above coefficients and data on pastoral acreage see C.M. Lewis 'The British-owned Argentine Railway Companies, 1857-1947' PhD thesis, University of Exeter 1974, p. 409.

BIBLIOGRAPHY

A) *Primary sources*

  I: manuscripts

   a) Argentine archives

   1) Archivo General de la Nación, Buenos Aires
   Documents   1852/10/28/2/4/1723b; 1852/10/28/2/1/1431;
               1853/10/28/3/7/3919; 1853/10/28/3/13/4497;
               1854/10/28/4/14/6671; 1859/10/29/3/2/1660

   2) Ferrocarril Nacional General San Martin (ex Buenos Ayres and Pacific Railway Company Limited), Buenos Aires
   Buenos Ayres and Pacific documents 'Local Board Meetings' (uncatalogued); 'Meetings of Chief Offices, Revenue, Budget, Capital Expenditure, Various: sessions 1–30' (uncatalogued)
   Villa Maria and Rufino correspondence 'Letter Bundle A – [no terminal designation]' (uncatalogued)

   3) Ferrocarril Nacional General Roca (ex Buenos Ayres Great Southern Railway Company Limited), Lomas de Zamora
   Mechanical Department records 'Descripciones' (uncatalogued)

   4) Gibson archive, Corrientes
   Sir Herbert Gibson's papers 'Diaries' (uncatalogued); 'Press Cuttings' (uncatalogued); 'Correspondence with Fillett Holt' (uncatalogued); 'Correspondence with J.M. Eddy' (uncatalogued); 'Great Southern Rly.' (uncatalogued)

   5) Museo Ferroviarrio, Buenos Aires
   Buenos Ayres and Rosario Railway Company Limited 'Letter Books (accounts)' (uncatalogued)
   Central Argentine Railway Company Limited 'Account Book A 19'

6) River Plate Trust, Agency and Loan Company Limited, Buenos Aires
Central of Chubut Railway Company Limited Files 706; 707; 914
Cordoba Central Railway Company Limited Volumes 225; 226
East Argentine Railway Company Limited   Volumes 249; 250;
                                                  251; 254;
                                                  328; 351
                                          Files   405; 406
Entre Rios Railway Company Limited   Volumes 184; 185;
                                                  186; 188;
                                                  190; 193;
                                                  196; 197

b) British archives

1) Baring Brothers, London
Files HC 3.142; 149
          4.1.29; 39; 44; 48; 52; 53; 65; 67; 68; 71; 78; 85; 86; 95;
          96; 121; 122; 124; 126; 132; 135; 137; 138; 141;
          142; 154; 159; 160; 162; 164; 165; 168; 170; 190;
          193; 194; 196; 197; 199; 200
          7.55
          8.1
          17.429
     LB 87

2) Public Record Office, London
Board of Trade Papers   BT 31/2864; 6982; 17405;
                                 27644; 28900; 31490;
                                 35228
Foreign Office Correspondence FO 6/189; 191; 192; 196; 198;
                                 199; 200; 201; 202; 211;
                                 251; 254; 256; 264; 268;
                                 269; 274; 277; 278; 315;
                                 318; 320; 321; 326; 328;
                                 329; 333; 334; 335; 339;
                                 340; 344; 347; 353; 359;
                                 366; 367; 368; 371; 372;
                                 375; 376; 379; 380; 385;
                                 398; 399; 402; 405; 408;
                                 410; 415; 418; 419; 420;
                                 421; 423; 424; 425; 429;
                                 430; 431; 440; 442; 448;
                                 450; 458; 460
                                 368/2; 86; 268; 506; 507;
                                 649; 1203; 1207
                                 371/5; 194; 825; 4415; 4417;
                                 5521; 5526

3) Stock Exchange, London
Quotations Department Records 21 A 775; 796
                                22 A 1110
                                 6 B 154
                                14 B 97
                                16 B 314
                                30 B 58

II: printed material

*1) Railway documents
Argentine Great Western Railway Company Limited *Report(s)* 1889–1901
Argentine North Eastern Railway Company Limited *Report(s)* 1890–1914
Buenos Ayres and Campana Railway Company Limited *Report* 1880
Buenos Ayres and Ensenada Port Railway Company Limited
    Report(s) 1880; 1886; 1889; 1890; 1895; 1896
Buenos Ayres and San Fernando Railway Company Limited
    Prospectus
Buenos Ayres and Pacific Railway Company Limited *Report(s)* 1893–1914
            Proceeding(s) 1904–1914
            Memorandum and articles of association, construction,
               contract, and translation of concession
Buenos Ayres and Rosario Railway Company Limited *Report(s)* 1884–1908
            Tarifas kilométricas: 1° de julio de 1908
Buenos Ayres Great Southern Railway Company Limited *Report(s)* 1866–1914
            Proceeding(s) 1901–1914
            Memorandum of association and articles of association
Buenos Ayres Northern Railway Company Limited *Report* 1884
Buenos Ayres Western Railway Company Limited *Report(s)* 1891–1914
Central Argentine Railway Company Limited *Report(s)* 1870–1875; 1879–1882; 1900; 1909–1914
            Letters concerning the country of the River Plate being
               suitable for emigrants and capitalists seeking to settle in
            Tarifas generales: mayo de 1909
Cordoba and Rosario Railway Company Limited *Report(s)* 1890–1900; 1903; 1905
Cordoba Central Railway Company Limited *Report(s)* 1890–1914
East Argentine Railway Company Limited *Report(s)* 1879–1885

**Report(s)* signify the annual and half-yearly reports and statements of account presented by dirctors to shareholders.
Proceeding(s) signify the account of events – often in abridged form – that transpired at ordinary, annual general meetings.

Entre Rios Railway Company Limited *Report(s)* 1893–1914
Villa Maria and Rufino Railway Company Limited *Report(s)* 1892; 1894; 1900

2) Official publications

(a) Argentine

República Argentina *Registro nacional de la República Argentina; 1894* (Buenos Aires 1894)
República Argentina, Congreso National, Senado *Diario de sesiones de la Cámara de Senadores* 1888, I; 1907, I; 1918 I
    Càmara de Diputados *Diario de sesiones de la Cámara de Diputados* 1863, I; 1864, I; 1870, I; 1873, I; 1874, I–II; 1875, I–II; 1876, I–II; 1877, I; 1878, II; 1883, I–II; 1888, I–II; 1891, I–II; 1896, II; 1898, II; 1899, II; 1907, I; 1916, II & VI
República Argentina, Ministerio de Hacienda, Dirección General de Estadístaca de la Nación *Extracto estadístico de la República Argentina correspondiente al año 1915* (Buenos Aires 1916)
República Argentina, Ministerio de Obras Públicas, Dirección General de Ferrocarriles *Estadística(s) de los ferrocarriles en explotación durante el año 1893 (–1935)* (Buenos Aires, 1895–1938)
República Argentina, Ministerio de Relaciones Exteriores y Culto *Constitution of the Argentine Republic* (Buenos Aires 1926)
Provincia de Buenos Aires *Registro oficial de la provincia* 1854; 1857; 1859; 1862; 1863; 1864; 1868; 1869; 1870; 1871; 1908

(b) British

Parliamentary Papers: Accounts and Papers 1857/8, LIV–LV; 1859 (Second Series) XXVIII & XXX; 1860, LXIII–LIV & LXVIII; 1861, LVIII &LX; 1862, LIV & LVIII; 1863, LXV & LXX; 1864, XXX, LVII & LXI; 1865, LII; 1866, LXVIII & LXIX; 1866, LXXI & LXXIV; 1867, XXXVIII part 2 & LXIX; 1867/8, LXX; 1870, LXV; 1872, LIV, LVII, LIX, LXI & LXX; 1873, LXV & LXVII; 1874, LXVI & LXVII; 1875, LXXIV & LXXVI; 1876, LXXIII & LXXV; 1877, LXXXI & LXXXIII; 1878, LXXII–LXXIII & LXXV; 1878/9, LXXI; 1881, LXXXIX; 1882, LXIX; 1883, LXXI & LXXIII; 1884, LXXX & LXXXVIII; 1884/5, LXXXVIII; 1887, LXXXIII; 1888, C; 1889, LXXVIII & LXXXVI; 1890, LXXII–LXXIV; 1890/1, LXXII, LXXIV, LXXXII, LXXXIV–LXXXV; 1892, LXXIX–LXXXI & LXXXV; 1893/4, LXXX–LXXXIII & LXXXXVIII; 1894, LXXXV & LXXXIX; 1895, LXXXXVI & CII; 1897, LXXXIV, LXXXVIII–LXXXIX; 1898, LXXXXII & LXXXXIV; 1899, LXXXXIII, LXXXXVI & LXXXXVIII; 1900, LV & LXXXXII; 1901, LXXXI; 1904, LXXXXVII; 1905, LXXXVII; 1906, CXXII; 1907, LXXXVIII; 1911, LXXXX; 1912/3, LXXXXIV; 1914, LXXXIX; 1914/16, LXXI
Board of Trade, Department of Overseas Trade *Report(s) on the*

financial and economic conditions of the Argentine Rupublic (London 1921 & 1922)
   Report(s) on the financial, commercial and economic conditions of the Argentine Republic (London, 1923–5)

(c) *miscellaneous*

United Nations Organization, Economic Commission for Latin America *Análisis y proyecciones del desarrollo económico. V. el desarrollo económic argentino* (New York 1959)
   The rail-rolling stock industry in Latin America (New York 1956)
United States of America, Department of Agriculture *Year book of the United States Department of Agriculture, 1904* (Washington 1905)
   Department of Foreign and Domestic Commerce *The railroads of South America: Part I, Argentina* (Washington 1926)

B) *Secondary sources*

I: *newspapers and periodicals*

Bradshaw's Railway Manual, Shareholders' Guide and Directory XIII–LXXV
Burdett's Official Intelligence III–XIII
The Brazil and River Plate Mail I–XVI
The Railway Times XXIII–CIII
Revista de economía argentina I–VIII
The South American Journal XVII–CXII
The Statist XXV–CX
The Times

II: *select monographs and articles*

Alberdi, Juan B. *La vida y los trabajos industriales de William Wheelwright en la América del Sud* (Paris 1877)
Barres, F. *Reseña de los ferrocarriles argentinos: principales antecedentes legales y estadísticas, 1857–1944* (Buenos Aires 1945). Compiled from *Boletin de la asociación internacional permanente de congreso panamericano de ferrocarriles*
Bunge, A.E. *Ferrocarriles argentinos: contribución al estudio del patrimonia nacional* (Buenos Aires 1916)
Carcano, R.J. *Historia de las medias de comuniacación y transporte en la República Argentina* (Buenos Aires 1893)
Carter, J.R. *South American railways: Argentina and Uruguay* (London 1891)
Cootner, P.A. 'The role of the railroads' *Journal of Economic History* XXIII 4 (1963) 477–521 (hereafter *JEH*)
Cortés Conde, R. & Gallo, E. *La formación de la Argentina moderna* (Buenos Aires 1967)
Cuccorese, H.J. *Historia de los ferrocarriles en la Argentina* (Buenos Aires 1969)

Díaz Alejandro, C.F. *Essays on the economic history of the Argentine Republic* (New Haven 1970)
Duncan, J.S. 'British railways in Argentina' *Political Science Quarterly* LII 4 (1937) 559–82
Fair, J. *Some notes on my early connection with the Buenos Ayres Great Southern Railway* (Bournemouth 1899)
Ferns, H.S. *Britain and Argentina in the nineteenth century* (Oxford 1960)
Fishlow, A. *American railroads and the transformation of the ante-bellum economy* (Cambridge, Mass. 1965)
Fogel, R.W. *Railroads and American economic growth: essays in econometric history* (Baltimore 1964)
Ford, A.G. *The gold standard, 1850–1914: Britain and Argentina* (Oxford 1962)
Hadfield, W. *Brazil and the River Plate in 1868* (London 1869), *Brazil and the River Plate, 1870–1876* (London 1877)
Irazusta, J. *Influencia económica británica en el Río de la Plata* (Buenos Aires 1963)
Jenks, L.H. 'Railroads as an economic force in American development' *JEH* IV 1 (1944) 1–20, 'Britain and American railroad development' *JEH* XI 4 (1951) 375–88
Kuczynski, R.R. 'Freight rates on Argentine and North American wheat' *Journal of Political Economics* X 3 (1902) 333–60
Lloyd, R. (ed.) *Impresiones de la República Argentina en el siglo veinte* (London 1911)
Mabragaña, H. (ed.) *Los mensajes: historia del desenvolvimento de la nación argentina redactada cronologicamente por sus gobernantes, 1810–1910* (Buenos Aires 1910)
Mulhall, M.G. & E.T. *Handbook of the River Plate, comprising Buenos Ayres, the Upper Provinces, Banda Oriental and Paraguay* (Buenos Aires 1869), *Handbook of the River Plate Republics* (London 1875)
Ortiz, R.M. *El ferrocarril en la economía argentina* (Buenos Aires 1958), *Historia económica de la Argentina, 1850–1930* (Buenos Aires 1955)
Pendle, G. 'Railways in Argentina' *History Today* VIII 2 (1958) 199–225
Platt, D.C.M. *Latin America and British trade, 1806–1914* (London 1972)
Pulley, R.H. 'The railroad and Argentine national development, 1852–1914' *The Americas* XXIII 1 (1966) 63–75
Ramos Mexía, E. *Mis memorias, 1853–1935* (Buenos Aires 1935)
Rippy, J.F. *British investment in Latin America, 1822–1949* (Minneapolis 1959)
Robbins, M. 'The Balaclava railway' *Journal of Transport History* I 1 (1953) 28–43
Rögind, W. *Historia del ferrocarril sud, 1861–1936* (Buenos Aires 1937)
Scalabrini Ortíz, R. *Los ferrocarriles deben ser del pueblo argentino*, (Buenos Aires 1946), *Historia de los ferrocarriles argentinos* (Buenos

Aires 1958), *Politica británica en el Río de la Plata* (Buenos Aires 1940)

Scobie, J.R. *Argentina: a city and a nation* (New York, 1964), *Revolution on the pampas: a social history of Argentine wheat, 1860–1910* (Austin 1964)

Solberg, C. *Immigration and nationalism: Argentina and Chile, 1890–1914* (Austin 1970)

Smith, P.H. *Politics and beef in Argentina: patterns of conflict and change* (London 1969)

Spawn, W.M.W. *Government ownership of the railroads* (New York 1928)

Taylor, W.H. & Rankin, R.M. *Ferrocarril de Buenos Aires al Pacifico: reseña historica y características de la empresa, 1882–1933* (Buenos Aires 1933)

Di Tella, G. & Zymelman, M. *Las etapas del desarrollo económico argentino* (Buenos Aires 1967)

Di Tella, T. & Halperin Donghi, T. (eds.) *Los fragmentos del poder: de la oligarquia a la poliarguia argentina* (Buenos Aires 1969)

The Times *The Times book on Argentina* (London 1927)

Tornquist, E. *The economic development of the Argentine Republic in the last fifty years* (Buenos Aires 1919)

Vázquez-Presedo, V. *Estadísticas históricas argentinas: primera parte, 1875–1914* (Buenos Aires 1971)

Williams, J.H. *Argentine international trade under inconvertible paper money* (Cambridge, Mass. 1920)

Wright, W.R. *Foreign-owned railways in Argentina: a case-study of economic nationalism, 1857–1947* (Austin 1974)

INDEX

agricultural colonies, 28, 38, 132
Alberdi, Juan Bautista, attitude to railway promotion, 6, 7
Altamirano, 35, 36
amalgamation, *see* individual railway companies
Argentine domestic investment in railways, 9, 19, 20, 21, 128, 129, 155, 215–6, 227 n.105
Argentine Great Western Railway Company Limited: amalgamation, 165, 169, 174, 178–9; capital, 138, 169, 171; competition with other companies, 169–74; extensions, 169, 171–2, 178; guarantee, 117, 122, abrogation, 122; mileage, 138, 169, 205; purchase of state railway, 164; stocks and shares, 179; tariffs, 168–9, 170, 173, 174; traffic, 172, wine, 93, 172, 174
Argentine North Eastern Railway Company Limited: amalgamation, 183–8; capital, 82; competition with other companies, 182–4, 186–7; dividends, 199; extensions, 183, 187; guarantee, 117, 119, 122; mileage, 197; stocks and shares, 82, 185, 202–3; tariffs, 170, 184; traffic, 191
Armstrong, Thomas, 19, 20, 21
Arreglo Romero, 119, 120
Avellaneda, Nicolás, president, 33
Azul, 24, 36

Bahía Blanca, 51, 80, 94, 175, 176, 206, 207, 212
Bahia Blanca and North Western Railway Company Limited: amalgamation, 176–7; capital, 82; concession, 175; guarantee, 119, 122, abrogation, 122; mileage, 176;
stocks and shares, 82
Baring Brothers, 15, 20, 25, 60, 65, 108, 109, 110, 114, 123, 130
Baring Crisis: causes of, 69–70, 79–80, 84, 86, railways as cause of, 69, 70, 73–4, 77, 79, 80, 82–4, 86, 111, 112–3, 116–7; effect upon railways, 67–8, 71–2, 73, 93, 94–5, 96–7, 124, 137, 143, 147, 150, 162, 166, 176, 183, 193, 195
Boca railway, *see* Buenos Ayres and Ensenada Port
Bolivia, 31, 57
Bouwer, Nicolas, 25, 60–1, 69
Brazil, 8
Buenos Aires, city, 6, 92, 188, 206, 207; port improvement projects, 34
Buenos Aires, province: guarantee policy reformulation, 106–7; pressure on private railways to construct extensions, 9, 35, 50–2, 59
Buenos Aires Provincial Bank, 55
Buenos Ayres and Campana Railway Company Limited: capital, 41, 230 n.159; competition with other companies, 33, 34, 107, 108; concession, 33, 52; extensions, 33, 53; guarantee, 33, 105, 112, abrogation, 53; inauguration, 33; mileage, 105; reorganization, 53; *and see* Buenos Ayres and Rosario
Buenos Ayres and Ensenada Port Railway Company Limited: amalgamation, 190; capital, 58, 230 n.159; concession, 9, 14–5, 34; construction, 34; extensions, 139, 141; guarantee, from contractor, 34; mileage, 205; revenue, 59, 76
Buenos Ayres and Pacific Railway Company Limited: amalgamation, 165, 166–8, 174, 176, 177–9; capital,

54, 56, 67, 138, 180, 196, 200–1; competition with other companies, 57, 58–9, 62, 70, 165, 169, 171–2, 173; construction, cost of, 54, 56; dividends, 199, 200; extensions, 56, 141, 173–4; financial reorganization, 89; flooding, 77, 201; guarantee, 54, 117, 119, 122, abrogation, 122; mileage, 138, 197, 205; opening delayed, 55; revenue, 77, 200–1; stocks and shares, 54, 179, 200, 202–3, 204; tariffs, 170; traffic, 93, 191

Buenos Ayres and Rosario Railway Company Limited: amalgamation, 58, 148–63, 165, 192; capital, 53, 62, 66, 138, 156–7, 160, 196; competition with other companies, 52, 53, 57, 58–9, 62–6, 136, 148, 149, 150, 151–2, 153, 156; construction, 53, cost of, 62; dividends, 53, 77, 85, 95, 96, 199, 218; extensions, 61–2, 141, 150, 155, 162–3, 205; mileage, 66, 138, 197, 205; revenue, 85, 157–8; stocks and shares, 53, 62, 156–7, 202–3; tariffs, 154, 170; traffic, 93, 154; *and see* Buenos Ayres and Campana

Buenos Ayres and Valparaiso Transandine Railway Company Limited: amalgamation, 169, 174, 178; guarantee, 174, 180, abrogation, 122; tariffs, 170

Buenos Ayres Great Southern Railway Company Limited: amalgamation, 176, 190; capital, 16, 39, 51, 66, 80–1, 94, 138, 196, 210–1, 230 n.159; competition, with bullock carts, 24–5, 35, with other companies, 14–5, 35, 176–7; concession, 13, 14, 16, 20, 99–100; construction, 13, 14, 36, cost of, 14, 36, 38–9, 42, 229 ns.142 *and* 143; disputes with government, 15, 35, 46, 50–1, 196; dividends, 16, 46, 48, 77, 81, 85, 95, 96, 138, 199, 217, 218; extensions, 23–4, 35, 36, 38–9, 50–2, 66, 76, 80, 94, 139, 141, 196; guarantee, 14, 16, 99–100, 102, 105, 112, abrogation, 16–7, 107, extension stock guarantee, 39, 80–1, sub-guarantee, 16, 20; management, 21; mileage, 13, 22, 39, 52, 66, 105, 139, 141, 197, 205; reserves, 46, 48; revenue, 48, 75, 85, 89, 90, 92; rolling stock, 36, 205, 208–9; stocks and shares, 16, 20, 49, 51, 80–1, 201–4, 218; tariffs, 23, 25, 51, 61, 170; traffic, 24, 27, 50, 75–6, 89–91, 191, passengers, 27, 92, wool, 28, 90, 91

Buenos Ayres Northern Railway Company Limited: capital, 18, 41, 108, 230 n.159; competition with other companies, 34, 107, 108; concession, 9, 17; guarantee, 18, 103, 108, 109, 112, non-payment, 58, 103, 108, suspension of, 103, 108; inauguration, 17–8; lease, 64, 162, 165; management, 18, 108; mileage, 22, 205; *and see* Buenos Ayres San Fernando

Buenos Ayres San Fernando Railway Company Limited: concession, 9, 105; construction, 17; guarantee, 105; mileage, 52; reorganization, 17; share quotation suspended, 17; tariffs, 22–3; *and see* Buenos Ayres Northern

Buenos Ayres Western Railway Company Limited: amalgamation, 176–7, 190; capital, 130, 196; concession, 130; dividends, 95, 96, 199; extensions, 196; mileage, 139, 197; purchase of *Oeste*, 130, 139, 240 n.13; stocks and shares, 202–3; tariffs, 130, 170; traffic, 92–3, 191; *and see Ferrocarril Oeste*

bullock carts, competition with railways, 22–3, 25–6, 35

Buschental, José, 8, 10

Campana, 33

Central Argentine Railway Company Limited: amalgamation, 58, 64, 148–63, 193; capital, 10, 19, 38, 40, 65, 80, 138, 156–7, 161, 230 n.159; competition with other companies, 52, 57, 58–9, 61–6, 70, 74, 136, 148, 149, 150, 151–2, 153, 156, 163, 165, 171, 173; concession, 8–9, 10, 12; construction, 17, cost of, 10, 12, 39–40; dividends, 47–8, 77, 85, 95, 96, 199, 218; disputes with government, 40, 135; extensions, 38, 51, 56–7, 64–6, 136, 139, 141, 150, 155, 162, 205, refusal to construct,

30; guarantee, 10, 12, 40, 112, 113, abrogation, 40, 47, non-payment of, 102–3, 109; inauguration, 8; land grant, 10, 12–3, 17, 97–8; management, 65, 141, 149, 150–2; mileage, 57, 65, 138, 197, 205; relationship with state railways, 31; revenue, 46–7, 76, 85, 89, 90, 157–8; state aid, 19, 32; station facilities, 39; stocks and shares, 19, 49, 156–7, 159, 202; tariffs, 22, 93, 170; traffic, 154–5, 191
cereal cultivation, 27–8, 87, 88, 90, 92, 93, 154, 155, 191, 198, 205–6, 210, 211, 220; *and see* agricultural colonies
Chascomús, 13, 22, 34, 35
Chile, 8, 54, 70, 94, 135, 136, 164, 165, 168, 174, 180
Clark, J.E., 54, 239 *n*.3
Colombia, 8
competition amongst railways, *see* individual companies
Concordia, 33, 182
Córdoba, 8, 10, 22, 30, 54, 57, 62, 70, 135
Cordoba and Rosario Railway Company Limited, amalgamation, 189
Cordoba Central Railway Company Limited: amalgamation, 189; capital, 79, 82; dividends, 199; extensions, 141, 196, 207; guarantee, 117, 121, 122; mileage, 197; purchase of state railway, 136–7, 189; stocks and shares, 82, 189, 190, 202–3; traffic, 191

diplomatic intervention, 109
directorships, interlocking, 142, 149, 160, 166, 169, 174, 185, 187–8, 190
Dolores, 24, 35, 36
double-tracking, 210
Drabble, George, 20, 50, 62

East Argentine Railway Company Limited: amalgamation, 183; capital, 41, 230 *n*.159; competition with other companies, 182–4; concession, 33; construction, 33, cost of, 41; gauge, 41; guarantee, 33, 40–1, 108, 112, 114, 117, 122, abrogation, 122, non-payment of, 58, 103, 104, 108, 109; mileage, 33, 197, 205; protest to London Stock Exchange, 58; rolling stock, 113–4; stocks and shares, 185; tariffs, 168–9, 170, 184
economic crises, 45, 55–6, 61, 110, 129; effect on railways, 25, 27, 37, 38, 43, 55, 66–8, 95, 105, 108; *and see* Baring Crisis
economic nationalism, 55, 97, 118, 126–7, 143, 145, 192, 228 *n*.118, 239 *n*.1
electrification, 211
Ensenada, 34, 190
Entre Rios Railway Company Limited: amalgamation, 183, 184, 186, 187–8; capital, 131; competition with other companies, 184, 186–8; dividends, 199; extensions, 184, 186–8; guarantee, 117; mileage, 182, 197; purchase of state railways, 131–2, 136; stocks and shares, 202–4; tariffs, 132; traffic, 191
expropriation of private railways, 9–10, 14, 122, 130, 195; threats of, 35, 36, 40, 50, 56, 58
external borrowing, 19, 60, 61, 83, 110, 122, 129, 130, 131, 133, 135, 137, 139, 143, 144, 215

Fair, John, 20, 216
Farquhar Syndicate, 187, 189, 190
Ferrocarril Oeste (Buenos Aires Provincial Railway): accident, 6; capital, 9–10, 130, 138, 144; competition with other companies, 33, 35; concession, 8; construction, cost of, 42–3; deterioration, 42, 127; expropriation, 9–10, 14, 42; extensions, 29, 35, 38, 138–9, 141, 205; government aid, 9; horses, use of, 9; inauguration, 6, 8; mileage, 7, 22, 29, 138, 139, 140, 205; profitability, 128–9; sale, 127–30, 138, 240 *n*.13; tariffs, 23, 26, 129
foreign commerce, 27, 28, 49–50, 55, 57, 60, 87, 110, 210, 220; effect of railways, 26–7, 31, 57, 210; with neighbouring countries, 31, 57, 165; *and see* meat trade
French investment in railways, 69, 133, 142, 152

258 INDEX

gauge: adverse effect of breaks, 31, 133, 142, 165, 169, 207; determinants of, 31, 41, 216, 230 n.161; impact upon amalgamation, 182
gold premium, 46, 56, 79, 80, 127
government railway policy, 7, 8, 43, 52, 59, 60, 73, 93, 117–8, 124–7, 132, 138, 142–3, 144–5, 173, 175–6, 177, 192, 193–5, 200, 239 n.3; *and see* guarantees, *Ley general de ferrocarriles*, state railways
Gowland, David, 19, 20, 21, 216
grain elevators, 155, 156, 211
guarantees, 10–1, 14, 33, 44, 60, 69, 71, 73, 80, 82–3, 86, 97–123, 189, 204, 215, 216, 238 n.49; abrogation, 16–7, 97, 116–23, 124, 166

immigration, 50, 88, 220; *and see* agricultural colonies
interventores, appointment of, 115

Juárez Celman, Miguel, president, 113, 126

labour disputes, 193, 201
La Plata, 92, 212
Ley general de ferrocarriles (General Railway Law), 114–5, 144, 193, 194
London Stock Exchange, 17, 58, 77, 108, 109, 110, 114, 160, 201; share quotations on, 16, 48–9, 78, 118, 202–3

market integration, 6–7, 21, 23–4, 27–8, 38, 52, 53, 57, 59, 68–9, 71–2, 88, 141–2, 146–8, 179–80, 186–8, 198, 207, 212, 220
meat trade, 49–50; *and see* foreign commerce
Mendoza, 54, 56, 57, 164, 171
Merlo, 35
Mitre, Bartolomé, president, 13, 18
Mitre Law, 193–5, 196
Monte Caseros, 33, 182
Moreno, 9

National Railway Board (*Dirección general de ferrocarriles*), 10, 114, 118, 119, 144–5, 173

Parish, Frank, 42, 53, 62, 74, 149, 154, 159, 160, 166

passenger traffic, significance of, 92–3, 153, 211
Pellegrini, Carlos, president, 61, 117
Peru, 8, 31
peso, depreciation of, 25, 61, 77, 88, 110
Phillips, John Wynford, Lord St Davids, 168, 182
political instability, hindrance to railway promotion, 8, 13, 43–4, 46, 56, 88; *and see* revolutions
Porteña, La, first locomotive, 6, 8, 42
port facilities, 34, 206, 207, 210, 211

radial networks, 59, 175–7; *and see* market integration
Railway Committee, 118, 120
railway company–government relations, 2–3, 6–8, 10, 14–5, 29, 43, 50–1, 58, 62, 94, 101–5, 107–23, 129, 133, 135, 144–5, 149, 160, 161, 171, 172, 173, 174, 177, 186, 191, 192–5, 196, 200, 204, 212, 228 n.118, 238 n.49, 242 n.20
railway mania, 45–6, 55, 60–72, 82–3, 84, 86, 124
railway profits, 48, 84, 85, 89, 95–6, 126, 128–9, 131, 134, 156–7, 168, 196, 199, 204, 211, 212, 214, 215–7, 220, 234 n.16; *and see* individual companies, dividends
railways, general: construction, cost of, 10, 12, 14, 18, 31, 38–43, 54, 56, 62, 139, 225 n.20, 229 ns.142 *and* 143, 239 n.1; contracts, corruption, 15, 31–2, 86, 102, 103, 109, 126; investment in, 41, 50, 69, 71, 80, 82, 94–6, 116–7, 193, 196, 216, 219; investors in, 18–22, 26, 42, 45, 65, 168, 215–6, 219; mileage, 36, 41, 67, 68, 69, 71, 72, 112, 134, 135, 137, 138, 141, 196, 197; state aid, 9, 11, 17, 19, 21–2, 30, 32, 36, 38, 43, 53, 94, 136, 164, 216, 241–2 n.4, 245 n.49; and development, 1, 2, 5, 6, 20–1, 49, 57, 89, 98, 101, 141–2, 186, 219–20; and political integration, 6–7, 22
revolutions, 22, 67, 88, 117
Riestra, Norberto de la, 12, 15, 19
Robertson, David, 15, 21
Roca, Julio A., president, 22, 43, 46, 61, 126

rolling stock, 16, 24, 25, 36, 64, 108, 113–4, 137, 204, 206, 238 n.49; ratios, 204–5, 206–7, 208–9
Rosario, 8, 10, 22, 53, 54, 57, 64, 132
Rosas, Juan Manuel de, 1, 8
Rothschild Committee, 118, 119, 120, 136

Sáenz Peña, Roque, president, 117
San Juan, 54, 164, 171
San Luis, 54, 57
state railways: national and provincial, 36, 43, 112, 122, 126, 127–37, 172, 192, 205, 215; denationalization, 125, 127–37, 139, 141, 142, 144, 164, 241 n.41; *Andino* (Andean), 30, 56, 134, 135, 136, 164, 165, 166, 168, 171, 173, 175, 205; *Central Norte* (Great/Central Northern), 31–2, 62, 134–7, 141, 189; *Primer Entrerriano* (Entre Rios Central) 30, 132, 134, 136; *and see Ferrocarril Oeste*
stock raising, 25, 28, 90, 92; products transported by rail, 25, 92, 191; *and see* meat trade, wool
sugar, 92, 93, 191

Tandil, 24, 80
tariffs, rail: differential, 51, 171, 184, 209–10; government regulation of, 100, 130, 194, 244 n.13; *and see* individual companies

taxes, railways exempt from, 130, 132, 194, 195
travelling times, reduction effected by railways, 22, 54, 206
Tucumán, 8, 57, 62, 64, 135, 136

unprofitable construction, 32, 43, 58, 68–71, 84, 86, 89, 104, 108, 131, 133, 134, 137, 142, 156, 166, 189, 217
urbanization, 88, 92, 198
Urquiza, Justo José de, president, 19, 52

Villa Maria and Rufino Railway Company Limited, amalgamation, 165, 166–8, 178

watering of capital, 18, 40, 41–2, 54, 56, 109, 159, 160–1, 180, 185, 239 n.1, 242 n.25, 243 n.35
Wheelwright, William, 12, 14, 19, 34
wine production, 88, 92, 93, 171, 172, 174, 178, 179, 191, 220
wool, 28, 90
working ratios, 58, 59, 76, 100–1, 115, 116, 119, 213, 214, 219
workshops, 205

zoning, 37, 48, 93, 94, 124, 143, 146–7, 162–3, 171, 179, 188, 190, 192, 199, 207, 214, 216